Through Different Eyes

For Eileen —
dear friend — who helped
me find my voice —

Barbara

Through Different Eyes

An Immigrant's Heroic Journey
1889-1909

J. BARBARA ALVORD

Front cover: Libbie Marie (left) and Anna Barbara (right), circa 1916

Library of Congress Number:		2003097464
ISBN:	Hardcover	1-4134-3489-4
	Softcover	1-4134-3488-6

This book was printed in the United States of America.

To order additional copies of this book, contact:
Xlibris Corporation
1-888-795-4274
www.Xlibris.com
Orders@Xlibris.com

21127

Contents

Author's note 9
Prologue 13

PART ONE: THE PEASANT LIFE

Chapter One: A Child Learns Her Place 23
Chapter Two: School and the Good Nuns 40
Chapter Three: Working Out 55
Chapter Four: The Chosen One 66

PART TWO: THE LONG TREK WEST

Chapter Five: Over Land and Sea 75
Chapter Six: Weeks at Ellis Island 105
Chapter Seven: Six Weeks in New York City 122
Chapter Eight: Into the Heartland 170

PART THREE: IN AMERICA

Chapter Nine: The First Hard Years 191
Chapter Ten: A Better Life 244
Chapter Eleven: The Gathering of Family 298
Epilogue 331
Acknowledgments 337
Resources: Through Different Eyes 339

For my son, Kel

Author's note

*T*HROUGH DIFFERENT EYES is a creative biography about the life of Anna Barbara Mrkvička Kups.

Imaginative license has been taken to put flesh on the bones of facts and stories known of her immigrant journey and her life. A few minor characters are fictionalized to help explain the culture and era within which she traveled. Some factual names have been replaced by pseudonyms to protect descendants' privacy.

Czech surnames are represented in Anna's story by a single form rather than the masculine and feminine forms traditionally used in the Czech language. It is an attempt to simplify the identification of characters and to represent the modification of surnames that immigrants often experienced when they were processed through Ellis Island and assimilated into the American culture.

"Who has fully realized that history is not contained in thick books but lives in our very blood?"

Carl Gustav Jung (1875-1961)

Prologue

I T WAS POURING rain that day in April 1992, as I stood on Ellis Island in New York City Harbor under a large red umbrella, dodging raindrops. I struggled to stay dry and to trace "Anna Mrkvička Kups" engraved alongside thousands of other immigrants' names on a copper-colored steel panel. The list wove around the rock Immigrant Wall of Honor that curls among the Island's memorial buildings. With pencil lead I rubbed images of the name onto scraps of paper dug from my purse, so that other family members back home in Iowa could see for themselves the chiseled proof of "Anna" on the memorial. The Statue of Liberty loomed from a film of wet haze on nearby Liberty Island. "The Grand Lady," as my grandmother Anna always referred to her, lifted her torch more than three hundred feet into rain-soaked skies.

I knew that in May of 1903, the very month and year my maternal grandmother left her home in Bohemia for America, the famous poem by Emma Lazarus was inscribed at the base of the Statue. As I stood in the rain 89 years later, gazing over the water at the grandeur of the majestic white form, I wondered if anyone had been able to explain the English words of the poem to the young peasant girl who could not speak or read the language when she steamed on a passenger ship into the harbor. Like most travelers huddled beside her on the steerage deck that day, she had left the political unrest and extreme poverty of the laboring class in Europe to seek hope for a better future in the democracy and freedom of a new land. All gathered with her would have hungered to understand the poem's last lines:

> Give me your tired, your poor,
> your huddled masses yearning to breathe free,
> the wretched refuse of your teeming shore.
> Send these, the homeless,
> tempest tossed, to me.
> I lift my lamp beside the golden door!

I remembered my grandmother telling me that everyone crowded to the side of the steamship the day The Grand Lady came into her view after six long swaying days and nights at sea. Some near her cried "Freedom!" Some fell to their knees praying, or hugged and kissed their loved ones. Nearly ninety years later I could almost see the great four-stack ship S.S.Kronprinz Wilhelm floating in the mist. I could almost hear the cacophony of countless foreign voices on its deck.

In all the hubbub, Anna would have pondered the symbolism of the Statue as I did that day decades later. Near the shadow of the New York City skyline she gazed amazed at it all, a young stranger entering a foreign land without her parents or siblings to support her. Anna Barbara was just fourteen years old when her mother and father, *Marie* and *Karel* Mrkvička, chose her to accompany her paternal step grandfather, *Josef* (Joe) Valenda, who also was her godfather, to the United States. She was the eldest surviving child of their growing family. With Joe Valenda she was to join one of Joe's sons farming the fertile midwestern plains of Linn County, Iowa, near the town of Center Point.

So that the older man would not have to travel alone, Anna's parents decided that their daughter would accompany him, and then would work for her keep at the Valenda farm. The young girl had no choice in her parents' decisions, but it was understood that she would try to find a way to help bring the rest of her family to join her later.

The terrified young girl hid in a nearby rye field for a time when the hour approached to board the train and leave her small Czech farm community of Velký Lunec, located within walking distance of historic Kutná Hora. The familiar forests and fields and the shadows of the spires of medieval Saint Barbara's Cathedral had cradled her all her life. Nevertheless, at fourteen she was sent away from family and everything familiar into the unknown.

As I stood at the Wall gazing through the sheets of rain at the Statue and remembering my grandmother, I felt an aching sadness. Images of the Gramma Anna of my childhood floated through the mists, images of the tiny woman who was incredibly quick on her feet, and who seemed invincible to me as a young girl, even though I towered a head above her at my own age fourteen.

I remembered the hard working little woman of strong will who could be feisty, argumentative and opinionated, but who always remained staunchly steadfast in her loyalty to her family. It was she who gifted me, her firstborn American grandchild, the unconditional love that sustained me during difficult years of a Depression-era childhood.

My mind turned to the earliest image of my grandmother and me together, when I first noticed her unusual eyes. I was sitting on her lap at the age of three or four, and I realized that her two eyes were unusual, each a slightly different color. I was very close to her face and rubbing her cheek with my fingers as small children do. I saw that one of her eyes was light green-gray, or hazel; the other was pale brown.

I was fascinated with that, as children are with such things. My eyes and those of my mother were dark brown. I remembered asking "Gramma" whether the world looked different to her through her two different-colored eyes. "No," she replied, laughing, "they don't."

There in the rain on Ellis Island, remembering those different eyes, they began to symbolize for me what I knew about Anna Mrkvička Kups and her two visions of the world—one Czech, the other American. She strove to bring them into focus all her life. She brought from her homeland a scarring experience with poverty and hunger. It resulted in her driving will to work hard to bring her family together in a democratic America, to live in a place of her own, to have ample food always on her table, and to save money to take care of herself and her husband in their old age.

My sadness there on Ellis Island came from a realization that my grandmother's courageous story of grit and determination was disappearing from the archives of my family's memory. To my son and grandson, who came along too late to know her, she was a distant character looking out from fading snapshots in disintegrating photo albums, a ghost with an unpronounceable Czech name in a genealogical family tree. She was a stranger who in some yesteryear had transplanted our family lineage from the beet fields of Europe to the corn rows of Iowa.

In today's affluent United States, understanding of the European poverty and struggle of Anna Mrkvička's heroic immigrant journey nearly a century ago was slipping away generation by generation. During our current era of incredible technology and a glut of material goods, imagining the life of a small peasant girl in mid-Europe, who sometimes had to wrap gunnysacks around her bare hands and feet to walk to school in the winter, seems incomprehensible. And some of Anna's descendents have preferred not to remember the grim realities of the old world shadows in their past altogether.

My grandmother's firstborn American daughter, my mother, Libbie Marie, strove to disassociate herself from her Czech heritage in her teenage years; it is a pattern not uncommon in second-generation immigrant families. In 1920s jazz age rebellion she tired of straddling the old- and new-world cultures that conflicted Anna's home. Libbie wrestled desperately for a time to become what she saw as "American."

By the time I, Anna's firstborn American grandchild, "Barbaruška," was a young adult, the grandmother who had given me a love I shall never know again seemed quaint to me, her European ways old-fashioned, her wants in life limited and out-of-date compared to the grandiose and unrealistic dreams I dreamt. As generations of us grew away from little Anna's roots, we asked less and less about her life story. We gradually lost sight of the significant gift of her incredible immigrant experience and what it meant to our American lives.

Out of the mists of the Grand Lady that day on Ellis Island in 1992 grew my resolve to retrace how Anna Barbara Mrkvička launched both her and my American lineage, how she survived day to day during the often brutal times for immigrant workers like her in America the first half of the twentieth century. My quest for information uncovered countless stories written about other foreigners in Iowa who "achieved" by American standards. Many became landholders, business owners and community leaders. They have left us wonderful written histories that reveal the extraordinary opportunities of this amazing country.

But peasant Anna's story carries with it a different kind of struggle. It mirrors those of the rest of the mass of immigrants whose children and grandchildren usually evolved into the blue collar workers of America, those whose ancestors came to work here with little or no education, and who had scant support during their adjustment to a capitalistic democracy about which they understood little. Their families' climb from poverty to an educated, better life, often has been incredibly long and fraught with heartbreaking setbacks along the way.

When Anna entered America the Industrial Revolution was playing havoc with those like her who worked for a living with their backs and hands. It was the time of the tragic Triangle Shirt Waist factory fire in New York City, and strident, angry union/management confrontations. Anna and other women strained side by side with men in farm and factory, often in deplorable conditions, but as women workers they faced unique social inequities.

Women had only restricted legal rights when my grandmother arrived in 1903; they had not attained the right to vote and they had little political influence. In addition, social roles defined their lives as subservient to men. Knowledge of family planning was guarded and taboo. Suffragettes were angry and marching for an educated, empowered life for twentieth century women.

Anna was the first in her family in Bohemia able to attend primary school, and she was allowed regular education only until the age of twelve. Then she was removed by her mother to work as a domestic full time. Her wages went to support her family. Neither of her two children completed high school. Her daughter left the twelfth grade to marry; her son quit to help his parents financially during difficult times.

My grandmother would have been amazed to know that after she died in 1956, her first born American granddaughter did earn degrees at a university, and that I chose to study the English language that was such an aggravation and challenge to her at every turn of her immigrant life.

The more I had the opportunity to be educated about the differences between my and my grandmother's choices in our lives, the more I was driven to try to truly understand Anna Mrkvička's struggle. I wanted to know more about how she obtained the courage to withstand the many challenges and disappointments she faced.

Since that spring day at Ellis Island in 1992, I have immersed myself in a journey of my own, one to trace my grandmother's historical footsteps. I reconnected with long-ignored relatives and quizzed them about their memories of events surrounding Anna. I sat for countless hours scanning old newspapers and records in the archives of historical museums and courthouses, and searching the Internet for snippets of insight.

I experienced the realities of my grandmother's six-week stay in the Lower East Side of New York City at the dawn of the twentieth century by visiting the Tenement Museum there. Walking the creaking wooden floors, I saw for myself the tiny and windowless rooms, the crowded, bleak conditions the fourteen-year-old herself saw during her first weeks in America. Nonetheless, she always referred to her stay in New York City as "wonderful," which says a great deal about the life she left in Bohemia.

Out of the mists of Ellis Island Anna's story slowly took form. Each revelation illuminated how my grandmother's old-world attitudes and values flowed into the marrow of my family's American bones, how her move from Europe to America impacted those of us who came after her.

Then in 1998 I was able to travel to Kutná Hora, forty miles from Prague in today's Czech Republic, to wander the very paths my grandmother walked as a young girl. When I strode the cobblestone streets of that centuries-old village, I imagined her quick steps beside me as she explained each scene from her youthful memories–the patricians' villas she had admired with awe, the spires of Saint Barbara's Cathedral she could see from her nearby farming hamlet, the town's communal well she passed daily as she went to school. And I could hear her words of excitement in the courtyard of the historical Town

Hall, where she watched with her brother and sisters as neighbors, relatives and her parents danced the polka on balmy summer evenings. It was there in Kutná Hora that I followed a Czech guide down the stairs of the very fourteenth century "Italian Court" Town Hall so familiar to Anna. I was led to a records room currently deep in the bowels of the beautifully hand-painted old structure. My research had disclosed that the farm settlement of Velký Lunec, Anna's birthplace, no longer existed geographically. But the woman clerk in that cluttered records room reached among stacks of canvas-bound, hand-written ledgers to pick out a gray book filled with old Catholic baptism records, "Velký Lunec" scripted on its spine.

Over a wooden table the woman rapidly flipped through pages of that book with her adept fingers, looking for the name and birth date I had given her. Finally she said, "1889 . . . Mrkvička, Mrkvička, Mrkvička," reading names of the clan sheet by sheet. Then, "Ah, yes! *Anna Barbara Mrkvička,* April 6, 1889," and she laid the book before me. The ink was faded but the names of the priest who baptized baby Anna and the midwife who pulled her from her mother's womb were strong and legible. Dates and notes about witnesses and family members were scrawled clearly across the page.

My journey to understand Anna had led me from seeing her name etched in steel on Ellis Island in 1992, to seeing spread before me in the Czech Republic the hand-written historical record of her entrance into the world in 1889. I finally learned the identities of persons who helped usher her into her incredible life journey over a century ago. That discovery became a vital piece of the puzzle that was my grandmother, and it cried out to me a challenge to tell to others what I have learned about her courageous journey.

This story is written in homage to all of the unsung immigrants like Anna Barbara Mrkvička who have struggled through the centuries to build new lives for their families in America, and to the millions whose heroic journeys have disappeared forever into the shadows of time.

PART ONE

THE PEASANT LIFE

Chapter One

A Child Learns Her Place

ANNA'S BARE FEET flew over the damp spring earth on the forest path to *Babička Marie*'s hut, slapping through mud as she quickly crossed a trickle of stream. As a special treat for her daughter's sixth birthday, *Maminka*, her mother *Marie Barbora*, had allowed her to go by herself through the woods to visit the child's great-grandmother.

Marie was thankful that her eldest living child had survived six hard winters in her crowded one-room home. She remembered the comforting arms *Babička Marie* Mosedič had extended to her during her own childhood, so she had allowed her daughter to visit the old women in the nearby hamlet as a special birthday treat. It would be welcome relief for her from house chores and caring for her younger sisters.

The little girl ran as fast as she could so that she would be able to visit *Babička* and dash back to her mother before dark. Shadows from the sun filtering through the tall pine trees fluttered over her drab wool dress as she sped along the trail. She had not admitted to her mother that she was afraid of the spirits in the forest. She tried to push from her thoughts stories *Otec* (father) and her uncles noisily told her and her sisters evenings by flickering firelight. As the men drank more and more beer, their stories of tree goblins and scary ghosts grew ever more frightening.

When she had left the communal building and her parents' room, she had stopped at the niche of the Virgin Mary by the east door. There she stood on tiptoes to touch the statue and cross herself quickly, pleading for safekeeping through the woods.

Everyone told her that at six she was a big girl, but she knew she wasn't big at all. Most other children her age in her Velký Lunec farming compound were taller and stronger than she was. She could barely reach up to put soup bowls on the table for her mother at suppertime.

As her little legs scampered towards *Babička's* cottage, her mind wandered to how she would help *Maminka* and her father at planting time. She had been told just that morning that she was now old enough to start work in the fields with them. She was to join other children to scare jackdaws from newly sown seeds and to carry water to farm workers.

She thought she could shoo the birds away easily enough. She had been minding *Maminka's* flock of geese in the common fields for over a year. But she was afraid that she wouldn't be able to carry the heavy wooden buckets of water as was expected of her. They seemed as big as she was.

The girl also had been told that after harvest time something else important was to happen. *Maminka* said the village and church authorities had informed her that at six years of age Anna must start school in the fall at the nearby village of Kutná Hora. She must learn to read and write before her Confirmation.

All these things spun through the child's mind as she scampered through the light and shadow feathering over her thin, bare arms. Suddenly she realized that her feet were cold and her stomach was growling for supper. For comfort she searched through the trees for the nearby spires of Saint Barbara's Cathedral.

From a bluff in nearby Kutná Hora, in all their majesty, the amazing church buttresses looked down on her through gnarled branches. From Anna's earliest memories the Cathedral seemed perched there to protect her. The special name of the saint in whose memory the structure was built wove among those of the women of her family—her mother's "*Marie Barbora*," her own "Anna Barbara." If the Saint could keep the village silver miners of years past from harm, as she had been told time after time, surely she could help a lone little girl of six winters pass safely through the tree spirits this day.

Then the clearing surrounding *Babička's* hut came into view; countless hens and a lone gray goat wandered its grassy space. Anna raced to the door of the thatched-roof hut, scattering the chickens, then she squinted to find her great-grandmother in the darkness inside.

Babička Marie was sitting on her sleeping bench near the stone hearth that dominated one wall. She was settled in the light of the fire whittling the wooden cooking spoons she sometimes traded for other goods at Saturday market. Wood shavings spread around her like fallen brown flower petals.

Odors of damp thatch and dust and simmering stew filled the room. Children of the old woman's great-nephew, with whom *Marie* lived, crawled around her on the packed-dirt floor, two chickens among them. The children's parents were shepherds gone to the fields to watch sheep and milk cows.

The moment *Marie* Mosedič noticed little Anna her face wrinkled into a smile. "*Aničko, Aničko,*" she cried, clapping her hands as the girl ran into her arms. Anna's cousins crowded around as *Marie* planted a special, toothless kiss on the cheeks of her visitor. They all giggled with delight, but *Babička* noted once more how small this child of *Marie Barbora* was still, even so long after her birth. And the little one was chilled to the bone from her scamper through the woods.

The old woman took a rag heated on the hearth and wrapped it around Anna's feet, rubbing the girl's toes with her gnarled fingers to get them warm, pinching them and calling them little piglets.

Then she reached into a box on the table along the wall for fresh goat's milk and hunks of rye bread, and she dipped small portions of turnip and potato stew from the kettle hung over the hearth. Each child received a precious piece of the doughy food and a wooden bowl of soup. Then all but little Anna were shooed outside so that *Babička* could savor the time with her special birthday visitor.

Words tumbled from the child as she sopped bread in the soup.

Marie listened grinning, eyes wide, as her great-granddaughter told of her long run through the woods, and how she had escaped the tree spirits lurking in scary shadows. Anna passed on greetings from *Maminka*, and showed the old woman with her hands how her mother's belly was swelling with another baby that would soon join her and her younger sisters, *Antonie* (Antonia) and *Marie* (Mary).

Then the two settled into their usual ritual during Anna's visits. *Babička Marie* took a carved wooden comb from beneath the blanket on her sleeping bench and removed the wool hand-woven gray *bábuška* tied over her head. Before the warmth of the fire, Anna stood behind her to comb the old woman's long white hair. She gently moved the big comb from the top to the very bottom of the locks before her, chattering and asking familiar questions of the old woman.

At Anna's urging, *Babička* recounted the story once again of the girl's birth six winters ago. She described how *Karel* Mrkvička had hurried to her cottage through the woods that Saturday, April 6, the day before mass day, in the year of 1889. He had announced that his wife, *Marie Barbora*, was in the pain of birth. Accompanying *Karel* back to her granddaughter's home in a light spring rain, she had walked beside him listening to his worries about this pregnancy. Two winters before, his first-born son, *Josef,* had come early into the world, blue in death.

When *Marie* arrived at House #36 in Velký Lunec, the midwife, *Marie* Baba, from nearby Třechonín, was heating water in an iron kettle over a roaring fire in the fireplace and assembling string and knives to attend to the umbilical cord. Neighboring and family women sorted clean rags and swaddling cloth, or held *Marie Barbora*'s hands as she lay straining in labor on the straw-filled mattress of her marriage bed. The small room was stifling and crowded.

At that point in the story *Babička Marie* pulled little Anna from behind her to set her on her lap, smiling into the girl's bright eyes, now wide in anticipation. She had arrived at the part of the story she knew *Anička* awaited. She went on.

After hours of labor, a tiny but beautiful, healthy baby girl had been born, squeaking to announce herself. Her perfect little hands and feet jerked rapidly as though in a hurry to run through the life that lay before her. *Babička* tweaked her great-granddaughter's nose for good measure, laughing, then described the prayers of thankfulness to the Virgin Mary that had murmured throughout the birthing room. The new father, *Karel*, had lit his pipe and broken out warm beer for celebration for all assembled.

It had been three days later, April 9, when the baby was wrapped in a family christening shawl and Father *Jan* Dostál, village priest, baptized "Anna Barbara Mrkvička" into the family of the Lord. Godfather *Josef* Valenda, *Karel's* stepfather, joined another witness from Velký Lunec, Anna Vavička, to repeat baptismal vows to help raise the child as God's own.

With that closing of the story, Anna was satisfied. She crawled from *Babička's* lap to slide the wooden comb through the old woman's silver hair once again, now bursting to share all the important news from her mother's household. She was to work in the fields with the grown-ups this summer, and she was to go to school when harvest was over.

Babička Marie smiled and nodded with satisfaction. The old woman could neither read nor write. There had been no schools for peasant children during her childhood. It was hard for her to imagine that this little girl soon would know her numbers and how to read books, even the holy Czech *Bible*.

It was good news, but *Anička* needed a proper dress for school to replace the soiled, colorless one she wore each day. *Marie* Mosedič decided then and there to trade some of her carved wooden spoons at market for new cloth to make a suitable dress over the summer for her great-granddaughter's schooling.

Finally the child became courageous enough to whisper to *Babička* that she dreaded working beside and walking to school with the bigger boys and girls, who often teased her because of her small size. Sometimes they chased her and made her cry. The old woman drew her near again, telling her gently to talk her way out of problems as she could, and then to walk or run away as fast as possible just in case talking didn't work. Anna tucked *Babička's* advice close to her heart.

Too soon the light through the doorway dimmed as April sun began to set. It was time for the girl to leave the warmth of her great-grandmother's arms and hearth. *Babička Marie* tucked the comb back under the blanket of her sleeping bench and tied her old *bábuška* around her head once again. She hugged Anna tightly to keep her safe in the forest going home. Then the child reluctantly waved good-bye and disappeared into the woods, her small feet pounding the cold spring earth. She ran in haste to slip again through the forest spirits before they discovered she was passing by.

The home Anna scampered back to that day after her visit with her great-grandmother was simple and cramped. The girl's parents, twenty-six-year-old *Marie* and thirty-two-year-old *Karel* Mrkvička, had established their family in a long, low white-washed communal structure shared with other farm families. It was of log construction, its joints filled with clay, then covered with lime. Walls inside were white-washed but usually damp. Its corners seeped rain in summer and frost in winter.

Their Building, #36, stood in a cluster of living quarters, lean-tos, stables and cow sheds comprising the small farm hamlet of Velký Lunec. It was less than an hour's walk from the medieval town of Kutná Hora in Bohemia, itself about forty miles from Prague. Anna's community nestled around a small pond on a fertile Czech plateau southwest of the northern so-called "Giant Mountains" (*Krkonoše*). Ducks and geese swam in the water, oxen and cattle drank from the pond's rim, and in warm weather children plunged into its coolness and wiggled their toes in its muddy bottom.

A few families in Velký Lunec shared their living space with livestock. The Mrkvičkas owned no animals, and while some Czech peasants released from serfdom in the late 1700s had managed to accumulate small strips of land they could call their own, *Karel* and *Marie* owned no fields, garden plots or pastures. They were landless day laborers. *Marie Barbora's* children tended to their small flock of geese, which foraged for food in public areas.

Anna's building contained a central hall which ran the length of the structure; from it opened six doors to "family" rooms, three on each side. Each room housed a variety of intergenerational households. It may have included one family of parents and children, as did that of the Mrkvičkas, or it may have included a family plus a widowed aunt or an unmarried uncle. Often it included grandparents or cousins, retarded or crippled relatives. The rooms and living arrangements left little privacy for anyone. Raucous laughter and squalling babies in any one room could be heard by neighbors, as could angry shouting and family quarrels.

In 1895 Anna's crowded room housed her parents and their three small daughters: Anna age six, Antonia, five, and Mary, three. Their mother, *Marie Barbora*, was tired and short-tempered with her latest pregnancy and her added responsibilities with foster children.

For money or food staples *Marie* regularly suckled a series of abandoned or orphaned foster babies placed with agreeable peasant women by the church or civil authorities. That steadily increased mouths to feed in the household by one. The foster children usually stayed no more than two years, at which time they were placed with permanent families or moved on to orphanages.

The Mrkvičkas' room smelled of unwashed bodies and buckets under beds, utilized at night by children who could not get to the cobwebbed latrine outside. At most times stew simmered in a pot over the fire in a corner clay fireplace that provided for both cooking and heating. Food was kept in a wooden box to protect it from marauding mice and roaches. One lone window provided dim light, little ventilation.

Rough furniture was hand-made. Beds hewn of lumber and sticks from the forest lined the walls, one for the parents and nursing baby, one for all the other children. Straw-filled mattresses were thrown over rope taut and latticed on crude wooden frames beneath them. Fleas and bugs often were an aggravating problem. In the summer mattresses and scant bedding were laid out in the sun for airing and straw was freshened.

A table and splintered benches stood in the middle of the room. Bowls and spoons for eating were carved from wood and they were stacked on the table after being cleaned, readied for the next meal. *Marie* taught her children as soon as they were able to struggle regularly with a large hand-made broom, to sweep a dirt floor packed hard from the crowd of bare feet shuffling around the cramped space. Her girls were expected to gather water at the well and help keep their room as clean as possible.

Mother and father also trained their daughters at an early age to mind the family's meager flock of geese. *Marie*, in long cotton, linen, or woolen skirts, tied her Slavic *babuška* under her chin each farm day at four o'clock in the morning to go to field work side by side with her husband. She slung nursing babies over her back so that she could suckle them during the time she spent planting and harvesting sugar beets and wheat, or walking pastures to tend goats and oxen. She and *Karel* did not return to their one-room home and family until sunset. As young parents worked, aging relatives or neighbors looked after numerous small children left in the compound.

The Mrkvičkas were paid the equivalent of about thirty American cents a day for their work; all children were expected to help in the fields as soon as they were able. When there was little farm work in the winter, there was little family income.

Of course *Marie's* first-born daughter, Anna, was expected to assume great responsibility within the family. Besides working at age six with her parents in the fields, she helped tend younger children and she completed endless chores to feed and keep the household going day to day.

Only during the winter months, when fields were covered with snow and farming duties lessened, were children allowed relief from their work to attend school. Sunday mornings during farming weather adult workers were allowed some respite from work to attend Mass.

The Habsburgs ruling Bohemia were Roman Catholic. By Anna's time the monarchy had decreed religious toleration for Lutherans and Calvinists, but not for Bohemian (Moravian) Brethren. Austrian subjects were encouraged in many ways to remain loyal to Catholicism.

The meagerly-educated Mrkvičkas understood little of the history or forces that had shaped their difficult lives. It took all the energy of *Marie* and *Karel* to struggle through their hard-working peasant life, just as had their parents and grandparents before them. All of their ancestors had been tied to the land and food production, at one time as serfs. Generations survived as they could with little or no formal education and minimal shelter, toiling dawn to dusk to keep their families barely fed and clothed.

The Austrian Habsburg monarchy, the dynasty that had been in power over Czechs since the 1500s, still ruled the country during Anna's time. The geographical location of Bohemia, in the center of Europe and equidistant from the North and Adriatic Seas, made its citizens vulnerable to crisscrossed paths of booted, land-grabbing aggressors.

Throughout countless wars and skirmishes many young Mrkvička men died or were maimed when they were conscripted for armies pulled together to protect the powerful. The Czech National Anthem, "Where Is My Homeland?" (*Kde domov můj*) reflects centuries of alienation and unrest, along with the deep love Czechs developed for their troubled land.

Finally, by the 1800s, some members of the scattered Mrkvicka clan joined multitudes of their countrymen who made the difficult decision to emigrate. For the first time there was a way out, if they had the courage to cross the vast ocean to America. Many were weary of political and religious persecution and conflicts over Czech self-rule with the Austrian monarchs. Powerful Germans, who spread from their own country south into the rich Bohemian homeland, steadily pushed to control more land. A stream of Czechs began to flow from their villages west across the Atlantic Ocean to seek a better life.

Thousands left the country after hearing about the California gold rush in the 1850s. Many scattered to the farming fields of southeast Texas and to the meat packing plants of Chicago. Others found work in the mines and steel mills of Pennsylvania. And some began to farm the Great Plains in Nebraska, the Dakotas and Iowa.

So many Czech men and women left European provinces in the nineteenth century that Austrian authorities became alarmed; the privileged were losing their workers.

A government document circulated in Bohemia in 1855 warned Austrian citizens about going to America, saying travelers would be fed sickening biscuits on ships crossing the vast ocean. It further warned that jobs would be hard for them to find in the new country, and that emigrants would have to go hundreds of miles inland to escape the overcrowding on the eastern shore. Finally, Czechs were told that if they left Austria they'd lose their Austrian citizenship; they could not come back.

One Czech Catholic bishop was concerned about emigration for another reason. Budweiser Bishop J.V. Jirsit wrote and circulated "Should We Go To America" in 1867. He feared that Catholic Czechs would not continue worship in a new land without Czech-speaking priests to minister to them. His concerns finally led him to send priests to Saint Louis and Chicago to establish Czech parishes.

But whether Austrian religious and political influences liked it or not, letters from Czech emigrants in the United States to those still in Bohemia continued to arrive at impoverished peasant households. The letters lauded fertile land and new wonderful freedoms across the ocean. Such news was circulated from cottage to hut.

Transplanted Czechs who had settled in Iowa (nearly eleven thousand of them according to the U.S. Census of 1890) wrote back to their "old country" about similarities between the Labe River near Kutná Hora and the Cedar and Wapsipinicon Rivers wandering midwestern plains near Cedar Rapids.

Homeland rye and wheat and hops were compared to Iowa corn and wheat. The benefits of grazing farm livestock on soil rich from North American glacial residue were praised. And writers described how blue jays, crows and pheasants flew over clover and lilies of the valley in both lands early morning, how familiar fox, rabbit and deer wandered the fields and woods at dusk.

Handbills produced by U.S. railroad and steel companies circulated in European villages, inviting workers to lend their hands to help build America. One railway advertised for three thousand workers, pay $1.25 a twelve- to fourteen-hour day. "Information sessions" organized by Czech villagers to share their knowledge about emigration were held in homes and halls. Austrian authorities accused hosts of such meetings of "artificial stimulation of emigration fever," and forbid such gatherings by law.

Nonetheless, the potential to actually own property in a new land, and to live free from the imbedded class system of Europe, continued to be discussed by firelight in the crowded rooms near Kutná Hora. The idea of a different, democratic life tugged at *Marie* and *Karel* and many of their neighbors and relatives late in the nineteenth century, as their existence under control of the Habsburg monarchy droned on season by season.

In the summer *Marie Barbora* and Anna washed their ragged collection of dresses and pants in nearby streams and draped them on bushes to dry. They brushed out the wrinkles with their chapped hands the best they could. Because the brood of Mrkvička children had few changes of clothing, small bodies often were imprisoned in their room and bed until their clothes dried.

Children's clothing was seldom new. Faded dresses usually were passed to them from cousins or neighbors; Anna's clothing was worn in due time by younger sisters Antonia and Mary, until garments had been reduced to rags. The children did without shoes most seasons. Sometimes carved wooden clogs were worn in muddy fields by adults and children alike. In wintertime rags and gunnysacks often were wrapped around bare feet for warmth.

Wood had to be gathered daily for the fireplace. It was an extremely difficult task in winter months, and often Anna's duty. The climate in Czechoslovakia is similar to that of Iowa, sultry hot in the summer and frigid in the winter. Vicious storms blow through both lands.

In fact, *Karel's* father had been accidentally killed during one such storm near Velký Lunec before *Karel* was born. He had been reared by his mother and stepfather, Joe Valenda, who became Anna's godfather at her baptism. The Valendas and Mrkvičkas both lived in Velký Lunec.

With only one window and multiple bodies crammed inside its walls, the Mrkvičkas' one room was suffocating in summer. Regular bathing was difficult. The space reeked of sweat, dust, mold from the ever-damp thatched roof and charred firewood.

In the winter life was even more challenging. Cracks around the window were stuffed with rags and gunnysacks to try to keep out frost and snow, darkening further the cold gloom of shortened daylight. Dry wood for the fire was scarce. Goose down comforters, constructed by hand, were thrown on the beds. Sleeping crossways as many to a bed as their growing bodies allowed, children cuddled for warmth. Colds and croup were ever-present as they passed from one to another in the crowded conditions.

Marie Barbora, a midwife herself after her first pregnancy, treated her family with primitive cures: heated goose grease on the chest for lung congestion, poultices of moist bread and herbs for swelling and wounds. Rancid lard was rubbed on feet and hands cracked and hardened by weather and work, or smoothed on tender babies' bottoms. Death rates for peasant children were high. Accidents took their toll on all ages also. There were burns from scalding and wood fires, broken bones from feisty farm animals and falls while thatching roofs.

Occasionally packages of clothing arrived in Velký Lunec from relatives gone to America. Once a small sheepskin-lined winter coat sent to a neighbor fit only little Anna, so it was given to her. Villagers tried to work together to share whatever they could to get through their daily trials, although inevitably disagreements among them developed. One such fuss involved Anna and her sister, Antonia.

The Mrkvička children often were hungry. At mealtime father *Karel* ate first, and his wife and children shared what little was left. When Anna was five and Antonia three, they were so hungry one evening that they decided to go to a neighbor's pear tree and shake down fruit to eat. By the time Anna managed to climb to a lower branch, the neighbor's dog discovered the two intruders and raced at them fiercely barking. Anna scurried down and the frightened little girls were huddled together crying at the noise and the angry dog when the neighbor arrived and proceeded to slap them both soundly.

The next day Anna's mother was summoned to the Kutná Hora police station by the neighbor to answer for her daughters. Because it was the girls' first offense, *Marie Barbora* was spared a fine, but Anna and her sister were slapped again when their mother returned home embarrassed and angry. Peasant families owned little. Many times they chose to share readily what they had, but the stealing of food by anyone went against both the social mores and the laws of the community.

During Anna's sixth summer she had yet another brush with the law. Her mother sent her to a small square of public field to mind the family's meager flock of geese. Anna fell asleep and some geese wandered into a neighbor's grain to eat their fill. The neighbor filed a complaint with the police for restitution, and *Marie* and *Karel* were fined one hard-earned dollar that time, equivalent to more than three day's work. Anna was slapped once more. She learned her lessons well and never caused such embarrassment to her parents again.

During summer in the Mrkvička household food usually was adequate, if basic. There were sufficient potatoes and beets to hoard for winter months. Fresh cabbage, cucumbers and onions were available, as were nuts and squashes. Plums and berries grew along public lanes, so their picking was allowed. Family berry picking could be festive as members sang folk songs on an occasional beautiful day away from dreary daily duties.

The Czech "Prune Song" tells a story about the harvest time of plums, from which prunes are made. Its verses developed from the fact that the trees on private land needed to be guarded during the night from thieves when plums began to ripen, so that the fruit could be sold or used for *koláče* and dumpling making. *Marie* and *Karel* sometimes clapped their hands in rhythm as they sang "The Prune Song" with their children.

The last nights before the plum harvest in Bohemia, young men were sent from their homes to sleep under the sweet-smelling trees. It was one of the few times young people were allowed out after dark without adults. Of course liaisons occurred, and a myth of romance evolved around the ripening of plums under starlit skies.

Songs like the "Prune Song," about the beauty of spring and love, were treasured by hard-working Czech farmers. The perfume of June wildflowers, fragrant fruit trees and new green life in the fields were a welcome respite from the struggles of frigid winter.

Besides the purple plums and other summer fruit, mushrooms were available in damp woods during warm months, and they were free for the picking. Early on little Anna learned to hunt and discern only the mushrooms proper for eating during *houba* days in the spring. They usually were added as a special treat to the family's staple of goose or chicken soup stock, which almost continuously simmered over the fire. *Marie* bought a fresh chicken at market occasionally, or bartered for one with a neighbor. She periodically killed one of her own geese.

Wasting nothing, she and her daughters would roast the goose, put the leftovers and bones in the soup, and tie feathers in gunnysacks to dry. During the winter women gathered together for *dračky*, a feather-stripping party, where they plucked and separated down from feathers for comforters and pillows.

Peasants sometimes were allowed to share butchered pork or beef from the farms on which they worked. The air was so clear that sausage being cooked in neighboring villages could be smelled for miles. Round loaves of caraway rye bread purchased from a Kutná Hora bakery for ten cents were so large that they lasted the whole family for several days.

Through the centuries two factors had greatly influenced the lives of the Mrkvička clan. A Cistercian Monastery had been built in the 1100s in nearby Sedlec, establishing a strong religious presence in the area. Its famous Ossuary, containing thousands of Christian skulls and bones, was still a frequent site for prayers for the dead in Anna's time.

The other important factor in the history of Kutná Hora was the discovery of a rich cache of silver ore in the city in the 1300s, which made the locale a rich and bustling economic center of the Czech state. Five to six tons of pure silver extracted from the mines yearly made the Bohemian king the richest in Europe; therefore Kutná Hora served as a royal residence and a mint by the fourteenth century.

The "castle" built there for the king was designated the "Italian Court," so named to honor the Florentine experts hired to establish a minting process near the mines. The mint converted silver to the popular Prague coin, the *Groschen*, which circulated throughout Europe and added prestige to Bohemia. Eventually the name of the *tolar* silver coin minted there transformed into the name "dollar" of today.

By the 1800s, Anna's era, that same Italian Court had become the very Town Hall where the girl watched summer evenings as her parents danced the circle polka in its courtyard. It was where the Mrkvička children first heard the fiddles and concertinas that wove music magic into their lives. It was the very building where Anna's American granddaughter would find "Anna Mrkvička" written in baptismal records a century later.

By the fourteenth century the city's Catholic wealthy were inclined to build a cathedral in their city to showcase their importance in Czech society. Rich Kutná Hora patricians turned to Prague for guidance and hired the son of the famous architect who had designed the magnificent Saint Vitus Cathedral Workshop in Prague.

Saint Barbara's Cathedral was not ecclesiastical; there was no bishop seated at Kutná Hora at the time. The entire building endeavor was an unusual accommodation between secular and religious factions, which points out the influence of the wealthy silver mining patricians in the town.

When the cathedral was begun in the 1300s, Anna's Mrkvička ancestors were serfs, regarded as if they were property owned by manorial landowners and the rich silver mining patricians of Kutná Hora. They removed their hats and stepped off the road when the wealthy or noble rattled by in carriages. Parents had to ask a lord's permission for their daughters to marry. They were forced to billet troops wandering in war, and provide them with scarce food. They went hungry to pay whatever taxes the powerful demanded of them.

Some Mrkvičkas near Velký Lunec probably were conscripted to haul Saint Barbara's stone up the steep rock promontory on which the cathedral stands. Hundreds of serfs laboriously moved sandstone blocks from a nearby quarry to the building site over many years.

By the late 1800s, during Anna's childhood, Saint Barbara's Cathedral had looked down on all the daily activities below for centuries, stretching its pinnacles of stone crabs and flowers toward the skies. Daily the girl looked upward to the soaring spires for comfort.

In 1895, when the six-year-old started to school, scaffolding surrounded the structure's three unusual tent steeples; a newly-founded Wocel Museum Society undertook restoration of the amazing building. All the Mrkvičkas checked its transformation and noticed in awe its replenished stained glass when they walked to market once or twice a week.

So due to the background symbolized by the Cathedral and its previous wealth towering over their daily lives, nineteenth century Habsburg subjects like the Mrkvičkas lived in sight of imposing religious architecture and centuries-old reminders of their faith almost every path they walked.

Little Anna's fascination with Saint Barbara's Cathedral was not based on its unusual history, however, of which she would know little until she attended school. Her peasant interest focused on the compelling story of the virgin Saint Barbara herself, for whom the structure was named. Anna and her mother's middle names honored the saint, so the story was told and retold in her family. The little girl shivered whenever she thought of the young virgin and her fate.

Sketchy written accounts dating from the seventh century describe events that were supposed to have taken place about 300 A.D. Barbara's father, Dioscorus, is said to have been so protective of his daughter's beauty that he sealed her in a windowless tower when she was a young girl. During her imprisonment she converted to Christianity, enraging her father. He delivered her to the Roman governor, and when even under torture she would not recant, he took her to a mountaintop and cut off her head. At that point a lightning bolt from God supposedly killed him.

Because of the virgin's dark imprisonment and martyrdom, Saint Barbara became a Catholic patron saint for prisoners and miners like those who mined silver in the darkness beneath Kutná Hora at the time the cathedral was built. In their white-hooded robes, mine workers slid on their backsides hundreds of feet down to pitch-black honeycombed tunnels beneath the city. Once there they struggled in foul air and dusty candlelight to extract silver for rich patricians living in comfort above them. Some Mrkvička miners could well have joined them.

Men working the mines died young. Often rising water swiftly and silently crept through the porous rock mine tunnels to trap and drown them as they worked. The insidious water also leached arsenic from the mining process into surrounding drinking water, causing sickness and even the death of people drinking from the town well. Anna's ancestors could have been among the many who died of arsenic poisoning through the years, until authorities finally associated the mines with the water problem.

Down in the darkness, miners prayed to Saint Barbara, petitioning the virgin to watch over them. They asked that she give them the strength for the three-hour climb back up the dozens of ladders that lifted them from the tunnels at the end of the day to breathe sweet, fresh air once again.

Paintings illustrating the miners' dangerous work were brushed on the walls of the Minters' Chapel in the Cathedral after its construction. When Anna attended school she joined other Catholic school children to march reverently through the Cathedral to view its wonders, to pay homage to the Saint in whose honor it was built, and to learn the importance of Christianity and mining to their own salvation and the town's history. Girls like Anna with "Barbara" in their names glowed with pride.

The silver mines long ago had played out by the year *Marie Barbora*'s first child started her schooling. When *Anička* prayed to Saint Barbara in the dark of her one room at night, silver miners were no longer underground petitioning the patron saint. Even though only tales of the heyday of the town and its silver mining remained in Czech lore in the nineteenth century, sometimes Anna had vivid and troublesome nightmares about the saint's story.

The crowded conditions in which the Mrkvičkas lived often caused friction among members of the family, all worn down from over-work and a poor diet. In their cramped space tempers flared. Anna's father assumed his privileged role in a patriarchal society. He could be dictatorial and demanding, and he sometimes lost his temper with his wife and children, especially after bouts of drinking Bohemian beer.

When *Karel* switched Anna for her errors, the little girl trembled, thinking of young Virgin Barbara at the hands of her father. Images of *Otec* cutting off a chicken's head with one whack of a hatchet reminded the girl of the Saint's gruesome fate, and filled her with terror. With eyes clinched the small girl pleaded with Saint Barbara for safety in a scary world where forces controlling her life were much, much bigger than she was.

So at the end of the nineteenth century the stately cathedral in Kutná Hora hovered like a ghost from the past over the lives of the Mrkvičkas and Velký Lunec below. Its story and symbols sometimes troubled those who walked among its long stretching shadows, but its majesty nonetheless gave them pride. It gave them the solace of the steadfastness of the church. It gave them a constant anchor to the history of their homeland's rich religious and mining past.

As a small child Anna Mrkvička developed within a well-established historical and social setting, but her formal education gradually would separate her from the lives and expectations of her parents. Her experiences with the regime of the nuns in Kutná Hora's Catholic school stretched her imagination very quickly. Her different eyes began to view life differently than the eyes of her parents.

Chapter Two

School and the Good Nuns

ANNA HAD HARDLY slept the night before the warm September day in 1895 that was to be her very first day at school. She rose early, washed carefully after gathering fresh water from the well, and proudly donned the new blue linen dress *Babička Marie* had stitched for her. Then she laced worn, scuffed boots up her ankles. They had been donated by a neighbor and they were a little large, but she was glad to cover her small, already-calloused feet. The ill-fitting heavy footwear forced her to drag her heels with every step.

The crowded Mrkvička living space was busy and noisy as *Marie Barbora* placed gruel on the table and made clear to the children their duties for the day. Anna tugged at her mother's worn dress to get her attention. Her fine brown hair needed fixing before she could go to school.

As *Marie Barbora's* rough hands quickly combed and laced strands back and forth in one long braid, tying it with string, her eyes scanned closely the hands and face of this small daughter of hers, to see that she was clean. Then she admonished her child to be a good girl and to mind the nuns before she kissed her good-bye quickly on her forehead and nudged her toward the door. The girl in turn hugged her little sisters before she walked into the morning toward her new adventure.

She hadn't told her mother how fearful she was to be the smallest among bigger children and the black-robed nuns. Instead she moved quickly to join familiar students leaving the compound, to walk with them the half hour toward Kutná Hora and the town's Catholic school. Of course she had to endure the ritual of initiation for being the youngest in the group.

Bully *Jan,* whose pants were always stained in front from too-late forays to relieve himself, taunted his little neighbor as he usually did.

"Sister *Marie Helena* will whack you with a ruler if she doesn't like you. And she doesn't like little runts."

"Shut up, *Jan,*" said *Tereza,* a pale girl who lived with her grandparents on the other side of the pond. She clenched her left hand in a fist most of the time, but once she opened it in a gesture that revealed her fourth and little finger joined together by a web. Anna moved to walk to *Tereza's* right in case the older girl reached to take her hand, but she was thankful someone was sticking up for her with *Jan.*

By the time the group neared Kutná Hora, it melded into lines of other children from nine farm villages. Once in town the children saw nuns already were standing at the front door of the stone schoolhouse clanging hand bells for attention. At the sight of the black-robed Sister *Marie Helena,* pointed out to her by the still-taunting *Jan,* Anna wanted to shrink even smaller than her size.

A group of grim, no-nonsense nuns soon marched their charges inside through a hallway, sorting students by age and grade into different classes. Anna walked into a room behind a boy with a clubfoot who clumped over wooden floors as the other children steered around him. She began to lift higher her own oversized shoes, lest anyone think that she, too, had misshapen feet.

Once in her room Anna was placed in the front row of splintered double desks with other shorter, younger students. She sat next to a barefoot girl named *Josefína.* The two would share a slate on which to write and any of the few tattered books available to students.

When preliminaries were finished, all classes were taken to chapel for the morning prayers that they would experience daily for the rest of their schooling. Anna knelt and folded her hands in prayer as "Hail Mary, full of grace . . ." was recited, but she peeked once at the elaborate carved wooden crucifix hung at the front of the chapel. Jesus' head was encircled with a carefully whittled dark oak crown of thorns. She had watched *Babička Marie* whittle spoons many hours, and she realized how hard it must have been to carve the pointy ring of thorns. Seeing the agony on Christ's face, she thought she could feel punctures from the spiky crown on her own forehead.

Very quickly that day Anna learned to adjust to the realm of the nuns, their rules and expectations. *Marie Barbora* and her husband already had taught her discipline and obedience to authority. "Yes, Sister" and "No, Sister" became part of her vocabulary by the end of the day, as her head filled with the amazing new things that spun out of those first hours of school.

What captured Anna's attention most mid-afternoon was Sister *Marie Helena* explaining exactly where the six-year-old "was" in the world. Where she really "was." The little girl never had seen a map before. The hand-painted one hammered to the schoolroom wall intrigued her. The Austrian-Habsburg Empire was a large and prominent shape spread on it, green with shaded browns for mountain humps. The wimple-clad Sister tapped her pointer to a spot with "Kutná Hora" printed beside it, looking sternly at her pupils to announce, "This is where you sit in God's world. Right here!" Anna was fascinated, her different eyes wide.

Then the nun showed the class where Prague was located nearby, at the center of Europe, and she continued to identify countries and continents as they spiraled out from Kutná Hora, where Anna "was." She tapped on Germany, France, and the British Isles. At last her pointer moved across a painted blue sea dotted with inked images of billowy sailing ships afloat on inverted v-shaped waves. She finally banged her stick on a strange brown shape called the United States of America.

Anna glanced back and forth between the spot that was Kutná Hora, her spot, and the brown shape across the blue Atlantic Ocean. So that was the America grown-ups talked about so much by firelight. It didn't look so far after all from where she "was" on the colorful map.

From that time forward in her mind the United States was a strange and irregular brown blob beyond bright blue seas.

The good nuns were determined to teach the rag-tag peasant children in their charge to understand their place in God's world, to read and write properly, and to be ready for their first Holy Communion and a life with Christ. When children came to school with dirty faces and necks they marched them to the water pail by the door and scrubbed their faces with a damp, rough cloth until their skin was blotchy and red. Anna determined to rise early enough each morning to fetch water from the well and wash herself as best she could so that she didn't have to go home and explain a red face and neck to her parents.

The little girl quickly became one of the Sisters most attentive pupils. She completed assignments as rapidly as her feet flew through their daily tasks, soon realizing that she could partly make up for her small size if she could figure things out faster than the bigger students.

Her hand shot up to answer questions about numbers particularly; *Babička* and *Maminka* had taught her early to count her fingers and toes, spoons on the cooking bench, and the number of sticks and branches that fit inside the fireplace. She had been carefully instructed to count each goose she watched in the fields; none from the family flock dared be missing when she returned.

Religion at the school was the framework around which everything else was taught. Sister *Marie Helena* would ask of her class, "If Saint Sebastian has six pears and there are three crippled wayfarers for him to feed, how many pears would each poor wayfarer receive?" Anna quickly would work the problem with her fingers and stretch her arm high for attention.

Prayers began and ended each day. Holy days were memorized and honored; knowledge of the Saints was emphasized. Small holy cards with pale religious images, halos circling their heads, were given to students with ceremony when they did especially well at a task. Proud Anna carried hers home beaming and placed it on the rough-hewn windowsill near her bed for everyone to see. She later would carry it carefully to *Babička Marie's* cottage for her praise.

Study of spoken and written Czech and at least spoken German completed the curriculum. The German influence was so strong in Bohemia that Anna heard the two languages intermingled on the streets and markets near the school.

And extended time to spend in Kutná Hora became precious to the farm girl. Strolling cobblestone paths and streets with the nuns and her classmates, she studied a way of living Velký Lunec could not match. She was amazed by the stone patrician homes with carved or painted figures on their fronts, and by their beautiful glass casement windows. Some inside windowsills displayed sparkling garnet Bohemian cut glass, or crystal goblets inlaid with silver and gold, so different from the hand-carved wooden bowls and spoons on the Mrkvička table.

With awe Anna gazed at the costumes and hats of both women and men emerging from the wealthy homes to stroll narrow lanes. Of course she compared their clothing to the frayed hand-me-downs she and the other peasant children wore.

But she also began to feel fortunate for her healthy body after she noticed the town dwarf who swept the stone streets of Kutná Hora with a shortened broom. He stood little taller than she did, and he wore miniature pants on his short stocky legs. Her small size suddenly didn't seem so bad because she knew she was growing. Mother *Marie* measured the height of all her children regularly by the windowsill in the family's room. At six Anna had inched upward to peek almost over the sill and through the window. By next year surely she'd be able to look straight out to the path toward the latrine and not just upward to glimpse the treetops rustling in the clouds overhead.

With a new sense of self she walked by the police station, the colorful Kutná Hora markets near the town well, and the parish Saint James' Church. She breathed deeply the smell of fresh-baked bread from the town bakery. She liked seeing her warped reflection sliding along in the local lead-glass windows as she walked city lanes with her classmates. She looked up often to check that the pinnacles of Saint Barbara's Cathedral still peeked at her over buildings almost everywhere she wandered.

In good weather the small girl was amazed to be able to watch traveling puppet theater performances from Prague. Such shows were famous all over Europe. Sometimes they were brought to town by wealthy landowners to perform at their fine estates. Afterwards puppeteers often presented free performances to schoolchildren or to the public in the Town Hall courtyard or market square.

Angular, brightly painted wood-carved marionettes dressed in scarlet velvet and fine lace dangled from their strings in a portable box stage, their handlers shouting out dialogs of death, romance and royal intrigue. Sometimes their words were spoken in the Czech language, sometimes in German. Anna joined other dusty peasant children to giggle and clap her hands, covering her eyes during frightening scenes. If she couldn't understand the words, she guessed what was happening from the antics of the jerking wooden figures. To a small girl from a dirt-floored hut, seeing such play was wondrous indeed.

Anna soon came home to prattle to anyone who would listen about all that she saw and learned in school and Kutná Hora. *Babička* squeezed her with delight, her younger siblings listened with eyes wide, and her weary, uneducated parents listened tolerantly. Usually.

Sometimes, however, they became uneasy and annoyed that this little girl of theirs seemed to know so much more already from books and school than they knew about many things of their world. They were vexed that Anna's strong will began to blossom. That will often went crossways with that of her parents, especially her father.

Anna hurried Antonia along the path from school, overlooking her younger sister's complaints that she was walking too fast for her to keep up. It was a lush, warm day in May 1897. The shadows of gold-green maple leaves quickly ran over their faded dresses and worn shoes. Eight-year-old Anna was finishing her second year of primary school, Antonia her first. They had much to do before Mother and Father arrived home from work for supper.

When they arrived at their compound, they found five-year-old Mary watching toddler *Franta* (Frank), now two, at neighbor *Jelka's*. Frank was fussy and hungry. Little Mary was doing her best to keep him occupied. *Jelka* gave the girls a glowing stick from her fireplace so that they could go to their room to start a fire and prepare supper.

Once before their mother's hearth the small girls carefully laid sticks and dry grass around *Jelka's* starter for a fire, and all the children lined up to blow carefully on the glow until dancing sparks proceeded up the chimney. Even little Frank puffed his cheeks to help. It took his mind briefly off his empty stomach.

Then Anna searched the vegetable bin for three potatoes and a turnip, the set allotment for supper, to add to yesterday's meager leftover pot of soup. With the one worn knife belonging to the household she chopped vegetables carefully and evenly and tossed them into the pot. She dipped into the saltbox with her small hand to measure a mound of salt for the soup just the size of her inner palm, as her mother had taught her. Then she directed Antonia to fetch a fresh bucket of water from the well to add to the soup and to set aside for hand washing.

As she unwrapped a clean piece of cloth protecting a small heel of rye bread she was disappointed that there was so little left for tonight's supper; her parents were to go to market the next day for a fresh loaf from the village bakery. What was left was hard and dry. Anna's small fingers struggled to tear off a bit to give to Frank to quiet his fussing.

By the time the children heard their parents walking down the compound hallway, the small pot of soup was simmering over a healthy fire, Frank had been taken to the outhouse and cleaned up with a rough rag dipped in the water bucket, and Anna had readied a small poultice of moist bread for her mother's sore tooth; *Marie Barbora* had been suffering with it when she left for work at the farm in the early morning.

When the twenty-eight-year-old mother entered the room her jaw was swollen. With each pregnancy her teeth had deteriorated. Already she had had to have two molars painfully yanked from her mouth. She carried three-month-old foster baby, *Jindřich,* slung over her back, and he was whimpering for her breast again. She knew her milk was finally lessening after the birth of two-year-old Frank; the baby always seemed to be hungry. Anna gave her tired and drooping mother the poultice as she lay down on her bed to nurse the child.

Karel, hungry, washed his hands in the bucket quickly and sat down alone as usual for his privileged first portion of soup. Frank cried and pulled at *Marie* for attention. Everyone's stomach was growling at the smell of the soup filling the room. A question that had swirled fitfully around Anna's mind many times suddenly sounded though the crowded space. "Why do you always eat before us, Father? We're all hungry. There's little soup tonight and the bread's almost gone."

Marie Barbora stiffened on the bed as *Karel* put down his spoon and looked with amazement at his daughter. His rage began to build. Who was this child to challenge his place at the head of his own table? He jumped up and grabbed a startled Anna by the arm, throwing her into his chair. "If you're so hungry, *Anička*, eat!" he said ominously, and he began to force hot soup into Anna's mouth with his own large wooden spoon. *Marie* got up from her bed quickly, pleading for her husband to stop as she struggled to hold and nurse the baby. Her husband ignored her and continued to make his daughter swallow the soup spoonful by spoonful. The potatoes Anna had chopped so carefully were hot and burnt her mouth. Soon the girl was sobbing and vomiting. The other children clutched each other in a corner, terrified and crying for their sister.

Mother and children all were weeping when *Karel* finally threw Anna onto her bed and ordered his wife to clean up the mess and serve him fresh soup. With trembling hands *Marie* set *Jindřich* aside and followed the order. Then she and her children huddled together to watch the head of the house eat his fill.

When he was done he pushed his chair back and lit his pipe, motioning the others to proceed. *Marie* divided the few spoons of soup that were left among the other children. She had no stomach to eat a bit of it. Antonia, Mary and Frank stood by the table eating with difficulty, their large eyes darting back and forth from their defeated sister to their father.

Anna did not challenge *Karel* again. Bloody images of Saint Barbara and her father, Dioscorus, floated through her fitful sleep that long, dark night. Her younger sisters Antonia and Mary hugged her tightly.

Two years later, in 1899, Anna had survived her first ten winters, and the century in which she was born was drawing to a close. The Mrkvička's eldest daughter didn't understand how the turn of the nineteenth to the twentieth century was setting off celebrations and dire predictions all around the world, but she was beginning to understand more clearly the impoverished place of her family in the society around her, the only world she knew.

She listened carefully to the yearning for a better life and the talk of America that buzzed even more frequently around the fire at home. Children of her godfather, Joe Valenda, had left Bohemia and crossed the ocean seeking better lives. A son, *Petr*, occasionally wrote back to his father about his farm life in Iowa.

Also, information sessions had passed on to the people of Velký Lunec that other Czechs from nearby villages also had settled on the midland prairies of the United States, and that land there was good to them. The Iowa spoken of was almost in the middle of the brown blob of America that still was associated in Anna's mind with her schoolroom maps.

Even *Marie Barbora* and *Karel* had attended some of the emigration information meetings, swearing their children to secrecy lest the authorities learn of it. Anna didn't understand thoroughly what all the secrecy was about, why she and her Czech neighbors had to plot to try to talk about faraway America.

History at her school was told to her through Austrian loyalty. The good nuns explained to their students about King *Josef* Habsburg II and how he had been so kind to release peasants like their families from serfdom over a hundred years before. They did not tell their young charges, however, about the long struggle of Czech intellectuals throughout the nineteenth century to set up their own Parliament, to have some say over how they were treated as Habsburg subjects. Czech men were not yet allowed to vote, dominated as they were by both an Austrian class system and aggressive Germans who influenced political decisions concerning Bohemia.

As the girl struggled to understand all these adult matters whirling around her, for the very first time she additionally had to cope with the death of someone very dear to her. Her beloved *Babička*, the kindly old woman who always had nurtured her little great-granddaughter with love and kindness, died.

Anna walked with her parents through the chilled autumn woods to *Babička Marie's* hut, her heart tight with sadness as she held hands with her younger sisters, Antonia and Mary, for comfort. Mary was wearing the blue linen dress *Babička* had presented to Anna four years earlier; Anna was clothed in yet another drab hand-me-down from a neighbor.

The eldest sister by now was old and wise enough to assure her younger siblings as they walked behind their parents that no wood spirits lurked behind the trees. Anna's childhood and such fears already had been put aside. The girl was developing a no-nonsense attitude toward the realities of her life, a fatalistic realization that she could do nothing about many events that were much bigger than she was.

At *Babička's* hut a small group of relatives and friends gathered at a night vigil for the dead, a practice which gave ample time to be sure that no breath remained within a body that appeared still in death. Feathers were placed beneath nostrils by next of kin to test that a body had actually breathed its last, but myths abounded about tapping coming from coffins as diggers prepared to close a grave too quickly.

With her family Anna entered the darkness inside the cottage, tears in her eyes. Balanced on the sleeping bench, *Babička's* body lay in a rough wooden box sawed and hammered together by her great nephew. The dank room smelled of the fresh cuts of pine. Silver coins covered the old woman's eyelids, a rite to prevent visitors from seeing their own mortality reflecting from the eyes of the dead.

Anna stood on tiptoes to see over the edge of the box, wincing at the sight of the strange waxen figure. It did not look like *Babička* at all. The great-grandmother's knotted hands finally were folded at rest over her heart as she lay there without her *bábuška* covering her head. *Marie* Mosedič had been laid out in her oldest dress, and ten-year-old Anna accepted readily the reason. *Marie's* great nephew would not want to waste the old woman's one good garment in the grave; it could be bartered or given to someone among the living.

Homemade beer and wine were passed around to the adults as children were shooed outside. Of the younger ones only Anna stayed inside to stand in a corner near *Babička's* coffin. Unnoticed, she pushed herself back out of everyone's way, wanting to disappear as she stood there hugging herself. She wished she could feel the old woman's hands reach up and pat her cheek once again. She longed to stroke *Babička's* long white hair with her carved wooden comb one more time.

Family and friends came out of the darkness all night, from Velký Lunec and beyond, to pay respects to old *Marie* Mosedič–their cousin, their sister, their mother and grandmother, their neighbor. Antonia and sister Mary rejoined Anna to huddle on the floor in the corner as the fire burned to a soft glow through the night. They all watched and dozed periodically, only to be awakened by old women in *bábuškas* wailing at the coffin, awkwardly saying their final good-byes.

When morning finally arrived, food that had been brought by visitors was shared: tough rye bread, goat's milk, *koláče*, gruel. *Milvoj*, the accordion player from a nearby village, appeared with his instrument at the door of the hut. The coins on *Babička's* eyes were removed. Father *Jan* Dostál, who for years had ministered to all the blessings and tragedies in Velký Lunec, arrived to pray as the coffin lid was closed and nailed shut. Anna covered her ears at the hammer's harsh noise and the raspy squeak of steel piercing wood.

Then the priest led the funeral procession through the woods to the cemetery. *Otec* and other men relatives carried the coffin on their shoulders as the accordion played *Babička's* favorite polkas. A straggling line of mourners followed hand in hand, occasionally grimly stepping in time with the music, tears flowing down their cheeks.

The gravediggers had done their work well. A hole in the black ground behind the small local chapel gaped open for a new coffin. After *Babička* and her box were lowered on ropes into place and the parish priest spoke "Dust to dust . . ." a crying *Marie Barbora* motioned for her children to join the others, to pick up bits of dirt to throw down upon the coffin.

Anna's small body shivered as her handful plunked down on the box. Imagining *Babička* alone in the ground that night in the dark was finally more than the little girl could bear. She and her sisters and brother moved into a circle, their arms clutching each other, wailing at the fearsome world. Even the pinnacles of Saint Barbara's Cathedral looking down on them in the distance gave no comfort.

Then suddenly a commotion startled the mourning crowd. A brightly-painted Gypsy wagon had stopped on a lane near the graveyard, and men at the back of the graveside gathering had begun to shout at the dark man and woman sitting behind their broken-down mules. "Go away!" they yelled, lifting their fists. "This old woman had nothing. Respect the dead! Go away!"

Mothers gathered their children close around them and the crowd began to leave the cemetery, again behind *Milvoj* and his accordion. Part of their minds was thinking of the music and *Babička Marie*; part of their minds was thinking of the Gypsies and the countless age-old tales of stolen children and grave robbing associated with them. Surely the dark strangers would not stay to search the grave of impoverished *Marie* Mosedič, they reasoned. A knot of men stayed behind to shovel dirt over *Marie's* coffin and to take turns watching the burial site until the suspicious wagon lumbered out of sight.

Tribes of Gypsies were no strangers to Bohemians. The dark-skinned people, believed to have traveled to Central Europe from Punjab and East Bengal in the 1400s, had wandered through the countryside in their brightly-painted wagons for centuries. They were different looking, different acting strangers surrounded with suspicion and myth.

In fact all strangers were suspect in closely-knit European ethnic cultures. Peasants wandered far and wide throughout Europe in the nineteenth century for many reasons: to flee war, famine, taxes, epidemics, and their crimes. Polish, Hungarian, Russian and Yugoslavian farm workers left their homelands on foot or mule to seek a better life or safety, often passing through centrally-located Bohemia.

Such outsiders seldom were welcomed. They competed with local peasants for what work was available. They were impoverished and had no place to stay or relatives to take them in. Sometimes villagers didn't allow them to use water from local wells. If the strangers happened to find shelter, they might open their door in the morning to find a stake pounded into the ground by the door sill, blocking their way in and out. The message was clear: "You're not welcome here!"

Add to this ethnic distrust swarthy-skinned, meandering tribes of Romany-speaking Gypsies, who claimed no homeland. Myths about their particular behavior grew and were embellished through the centuries.

They were a people who danced and reveled noisily around

campfires. Wearing gaudy jewelry and scarves, they read palms at the edge of the marketplace. They sometimes stole. *Babička* and Anna's elders had told these tales to her all her young life. And of course she had her own encounters with the mysterious people.

The summer Anna was seven her mother had sent her to care for their flock of geese in a public field about a mile from the main road. The girl also was to take along and care for her sister, Antonia, and her little brother, Frank, by then a toddler.

The children did as they were told and stayed in the field with the geese all day and into the afternoon. When young Frank became hungry and started to cry, Anna decided to head for home. It happened to be just the time a rickety Gypsy wagon lumbered over a hill near them. Anna froze, remembering the many stories about the Gypsy bands who reportedly grabbed away both children and livestock. She was terrified as the wagon, driven by a lone old woman with tangled black hair, creaked closer.

The seven-year-old grabbed her brother and sister and ducked down in the weeds and brush, praying alternately to Saint Barbara and the Mother of Jesus that the Gypsy would not see them. When Frank started to whimper as though he was about to cry again, Anna panicked. All she could think was "Stop crying, little baby. Stop!" She quickly put her hands over Frank's mouth and face, gripping tightly to keep him quiet.

The Gypsy wagon rumbled by on its large wooden wheels, its driver apparently not seeing the children. When it disappeared over a hill and Anna finally looked down again, she was aghast to see her hands still over Frank's face, his form gray and lifeless. The two little girls were frantic. They grabbed the boy's hands and legs and flopped him up and down between them, yelling, "Wake up, *Franto*! Wake up! Please wake up!" The little body finally started to gasp for breath.

But when the three scurried from the field and neared compound #36, shooing the waddling, squawking geese along as fast as they could, the wagon again came into view. This time the old Gypsy woman saw them with the geese and stopped, crawled down from her perch and moved toward them. As terrified as Anna was, she knew that she had to protect the flock or feel the wrath of her mother. Circling the geese as best they could, the children sobbed at the woman to leave them alone. Fortunately a neighbor heard their howls, ran from her house and scolded the Gypsy away.

Even in their fright the children had managed to save the geese, and for that *Marie Barbora* was thankful when she heard the tale. Neither Anna nor Mary told their mother about the incident with little Frank. That night two geese disappeared from the village pond, never to be seen again.

Thankfully there was occasional relief for Anna from tending geese and her heavy dose of other daily chores. One night a year, on Old Witch Night, she and the other Mrkvička children were allowed to don brooms and scamper giggling to and from bonfires in neighboring villages.

As almost all children do, Anna and her sisters played with mud pies. And they danced in circles chanting "Ring around the rosy; a pocket full of posies; ashes, ashes; we all fall down." She did not know that the jingle had been passed down generation to generation throughout Europe. Some experts believe that the rhythmic verse was created by children describing gruesome events of the fourteenth century Black Death: fever and rash, mourning, the burning of bodies.

The dances the family occasionally attended at the Kutná Hora Town Hall were festive times. No children were allowed to go in the courtyard with the adults to dance, but Anna listened to bouncing fiddle, accordion or concertina music outside the gate as she peeked in at the beer-drinking and revelry. In the street outside she learned with other children to dance the circle polka. New school friends from other villages joined in the fun.

Shy *Tereza* occasionally showed up, and Anna clutched the girl's good right hand as the two whirled around the cobblestones mimicking their elders.

Somehow Anna managed to attend school quite regularly until her twelfth year, except during eight weeks when the Kutná Hora School was closed due to a scarlet fever epidemic. In 1901, when she was twelve, she dressed in a borrowed white dress to be confirmed in the Roman Catholic Church with the rest of her class. She also was presented with an inexpensive, pale rose-colored rosary, which she hung next to that of her parents on a wooden peg near their clay fireplace.

By this time Anna could read and write Czech and she remained good with numbers. She had been taught well by her mother to clean and cook and manage the Mrkvičkas' modest household. *Marie Barbora* determined that it was time for her eldest daughter to help support her struggling family. The girl was adequately prepared to leave school and begin "working out."

After summer work in the fields Frank would join Antonia and Mary in primary school. Their mother was caring for yet another foster baby, *Anton* Procházka. Money would be needed for school clothing and shoes, of course, and food to get them all through the winter months.

Chapter Three

Working Out

*M*ARIE ARRANGED FOR Anna to begin to work days for a nearby Kopecký household for the equivalent of sixteen American dollars a year; the girl accepted the decision without question. Her peasant friends in school, including her best friend, *Tereza*, were entering their life of work also. All were expected to help their impoverished families.

Of course Anna was nervous starting her first job, but when she walked through the door of the Kopeckýs, into living conditions much more pleasant than she had ever seen, she was pleased and immediately anxious to do well. She had never been inside any households so unlike the dirt-poor rooms of her own family and relatives. A whole new way of living and housekeeping lay before her.

The girl quickly liked the mistress and her three boys, ages one to ten. Young Mrs. Kopecký was kind, but firm with directions, and on her part happy to find a girl worker who was quick to learn tasks new to her and careful to carry them out. She was surprised that a twelve-year-old of such small stature could work so rapidly. Additionally, Anna accepted directions well.

And the girl was pleasant to have around. Her round face held a ready smile that curved slightly to one side. Sometimes her very different eyes twinkled with mischief as she interacted with the boys, giggling right along with them.

The young mother worked side by side with fast-stepping Anna to complete household duties, teaching the girl more refined ways to care for a home and children. The master of the house helped his brothers in their father's family cobbler shop in Kutná Hora. Anna was quick to notice the fine shoes on each Kopecký foot, and to compare them with the shoddy boots in which her family walked. Sometimes she and her sisters had attended school barefoot. For a time one winter they had shared one pair of old boots among the three of them, two taking turns wrapping their feet in gunny sacks.

For the first time Anna Mrkvička spent her days cleaning and cooking in a single, separate house with sleeping rooms, a kitchen and parlor. She delighted walking on wooden floors covered with colorful rag rugs scattered here and there. With the home's many windows, the rooms were bathed with sunshine and color: the reds and brilliant blue of floor coverings, the yellow, orange and green of dried flowers and herbs hanging from kitchen rafters.

The girl especially enjoyed the pleasant aromas in the house. Whiffs of fresh baked breads and cakes filled the air, as well as the scent of herbs like rosemary, mint and chives potted near the east kitchen window. She breathed the smells in deeply as she dusted carved, painted cupboards that held pewter and porcelain dishes instead of wooden ones like those on her family's table. Her rough fingers stroked the smoothness of the plates and platters with pleasure.

A "holy corner" cabinet in a sitting room opposite the entrance to the house held a Czech *Bible* and pictures of Jesus and the Holy Mother Mary painted on glass. A carved wooden cross centered all the family valuables on its own shelf. Anna enjoyed wiping dust carefully from the beautiful things, seeing that they were clean and shiny.

While she still returned to her family's one crowded room at night to sleep, she was able to eat leftovers from meals she and Mrs. Kopecký cooked together, so she ate better and was hungry less. Sometimes she was allowed to take bits of food home to her parents.

Marie Barbora by that time was acting as midwife in her own and nearby villages. Usually her payment for working through long hours at the bed of a woman in labor was a chicken, sausage or cheese for her family's table. Sometimes used clothing was given her for her services, or boots that might fit one of the Mrkvička clan.

Of course when *Maminka* was away from her family's room at night, Anna, as eldest child, took charge of the younger children. Many times the girl worked long hours during the day, only to go home to added responsibilities in her parents' crowded room.

Young Anna soon looked forward to leaving the drab space of her family each morning. She liked going to her work, leaving the colorless room in Building #36 with its grayed mattresses and its hard dirt floor. She daily helped Mrs. Kopecký air out puffy white featherbeds by hanging them out of opened casement windows softened with delicate curtains. She polished the panes of glass regularly, enjoying both their sparkle and the feel of warmth from the sun on her face and arms.

As she completed her duties, Anna watched and played with the children. The sixteen dollars a year she earned for her efforts were paid directly to her mother. While the girl was pleased with her work, during those pleasant months at the Kopeckýs an important life-changing event occurred for her.

One warm summer Monday morning Anna and Mrs. Kopecký deftly dodged around each other in the hot kitchen, completing usual washday duties. They had hauled water from the well, heated it, and then bent over wooden tubs to wash and rinse skirts and aprons, shirts and children's diapers. Anna had walked the fifteen minutes from home to work feeling strange.

She seldom was sick, but this day nagging cramps rippled down her lower spine. Mrs. Kopecký noticed all morning that the girl grimaced and stretched herself up straight from the washtubs to rub her back with her wet knuckles. Before it was time to hang the clothes over a fence in the yard, Anna excused herself to make a quick trip to the outhouse. There she discovered that there was blood on her undergarments. She panicked.

When she didn't return to the kitchen for some time, her mistress walked down the path to call out "Anna? Are you all right, Anna?"

The door of the latrine opened slowly and the frightened girl stepped out, her face flushed with embarrassment. Hurried words of explanation to the older woman tumbled from her. She didn't know what was wrong, what to do.

"It's all right," Mrs. Kopecký said immediately in hushed tones, shy about the subject herself. Anna sensed a fatalistic sadness in the tone of her voice. The woman put her arm around her. "You'll be all right. You've just become a woman."

Walking her back to the kitchen the older woman explained in nearly a whisper that once a month Anna would experience a flow like that today, until the times she became pregnant with her own babies. "You must be very careful with young men now, Anna. You could become with child." The words made the girl more troubled.

A student named *Alena* in Anna's class the previous year suddenly had disappeared from school. Whispers were that she was carrying her father's child. The women in the compound gossiped about it at the communal well, but when Anna came near they immediately became quiet.

The crowded conditions in the Mrkvičkas' room had educated the children coarsely about the behavior of men and women in bed, but the pregnancies which resulted from the parents' sexuality always brought *Marie Barbora* to tears. Anna came to understand that her mother suckled foster babies as long as her breast milk allowed because she believed it would lengthen the time between babies.

The girl felt a heavy load settle on her shoulders as Mrs. Kopecký talked. With new and different eyes she sadly saw more clearly her mother's difficult life. She didn't want to think about being either a wife or mother herself.

Mrs. Kopecký went on to explain to Anna how to fasten folded cloths around her waist, and how to wash her soiled rags in a bucket behind the outhouse and hang them out of sight under bushes to dry. The girl had noticed such pails near her own compound, tucked away in the woods near a stream. Her mother wouldn't answer her questions about them. Whispers with other girls at school had shed little truth on what they were about. Anna felt unclean and ashamed of what had happened to her body, but she didn't know why. The confusion made her angry.

When she returned home that night and after supper whispered to *Marie Barbora* what had happened, her mother turned to look hard into her eldest daughter's eyes, then she began to cry and turned away. Not wanting to make her so sad, Anna never discussed the matter with her mother again, but when she shared her new secret with her two sisters, they were in awe, their eyes wide.

That night Anna prayed long and hard to Saint Barbara and the Virgin Mary about this strange new womanhood that had taken over her body. It had already changed and complicated her life. She didn't like being a woman very much.

And events began to nudge toward change for Anna's family as well. *Karel* Mrkvička's stepbrother and stepsister, the children of Anna's godfather, finally had established themselves in America. The son and his wife were renting a farm in fertile Iowa; the daughter, Anna Zieman, married to a German worker from a neighboring village in Bohemia, was working in the Lower East Side of New York City. A letter from the son announced to Old Joe that he would be able to send money for his father to travel to America and Iowa soon.

About that same time, eighteen months after Anna had gone to work for the Kopeckýs, *Marie Barbora* heard of a new, better-paying job she was eager to obtain for her eldest daughter. It was with the more prosperous land-owning Scavenisk family, and the pay would be an unbelievable $36 a year. When she announced to Anna that she was to go for an interview at the Scavenisks', however, the girl's strong will surfaced once again.

She liked working at the Kopeckýs', and she didn't want to leave that household. She was used to the routine there and the mistress had been kind to her. More money for her labor didn't matter to the girl because her salary was going to her mother anyway. *Marie Barbora* saw to it that her eldest daughter had adequate clothing and shoes to wear to work, but beyond that Anna received nothing of her wages.

The day the thirteen-year-old was supposed to go to the interview for the second position, she told her mother that she would gather wood for her before she went, but she managed to dawdle all afternoon in the forest to complete the task. Never did it take her so long to collect an armload of sticks and fallen branches.

On her way home a passing neighbor informed her that the $36 job with the Scavenisks had been given to someone else that afternoon. Anna knew that the news would upset her mother, and she was right. *Marie Barbora* was furious with her daughter, and for the first time Anna and her mother argued fiercely. Angry words careened around the walls of their one room; a maturing independence spurred the girl on. Anna knew she was valuable to the family, and she wanted her mother to listen to her feelings about changing jobs. She was frustrated that decisions about her life still were being made without her consent.

Finally, weeping and angry, Anna fled down the hall and out of the compound into a field to hide in a wheat stack. Hours passed. As it became dark she heard her mother wandering the edge of the village pond, calling out in a frightened voice "*Aničko! Aničko!*" but the girl felt a twinge of gladness that her mother was worried about her. She huddled deeper into the wheat stack, hugging her knees.

It was October, nearly All Saints' Night, and the chill and dampness of the autumn evening soon began to make Anna shiver; she finally crawled from the stack. Dreading another scene with her mother, she slowly walked toward Building #36. In the dusky shadows she met the village mailman, whom she had known all her young life. He could see the crying girl's distress, and at his urging she poured out her story of the lost job.

Of course the man who delivered the village mail knew everyone in the area, including the Scavenisk woman who was looking for a hired girl. He pitied the sobbing Mrkvička girl and her impoverished family, so he immediately went to speak with Mrs. Scavenisk. He instructed Anna to follow along through the growing darkness.

The girl waited anxiously outside as the postman entered the Scavenisk home and somehow was able to talk the mistress into reconsidering her decision and allowing one more interview for the job in question. When the man returned with the news Anna smoothed her hair and brushed wheat from her dress. She reluctantly was ready to right the error of her ways, to make peace with her weary mother.

The older man nudged her through the door to meet Mrs. Scavenisk. The anxious thirteen-year-old stepped into a house even more handsome than that of the Kopeckýs. Anna glanced around in awe, took a deep breath and talked as fast as she could to convince the woman that she was a good worker and would be the very best hired girl to keep her nice things clean and sparkling.

After asking several questions, and smiling at the young girl's eagerness to please, Mrs. Scavenisk told Anna that the job was hers. Her mother should come to her home without delay to finalize the matter.

Marie Barbora was delighted with the news, when her daughter finally reached home. Over the following days the two gradually recovered from their quarrel in their own ways, gingerly weaving back into the well-worn tapestry of family routines. But Anna had made her point. Her mother realized that after thirteen winters her eldest child was growing away from her influence. She had begun the blood flow of womanhood, and it seemed to have developed in her an even more determined and independent spirit. The mother pondered her strong-willed daughter's future.

In November of 1902 Anna sadly said good-bye to the Kopeckýs and took her capable hands and fast-stepping work ethic to the Scavenisk household. There she was challenged to learn to care for even finer possessions than those of her former mistress.

A well worn story circulated throughout the village about the established household and its land. It was said that generations before, a nobleman's daughter had been saved from drowning by a Scavenisk ancestor. In payment the lord had given the rescuing serf not only his freedom, but also a portion of his large holdings.

By Anna's time the family's home had been handed down for three generations, and had been added to by each family. The sprawling house consisted of a large kitchen with the biggest fireplace Anna had ever seen, a large parlor, and upstairs sleeping rooms under a dormered roof. A small summer kitchen was near the house, a laundry/bathing shed next to it. The villagers of Velký Lunec considered the family very well off.

Floors in the Scavenisk home were of fine wood, but in addition, colorful ceramic tile spread around the kitchen's fireplace. The holy corner in the parlor held a sculpted maple cabinet filled not only with religious items, but also with special *kraslice*, hand-painted Easter eggs. Anna's new mistress, who had moved to Velký Lunec at her marriage, had crafted them.

The eggs, hollow eggshells decorated with wax batik and brilliant scarlet coloring, were so fragile that Anna was not allowed to clean around them. On a shelf below the eggs rested Mr. Scavenisk's finely carved violin and bow. The new hired girl admired the treasures with wonder, but from afar.

Bedrooms upstairs had sturdy carved bedsteads dressed with fine linens, and out of sight beneath them were tucked porcelain chamber pots which Anna was expected to empty each morning. Before she left in the evening she filled pitchers next to ceramic bowls near beds so that the Scavenisks could wash themselves when they rose in the morning. Only after that task could she hang her oversized white maid's apron on a hook in the laundry shed until the next morning.

In the shed near a stove stood a large copper tub for bathing. Anna touched it with envy the first time she saw it. Imagining the feel of warm, clean water all over body, she thought sadly of her own struggle to keep clean using the household bucket in her family's crowded room.

At the Mrkvička compound the well water always felt cold; seldom was there time or energy to heat it. After *Otec* and *Maminka* washed in it, children took their turns in accordance with their ages, unless they decided to go out to fill fresh buckets. Babies had the last turn. There was no privacy.

In the summer as a child Anna had splashed and bathed in the village pond in warm weather, but she was too old to take part in that play any longer. The Scavinisks' copper tub became part of a frequent daydream that included her entire naked body lingering in the comfort of warm water as she luxuriously scrubbed herself from hair to toes.

Anna's new mistress saw that her home was kept spotless, but she also found time to attend *Sokol* meetings at the Town Hall in Kutná Hora. Mrs. Scavenisk explained to Anna that the organization emphasized exercises and sponsored gymnastics for boys and men and spiritual development for women. "*Sokol*" means "falcon" and symbolizes moral and physical fitness.

The girl was amazed to discover that some Czech women not only did not have to work to help support their families, but that they had time to attend social meetings in fine clothes. She had never heard of "exercise" beyond moving her body quickly through the hard work of each day. What a vast difference between the life of Mrs. Scavenisk and her bone-tired mother.

The thirteen-year-old was expected to keep linen and cotton dresses clean and pressed and ready for Mrs. Scavenisk to don for company and the *Sokol* gatherings. The girl spent hours Mondays hauling water from a nearby well and bringing it to a boil in a red hot laundry shed fireplace. Then she stirred clothing in soda crystals with a wooden paddle to help clean them. Her hands, already toughened to household work, even so turned red and rough, their skin cracked.

After washing, heavy linens and clothing were strung over wooden dowels in the shed to dry, and then stroked with a heavy iron heated over glowing coals to remove stubborn wrinkles. Anna learned after a few disasters how not to burn herself or scorch embroidered tablecloths and fancy ruffles on frilly dresses.

She also learned even more about food preparation, so much beyond the simple soups at her mother's hearth and the varieties of foods at the Kopeckýs. The kitchen was the realm of a live-in cook, *Anežka*, who grew vegetables in a nearby garden, stored food for the winter, and prepared all meals for the Scavenisk family of six: the parents, three sons helping to manage land holdings, and a twenty-year-old daughter.

Anežka had devised a moving spit along the hearth of the fireplace with the help of her blacksmith brother. A winding mechanism and a gate weight twirled the spit before the fire to roast pork and beef. Anna had never tasted anything like the meat from that spit; it was delicious. The cook also showed her charge how to fry bacon and sausage "down hearth" by raking hot coals forward from the fire and frying food in lard in an iron skillet with legs.

A collection of pots and pans Anna would polish regularly hung from hooks in the kitchen, and carved cookie molds were stacked near the oven. The cook taught the new hired girl how to prepare rolled egg noodles, special liver-filled *knedlíky* (dumplings), *bábovka* (poppy-seed cake), and varieties of cherry, raspberry and prune *koláče*. A smoke house near the kitchen processed hams. Anna was amazed with the amount and types of food available to this family, as her own sisters and brother often still went to bed hungry.

Saint Mikuláš Day was celebrated in the home in December as Mrs. Scavenisk supervised the laying of greens in the holy corner and the placing of candles in windows. Family members exchanged small gifts. The celebration especially touched young Anna, as Christmas was hardly recognized in her parents' one room.

Then after the New Year the wedding of the Scavenisks' daughter took place. Anna and the cook worked feverishly to prepare for the event, baking and cleaning for weeks beforehand. The thirteen-year-old was excited to be asked to help decorate with boughs and bows the buggy that would transport the bride and groom to and from the Nuptial Mass at Saint James Church in Kutná Hora.

She gasped when she saw the betrothed couple dressed in colorful traditional Bohemian wedding costumes that had been handed down from generation to generation. The bride wore a sky blue skirt and bodice over a white blouse with puff sleeves, and an extravagant apron stitched with silk embroidery and lace; the girl's grandmother and mother before her had worn it. The groom wore long dark blue trousers and a red embroidered waistcoat, also a family heirloom.

After the marriage ceremony a crowd of friends and relatives came to the home of the parents of the bride for food and joyous celebration. Anna watched it all eagerly as her quick steps completed her tasks from kitchen to serving table and back again. Mr. Scavenisk played his violin as couples wearing their bright red and black embroidered finery spun around the parlor. Women wore colorful woven shawls over their heads and shoulders. In a precious moment in the kitchen, the cook, laughing, grabbed Anna's hands and briefly whirled her over the colorful tiles around the fireplace.

In March the Scavenisks celebrated Saint Joseph's Day with a splash of the favorite Czech color, red. Cook *Anežka* colored beer red and baked red bread for a family celebration after mass. The thirteen-year-old viewed the spread of colorful food with excitement, her different eyes admiring her mistress as she wandered the gathering in her red embroidered shawl. At the Scavenisks' Anna observed the possibilities of a wider world than she had ever known. The stark room in which her family lived seemed more crude each time she returned to it, the hard-working struggle of her parents more suffocating. When she excitedly told her mother of the life she saw with her new mistress, thirty-four-year-old *Marie* responded little. Worn down by the daily difficulties of rearing her family, she held out little hope that her own life could ever improve. Anna's youth, however, allowed her to yearn for a better life, to not yet be resigned to her family's impoverished fate.

Chapter Four

The Chosen One

I T WAS TO be within six months of Anna's placement with the Scavenisks that a life-changing event occurred within the Mrkvicka family. Joe Valenda received a money order in an envelope mailed from his son in Iowa. It was Anna who read the Czech words in the accompanying letter to her godfather. The message explained that there was enough enclosed to take the old man by rail and ship to New York City to see his daughter, and then by rail again all the way to Iowa to son *Petr's* rented farm.

After much family discussion about the trip it became obvious that the aging Joe, who could not read or write, who signed "X" for his signature when need be, was very apprehensive about making the long journey across the ocean alone. As his anxieties increased, an unexpected opportunity emerged for his goddaughter, Anna.

Marie and *Karel,* with Joe's eager encouragement, weighed the possibility that their eldest daughter might accompany her godfather to America. Second daughter, Antonia, was by then also working out, and her income would replace some loss of Anna's wages.

Besides, *Anička* was a bright child who usually kept her wits about her. Her mistresses always had praised her work. She could read and write Czech and speak a little German. Hopefully she would be able to guide the pair through the trials of Ellis Island that they had heard so much about, and get the two finally to their destination.

The Mrkvička parents determined to gather somehow the $64 needed to send their daughter along with her godfather. They exchanged letters with the Valenda son and daughter. *Petr* wrote that if Anna came she could help his wife on the farm near Cedar Rapids in Iowa. He told his father and the Mrkvičkas to confirm their Austrian citizenship from their baptism records at the Kutná Hora City Hall. The pair would need proper identification papers all along their trip.

Also, Joe Valenda's daughter, Anna Zieman, wrote that her father and her stepniece, Anna, could stay with her and her husband and son in New York City for a few weeks before they departed for the Midwest. She would meet them at Ellis Island and she would try to help *Anička* find work to help pay for the rest of her trip west.

Marie Barbora hesitantly dared to nurse a glimmer of hope that perhaps her eldest daughter could find a way to help bring the rest of the family to join her in America later, just as Joe's children had done. Perhaps, just perhaps, the Mrkvičkas could change the pattern of their lives.

As Anna anxiously listened to developing plans to send her to Iowa, she struggled alternately with both excitement and gnawing fear. She couldn't imagine what the brown blob on the school map still representing the United States in her mind might hold in store for her. The thought of leaving her parents and her sisters and brother filled her with anxiety.

She had never slept in a bed by herself. She had never been further from her village than to Kutná Hora. She had walked everywhere she went her entire life, other than when she was pulled up occasionally to ride a cart behind oxen during her summer field work. An uncle once had let her ride on the back of his mule from barn to barn. She couldn't imagine what it was like to travel by train and ship all the way to the strange place called "Iowa" in America.

Anna knew that she would miss the pinnacles of Saint Barbara's

Cathedral looking down at her from the nearby bluff, and the familiar sights, smells and sounds of her small village. Nevertheless, the idea of the trip very quickly began to tug at her imagination. She hesitantly began to daydream about going to Iowa with Godfather Valenda; the journey became a mysterious, shadowy adventure dangling before her.

Marie Barbora had to negotiate through much fussing with the Scavenisk woman to have Anna paid off for the half year. Old Joe Valenda wanted to leave Bohemia in the spring of 1903. Even though the girl's mistress was very unhappy to lose such a good worker, and to have her full year's agreement with the Mrkvička mother broken, the money for Anna's work finally was placed in *Marie's* outstretched hand.

The money helped the family to gather coin by coin a sum that would cover the ship fare to transport Anna away from Building #36 in Velký Lunec and across the ocean on a very long trek westward. Hopefully the girl could work in New York City for additional money that might be needed to carry her by train to Iowa.

May 27, 1903, fourteen-year-old Anna was out of her bed before the sun crept through the window of her family's small room. Her quick feet padded to gather a wooden bucket of water from the nearby well so that she could carefully scrub her body and wash her fine, brown hair. Antonia and Mary jumped up to help her plait two braids down her back, tying them with string. Anna watched their reflection as she held a piece of broken mirror, the only one the family owned.

The younger sisters were already mourning this day's good-byes. Eight-year-old Frank sat on the children's bed unhappily watching the early preparations for his sister's leaving. Two-year-old foster child, *Anton* Procházka, toddled around the dirt floor, already grimy from his morning tumbles.

Otec had eaten and left the room to sit on a tree stump outside to smoke his pipe. The mother of the household busied herself with wooden bowls and bread and porridge for her family, sniffling quietly and wiping her eyes with a rag from the hearth.

At thirty-five her shoulders were stooped from carrying on her back through the fields the numerous small children of her household. The weary woman had recently realized that she was pregnant with yet another child to feed. And besides her own children, ten foster babies had already come and gone from her care since Anna's birth.

Her hands and knuckles were scarred and bruised, her teeth deteriorating yearly. Scuffed, run-over boots covered her feet and an old *bábuška* was tied over her hair, which was quickly turning gray. She wore a colorless dress ragged at the sleeves and hem. Similar threadbare family garments hung from nails and pegs around the wall. Three rickety beds now rimmed the small room where seven people slept and ate.

Watching her aging mother tearfully move around the hearth in such surroundings made Anna's heart ache. She knew that her trip to America was taking away much needed resources from all in the household. The girl had hardly slept her last night with her family, all of them crammed into a space smaller by half than Mrs. Scavenisk's kitchen.

Her mind had spun all night with a mixture of sadness and excitement, wonder and fear about the gaping unknown before her. Try as she could she could not grasp the vast distance that soon would separate her from her familiar village.

"Promise you'll send us a letter from America," thirteen-year-old Antonia pleaded as she helped her sister pack a small wooden trunk with a new brown linen suit, an extra pair of black stockings, and her old shoes. *Marie Barbora* somehow had produced two new outfits and good boots for the young traveler, along with a few coins for the trip tied with the girl's pale pink rosary in the faded *bábuška* that had once belonged to *Babička Marie*.

"I promise," Anna said as she slipped into a dress of plain blue and white checked gingham.

"Soon?" Mary, now eleven, murmured, fighting tears.

"Soon," Anna answered as she pulled on her other pair of black stockings and laced new brown high-top boots up her ankles. Her mother fussed with the children to come and eat. They each took their bowls and sat on the beds eating glumly.

It was the last meal for the family together, and Anna felt the simple food stick in her throat. As she looked at the unhappy scene around her she suddenly was overwhelmed with everything unfolding in her life. The fourteen-year-old jumped up quickly to run from the room, out of the building and into a nearby rye field.

Once standing alone in the spring dampness she looked up at Saint Barbara's Cathedral through salty tears. The pinnacles were anchored there as they always had been, but she knew in her heart that she would never see them again. They still would be there when she died as an old woman, wherever in the world that was to be.

Thoughts of her young life crowded together among images of the tall tent spires that reached upward in the early morning sky–memories of the feel of *Babička Marie's* warm and loving hands patting her cheeks, and of the nuns at school smiling at her when she came up with the right answers to their questions. She thought of her Confirmation and the mystery of her first Communion, her embarrassment at her first Confession. She remembered Mrs. Kopecký's kindness in the warmth of her pleasant kitchen and the amazing scarlet Easter eggs gleaming in the Scavenisks' holy corner.

Anna winced at leaving the sound of her sister Antonia's giggles as they lay whispering hand in hand in their bed, Mary's quiet nature and Frank's serious little face. She had been deemed old enough at six by the midwife to hold her younger brother in his swaddling clothes after his birth. She still could hear his mewling noises, feel his tiny wiggling body in her arms and the protective love that rushed over her.

Sounds hummed to her ears–roosters crowing, geese grousing, babies crying, the murmur of voices from the crowded rooms where impoverished farm women prepared meager morning food for their families. In the distance Saint James Church bells pealed softly, announcing seven o'clock. Anna counted every strike as she deeply breathed in familiar smells–the damp May field beneath her feet, the morning smoke from fireplaces, a whiff of dank manure from swine, horses and goats nearby.

Would it smell the same in Iowa? she wondered. What would be the scenes of her life in the middle of the "brown blob" of the United States? She had heard adults often say that streets were paved with gold in America. The only gold she had ever seen was a dainty locket Mrs. Scavenisk wore to *Sokol* meetings. She found herself thinking that it would take a lot of small lockets like that to pave a street.

In Iowa would she tend a house with fine wood floors instead of the dirt ones in Building #36? Would she sleep on featherbeds instead of a straw mattress and have embroidered cases on her pillows? Would she have a copper tub to bathe in? And would she never be hungry again, working the magic with food her mistresses had shown her, eating from her own bountiful table?

Then "*Anička, Anička!*" sounded in the distance from an anxious *Maminka*. Anna knew it was time for her to meet Godfather Valenda and go on her way. They had a train to catch for Prague. It would be her first ride behind the locomotives that traveled the tracks near Kutná Hora, blowing their baleful whistles. The box-like cars would take her a long way through Germany to the ocean where she would board what she remembered from the hand-painted map at her school–a ship with billowing sails floating on inverted v-shaped waves of bright blue.

Anna felt to her bones the weight of the many firsts that lay before her, but she took a deep breath and walked back to bid her family good-bye.

A knot of people had gathered outside the farm compound. Antonia held Anna's small trunk for her, eyes misty. Old Joe Valenda had arrived looking grim. He wore his worn gray cap on his head and a soiled black suit, tight around his bulk. He carried a basket holding his meager belongings. Neighbor women joined the family to bid little Anna Mrkvička farewell. Going to America was a dream for many of them. Each member of the village who found a way to make the long trip west was a celebrity.

There were last-minute hugs and kisses and an extra-long final hug between a weeping *Marie Barbora* and her eldest daughter. The mother's heart was torn with sadness and fear as she sent her first-born girl child away into an unknown world so much bigger than she was. At the last minute she pressed cold boiled potatoes and rye bread wrapped in a cloth into the girl's hands, to ease her hunger along the way. *Karel* stood awkwardly to one side.

Family tears that day swept fourteen-year-old Anna Mrkvička into the greatest undertaking of her life. With the feel of soft green morning around her, she bravely turned her back on her family and friends to leave her Czech homeland in Bohemia forever.

While sadness and uncertainly were laced into that leaving, those courageous steps away steered the young girl from a probable early marriage and continued hard labor at the bottom of the working class in her homeland. Her leaving also wrested her family and her children from what was to befall the war-weary province of Bohemia: German occupation and carnage that were to devastate the Czech people through two horrific World Wars, and eventually a devastating Communist occupation.

PART TWO

THE LONG TREK WEST

Chapter Five

Over Land and Sea

THE LOPSIDED PAIR—a pudgy old man shuffling beside a slight young girl—carried trunk and basket over the path from Velký Lunec to Kutná Hora to catch the train to cosmopolitan Prague. Everything that would happen from that point forward in Anna's life was to be new and strange to her.

A conductor in a dark blue uniform gripped the girl's hand as she climbed up high steps to board a creaking wooden coach car. Inside she and Joe Valenda bumped their way down a narrow aisle with their awkward baggage, settled themselves on uncomfortable benches among other anxious travelers.

As a warning whistle blew and steam puffed from the engine, the train slowly jerked away from the morning fingers of shadow stretching from the spires of Saint Barbara's Cathedral. The ancient pinnacles cast their images toward the vanishing cars as they rumbled away, as if to try to hold on to its departing people. A steady stream of men, women and children was leaving the centuries-old spiritual anchor behind.

Anna quickly found herself rocking side to side with the sway of the moving train. Her ears filled for the first time with the noisy clickity-clack of metal wheels as she clattered over shiny rails. The engine chanted "ta chugga, ta chugga," soot belching from its stack to filter back through windows opened to May warmth. Anna looked down with a frown to see black specks dotting her new blue gingham dress.

A uniformed conductor came through within minutes to collect tickets, which Anna and Joe were clutching tightly in their sweaty hands. Soon the fourteen-year-old settled down to survey the strangers swaying with her in the car—families, lone passengers, a few appearing to be just her age. Her attention then turned to scenery moving by the windows. She eagerly examined the hamlets and villages at which the train often stopped to pick up and deposit passengers. She listened as the conductor announced the names of each station. Her eyes and ears absorbed it all.

The view also revealed fields filled with farm workers whose backs were bent in the morning sun to seed and work the land. Some of them stopped to look at the train passing by; small children carrying water to workers put down their buckets to wave at passengers with both hands, just as Anna had when she fulfilled such duty near her working parents. Anna Barbara waved back, grinning her slanted smile.

In a couple of hours the villages seemed to blend together as cottages and houses beside the tracks began to form the crowded pattern of a large city. "*Praha* (Prague)" murmured through the car. It seemed to Anna that the packed collection of buildings went on for miles and miles.

She was excited to be entering the magnificent capital the good nuns had so often referred to in her classes. She remembered the first time she'd seen the dot on the wall map marked "*Praha*" in big letters. That dot certainly didn't reveal the sprawling largeness of the city or the coal smoke billowing from factories crowded near the railroad tracks.

When the train slowed, Anna sometimes could look from her seat directly through opened windows to the activities inside noisy buildings. She saw dark-clothed workers the age of her uncles and father scurrying among rapidly-moving, clanking machines, or hauling goods in wheelbarrows. What were those giant machines doing, making? she wondered.

Finally entering Prague's railroad yards, the moving cars often stopped to switch back and forth or to wait for numbers of other trains to pass. Through the open windows more soot drifted. Noise and odors of the city engulfed Anna and the other travelers–the bang of steel on steel, the hiss of brakes, the smell of big city grime and smoke.

At last Anna and Joe were carried to their train's slot in the central rail station in one of Europe's largest cosmopolitan centers. Their engine pulled its cars in line next to long rows of other trains. More knowledgeable travelers already were on their feet collecting their belongings when the train jolted to a halt. They fought to keep their balance as cars clanked together.

Once on the platform Anna did her nervous best to read signs for direction, anxiously shuffling along with her small trunk into the station among the largest crowd she had ever seen. Joe Valenda tried to keep up with her fast-moving feet. The girl often stopped to ask men in uniform for directions.

After lining up before a ticket window to check the schedule for the next train to Bremen, Germany, she learned that she and her godfather had a few hours before they departed. They had time to investigate the area around the station. Joe Valenda, stressed and frustrated in constantly changing situations completely foreign to him, grumpily peppered the fourteen-year-old with his concerns.

What the two did manage to see of Prague astounded young Anna. Hungry by now, the two found a place near the station to sit and munch the cold potatoes and tough bread *Marie Barbora* had sent along from her kitchen hearth. They sat eating and staring at colorful ceramic tile on streets and lanes, sophisticated people in fancy clothes and boots meandering through markets, businessmen hurrying by. The wealthy in fine suits and dresses wove among Czechs wearing colorful embroidered costumes indicative of various regions of the countryside. Among them all walked common farmers in soiled, baggy pants.

Foreign-looking people moved here and there–Jews in their black suits, hair braided; men and women dressed differently, from countries Anna knew little about: Poland, Hungary and Russia. Fresh food aplenty was rowed nearby on wagons and blankets, waiting for anyone with money to buy it. That alone amazed the fourteen-year-old as she swallowed bites of cold boiled potato.

She periodically and quickly walked back to check the time on the big overhead station clock; the girl was learning enough about traveling to be careful not to miss her next train. Godfather Joe, very uneasy to be for the first time in his life in a big city, reluctantly had to rely on a wisp of a girl to see him safely through his venture.

The travelers could not tarry long in Prague. They soon stepped aboard a second train that would carry them northwest more than three hundred miles through Germany to Bremen, a major North Sea port at the mouth of the Weser River. Once again the two were on a swaying train, travelers boarding and leaving their car.

Very quickly there were more German travelers joining them. Anna's limited German vocabulary put her at a disadvantage, but she could understand enough to respond correctly as stern men in uniforms came aboard all cars at the border between Germany and Czechoslovakia to review each passenger's national identity papers.

Soon the girl's stomach began to contract again with hunger. The cold potatoes had not been filling. After much discussion, she and her godfather decided that Anna should take a few of their precious coins and follow passengers at the next hurried station stop to purchase food. Godfather Valenda would stay behind to guard their belongings and their seats.

At the next stop the fourteen-year-old followed others from the train and watched what more experienced travelers were doing inside the station. She ended up wrangling with confusion to change Czech coins to strange German money. She felt unsure of the fairness of the transaction, but she carried back to Joe dark bread and cold boiled eggs purchased from a busy counter. It was all her new money would buy. The two downed the food quickly.

As the train moved on, closely packed passengers restlessly milled through the car. They often stood one behind another for a foul-tasting drink of water, or to use the smelly latrine. Once in such a line Anna and a young German girl behind her haltingly had a brief conversation, with much help from gestures. The girl's name was *Hilde*, and she was dressed in a dark blue suit and hat; Anna had immediately noticed the fine brown leather boots on her feet when she boarded the car. Her experience in the home of cobbler Kopecký would forever make her take notice of fine footwear.

Hilde explained to Anna as best she could that she was traveling by herself to America. Her uncle, who worked in the steel mills in the state of Pennsylvania, had sent her a second-class ticket on an ocean liner so that she could join his family. He hadn't wanted his dead sister's only daughter to cross the ocean alone in steerage, as he had years before.

It was the first Anna truly realized that she was to travel in a place on the ship separated from other passengers like *Hilde*. She had been admonished by her parents that she only had the money to purchase the least expensive ship ticket in third class, the area called "steerage." The young traveler returned to her seat puzzled as to what her coming trip across the ocean would be like. Already the lurching of the train was making her woozy. She had heard frightening stories about seasickness on the roll of the high seas. It was confusing to her, as the v-shaped waves on the schoolroom map didn't look to be high and dangerous at all.

The long train trip had become tiring by late afternoon, with its numerous stops and starts at places whose names Anna couldn't pronounce: Leipzig, Braunschweig, Hannover. Morning fascination faded into evening weariness.

As the day darkened, cool night breezes blew through the opened windows of the train. Strong men wrestled to try to close them, banging some shut; other windows were stuck and would not move, even though the men struggling with them cursed with exasperation. Anna didn't know German swear words, but she knew instinctively when such words were spoken in anger, no matter the language.

Conductors lit dim kerosene lamps that swung from the ceiling. Their flicker cast eerie light and moving shadows on the tired people below. The smells of lamp oil and unwashed bodies complicated the sick feeling in Anna's stomach. Already her gingham dress was wrinkled. The fourteen-year-old wiped her face and hands as best she could in a bucket in the latrine before settling down for the night, drying fingers and cheeks on her underskirt rather than the filthy towel provided.

Back at her seat by Joe Valenda, she plucked her brown suit jacket from her trunk and draped it over her like a blanket, scrunching down on the angles of the hard wooden seat to try to find a position comfortable enough to get some rest. It didn't work very well. It was not the straw mattress she was used to sleeping upon with her sisters Mary and Antonia, in the bed now miles behind her.

The girl and most travelers woke fitfully throughout the night as babies cried and mothers hushed and nursed them. One boy, looking to be about eight, Frank's age, had fits of dashing up and down the aisle, crashing into the shoulders and elbows of exhausted adults. Finally his sleepy father grabbed and slapped him soundly, waking everybody. The boy whimpered himself to sleep with his head on his worn-out mother's lap. Anna watched him awhile with drowsy eyes. She missed her little brother.

The squeaky wooden cars vibrated their way through German cities bustling with the work of the industrial revolution, even at night. Anna glimpsed for the first time the glow of electricity shining from factory windows. She saw rows of buildings fogging the sky with murky clouds of smoke, tightly packed workers' dwellings clustered nearby.

Once the next day dawned, she saw chicken coops crammed into tiny fenced-in yards and guard dogs barking at the train. The May soil of small garden plots already was turned. She was fascinated at the methods women found to dry their clothes in such crowded space. Some houses had poles like T's behind them, rope strung back and forth. There were none such T's in Velký Lunec.

Between villages more miles of country fields were alive with springtime planting. Anna's different young eyes, now tired from lack of rest, soon were looking through tears at scenes of countless peasant women like her mother, *bábuškas* on their heads, bent over their work in the dark fields. They often had babies slung over their backs, just as *Marie Barbora* usually did. She tried to imagine what her family was doing back in Building #36 her second morning away from them. She wondered if they missed her. Their lives seemed a world away already.

Anna and her grandfather at long last stepped from the train in the large port of Bremen on the Weser River. For the first time in their lives the smell of the ocean blew over them, even though the harbor was still miles from the open sea. After many inquiries within a sprawling station, and confusion with the language, the two made their way to the correct pier. Cawing sea gulls swooped overhead. In a crowded waiting room travelers of all sorts milled about or staked out a place for their families and belongings on one of the rows of long wooden benches. Anna made her way to a ticket window, bumped and jostled by people much larger than she was.

There she discovered with disappointment that they had missed the most recent ship to New York City. She also discovered that she and her godfather had hurdles to overcome as European emigrants before they would even be allowed to take the next ship to America, due in three days. The ticket master directed them to the Emigration Center. At Bremen they already needed special preparation to enter the United States, still thousands of ocean miles away.

In 1882 and 1890 the United States Congress passed laws to establish an Immigration Service and restrictive new regulations to govern foreigners entering the country. Before those years immigrants who survived the trip across the oceans to America were absorbed into the U.S. population with few questions asked.

The numbers coming to America grew so rapidly during the nineteenth century, however, that fear also grew about the "undesirables" pouring across U.S. borders. Pressure was put on Washington's Congress to tighten immigration policies. After 1890, laws attempted to make sure that foreigners entering the United States were sound of mind and body, and that they would not be a social burden to the country. Even in Bremen, Germany, Anna Mrkvička and Joe Valenda had to begin to prove to authorities that they were fit to leave Europe and enter America.

At the same time immigration was being questioned by so many in the U.S., the industrial revolution in the country had built a need for more workers than its population could provide. Car-maker Henry Ford's approach was typical of the times: pay workers a wage that would make them consumers of the products they helped manufacture. To keep capitalism on its upswing during the late nineteenth and early twentieth centuries, increased numbers of both workers and consumers were needed. So while immigration laws had become more restrictive by the time young Anna made her way west to America, the goal was to let healthy people like her continue to come into the country if at all possible, to work and to become consumers.

By 1903 processing centers like that at Bremen had been set up at European ports of embarkation to vaccinate and screen emigrants before they boarded ships bound for America. Transports carried goods below deck in steerage east from the States to Europe; often that same steerage area was adjusted to carry human cargo like Anna when it returned westward to the U.S.

With the tightening of America's immigration laws, shippers were required to carry back to their homeland from Ellis Island without charge anyone who was not accepted for entrance to America. People often spent every penny they had to get to the United States; if they did not pass entrance examinations once there, and were deported, U.S. authorities didn't want to have them stranded with no way to go back home. Foreign shippers cooperated with the U.S. Immigration Service to try to screen out questionable candidates before they boarded ships bound for the new world.

Anna and Joe Valenda entered this processing system when they arrived on the docks at Bremen. They would have to move through lines of people before they could board a ship. The two struggled with the language to answer all the questions asked of them at their initial meeting with Emigration officials. Anna fumbled with her limited German until the clerk yelled out "*česky?*" generally to other workers throughout the room. A man who understood the Czech language came over to make necessary inquiries of the two.

"Name? Age?" he asked, jotting answers in English onto manifest papers which would travel with all emigrants on their ships. The documents had to be completed by attendants with knowledge of the English of America, as U.S. Ellis Island Immigration officials would review them after the trip.

"Papers?" he asked, at which the two dug out their proof of Austrian citizenship, their documents from the Town Hall in Kutná Hora.

"Why are you going to America?"

Anna said she was going to live on a farm in the state of Iowa, and she explained her relationship to her companion traveler, her godfather. Joe dug from his pocket the names and addresses of his sons and daughter in the United States, written carefully by them and sent along in letters. The clerk wrote down all the information given him.

Then a man in uniform explained that Anna and Joe would have to have shots for typhoid before they would be allowed on a ship. They would be stuck in their arms with a needle, but it would be over quickly. He waved them toward yet another group of nervous people.

Once the two moved along the line of those being immunized, Joe Valenda began to balk and grumble. With each step they took forward he became more reluctant and agitated. The old man's eyes bulged as a young man ahead of them fainted the moment he saw the inoculation needle. Nurses and attendants knelt on the floor to revive him.

Anna looked on as a girl a bit older than she scrunched her eyes up tight as the needle pierced her arm. The fourteen-year-old steeled herself, trying to control the knot in her stomach. Neither Anna Mrkvička nor Joe Valenda had ever been treated by a doctor.

When Joe's goddaughter finally stepped up to the nurse, she took a deep breath and gritted her teeth as the pain of the needle plunged into her upper arm. Then it was over and she opened her eyes with relief, rolling down her gingham sleeve. She felt proud of herself that she hadn't cried out, or worse, fainted. Joe Valenda, right behind her, was breathing hard by this time and shaking his head with finality.

"No needle!" he said emphatically, his jaw set. He wouldn't move to the spot where Anna had received her shot, even though a nurse motioned him to step forward.

Anna tried to explain to him that it wasn't so bad; she lifted her sleeve to show him the tiny bit of blood from the prick in her arm, shrugging. "See?" she encouraged.

"No needle!" he repeated, not moving. The annoyed attending nurse hurried the man and girl into a separate room to see a young doctor, at which point Joe declared once again, "No needle!" shaking his head even more vigorously. The young doctor yelled "česky" to yet another doctor for assistance, one more near Joe's age.

The older doctor tried to reason with Joe in his native Czech language, to explain that the shots were necessary to avoid becoming seriously ill with typhoid on the closely packed conditions of the ship, but old Valenda remained adamant. "No needle!"

Anna's heart nearly stopped. What was she to do if this meant they could not go on to America? She watched the exchange between doctor and her godfather anxiously. Finally, with exasperation, the doctor gave up. If the Bohemian didn't care about his health, so be it. He took Joe's papers and scribbled something on them, waving the old man away with irritation. He would not require Joe Valenda to take the shot. The two travelers moved quickly on with relief as those on the medical team shook their heads and grumbled among themselves in German, "*česky*" peppering their words.

For three nights Anna and Joe slept on wooden benches at Bremen, crowded in the Center among testy travelers protective of their sundry possessions. Those who could not find space on a bench slept on the floor. Families huddled in piles scattered around the area. Anna tried to keep her feet propped up on her small trunk even as she slept, dozing off spasmodically, one eye on watch. Many of the people around her were filthy and ragged, and she maneuvered not to settle near them.

The majority of children wore hand-me-downs too large or small for their bodies. Buttons were missing from jackets with cuffs and hemlines frayed. Men wore an assortment of hats and caps even as they dozed.

During the delay the fourteen-year-old watched as some of the dirtiest waiting passengers were taken to be deloused. Anna was thankful that even in her wrinkled dress she didn't arouse suspicion of having lice on her body. She and her mother had battled bug infestations many times in their one-room living quarters—bedbugs, lice, fleas. At times each household in the compound had had to burn its straw mattresses, scrub clothes with harsh lye soap, roughly shampoo every itchy head.

At the Emigration Center, disinfectant baths and physicals were demanded of those who looked ill or especially dirty. A little girl with a wool hat over her head was forced by a nurse to remove it, showing her hair thin and bald in spots, her scalp covered with scabies. The bawling child was shuttled to a doctor behind a closed door, her angry, argumentative parents trailing along behind.

Joe Valenda remained apprehensive and combative when questions about his health history were asked of him. Anna struggled with her limited German, trying desperately to keep her godfather informed as to what was going on.

The two finally were waved on their way to the ticket center as at last the emigration screening ended. Once at the proper window Anna was allowed to purchase tickets to New York City in America on the

S. S. Kronprinz Wilhelm of the North German Lloyd line. She and Joe Valenda then were able to walk the piers freely, to watch amazing things taking place before them. Everything they saw was unknown to the two simple farming peasants familiar only with beet fields, rye stacks, sheep and goats.

Anna noted immediately that the broad gray river bay didn't look at all like the blue sea on the nuns' school map. Dirty port water lapped at the shoreline and the smelly and rotting wooden pier posts as gulls squawked overhead.

The girl was amused by the birds pecking around her feet and searching for dropped food. She and Joe both fed gulls a few pieces from their own precious purchased food. They were introduced for the first time to sandwiches sold from small carts–hunks of salty ham between thick slices of rye bread and slathered with horseradish mustard. With them they drank cheap German beer and ale, smacking their lips.

And their eyes were wide with the sights of the huge ships docking and their busy loading and unloading of large cartons of goods. Never had either of them imagined the size of the cargo ships they saw that day. Anna could not read many of the foreign names painted on their sides; they had come from all over the world.

The port was noisy with the screech of water birds, the blast of ships' horns, the toots of tugs busily nudging large steamers to their berths. It smelled alternately of smoke, grain dust and whiffs of fish and salt breeze.

On their third full day in Bremen the Kronprinz hove into view. The two travelers joined others who had moved into position with their baggage hours ahead of time to watch it dock. Anna and Joe stood gawking at its overwhelming size. The ship had four smokestacks, weighed over 4700 tons, and was nearly 450 feet long and fifty feet wide. It was equipped to carry about 120 first class passengers, eighty second-class passengers, and a thousand third-class steerage passengers like Anna and Joe.

The Lloyd Line ticket master spoke several languages sufficiently. He had told Anna in Czech when he sold her tickets that she would sail on a first-class ship that had been commissioned in 1901, only two years earlier. The Kronprinz even had won the Blue Riband on its westbound route the previous September. At 23.09 knots it had crossed the Atlantic "in five days, eleven hours and fifty-seven minutes," the ticket seller was careful to point out. He enjoyed bragging about it to his customers, telling them proudly that they would enjoy a fast trip to America on one of the most modern ships in any fleet. There even was running water and electricity on board. At that news Anna's eyes grew wide with disbelief.

As she and her godfather watched the Kronprinz dock, numbers of crewmen on the pier twirled hefty ropes from the ship around steel bolts as its huge anchor dropped to splash like a heavy boulder into the water. The girl wished she could share all that she saw with her sisters Antonia and Mary, little Frank, and her friend *Tereza*.

She already had learned much from her train trip across Germany, and she had managed to weave through the stringent emigration rules at Bremen. Her young eyes had been opened to a multitude of people different from those her parents ever saw in the small farm village near Saint Barbara's Cathedral. She especially missed telling her adventure to *Maminka*.

Not only had Anna taken her first train ride, she was about to embark on a nearly four-thousand-mile journey with hundreds of strangers through seven time changes, and sail over what would seem to be an endless body of frightening water. It was a far cry from the one-room home of the girl in the quiet fields of Bohemia. Her coming experience on the Kronprinz was to show the fourteen-year-old yet more lessons about the workings of a broader society and where she was placed within it.

All day and into the night the Kronprinz unloaded and loaded goods and supplies. The next morning attendants yelled out orders in several languages at numerous waiting rooms to those ready to board. After another restless night camped among the benches of the Center, Anna changed in a latrine to her good brown linen suit. She was, after all, boarding a ship to sail over the broad Atlantic Ocean, a grand, fast ship with running water and electricity.

She soon learned that even in her new suit she would not be among the first welcomed aboard the Kronprinz. Third class travelers were herded to a roped-off area set aside on the docks. From there they waited and watched first class passengers climb gangplanks upward to their accommodations in staterooms on the higher decks of the large ship. Anna wiggled to a point where she could see the entourage walk by.

World wise men wore vests and suits, sported trimmed mustaches, and had bowlers on their heads. The fourteen-year-old took notice that their shoes were polished as shiny as mirrors. Corseted women swished by in long skirts and stylish hats that sported quivering, rainbow-colored ostrich plumes.

A little girl minced by clutching her mother's hand. She was encased in numerous ruffled petticoats and a stylish bonnet, and she carried a doll wearing a dress matching her own. Anna had never seen such a doll, so unlike the carved wooden one *Babička Marie* had whittled, which she and her little sisters all had cuddled in their bed. Theirs had been wrapped in a frayed rag. This precious doll not only had a beautiful dress, it had pink cheeks and lips, and big brown eyes painted on its china face. Dark curls peeked from under a bonnet identical to that of its owner. Behind each first-class family, porters walked respectfully carrying fancy, brass-trimmed luggage.

After stateroom travelers were safely aboard, second-class passengers were allowed to enter the ship. Anna saw that they carried their own bags and trunks and were not so grandly dressed, their boots not quite so stylish or shining. She looked for *Hilde*, but did not see her among the people trudging by.

Steerage passengers groused and complained around the girl as they not-so-patiently awaited their turn to board. It seemed to take forever, but finally Anna and Joe heard an order in German to go aboard. They and the third-class mob inched forward so that they could enter a lower opening into the bowels of the Kronprinz.

The slight girl gripped her trunk tightly as men and women, their heads and shoulders well above her own, shoved and pushed to get ahead of her. They carried at their sides or over their heads their collection of baggage: canvas bags tied with rope, flour barrels stuffed with clothing, worn luggage fastened with old belts, boxes and baskets of all sizes.

Godfather Joe was agitated, muttering swear words in Czech at anyone within earshot. He did his best to keep near his goddaughter in the swarm of people, his girth not allowing him to dodge in and out of the openings little Anna managed more easily. Neither of the two peasants from Velký Lunec knew why people were hurrying, but once inside the ship they discovered a frantic free-for-all as families were separated to stake out bunks in their prescribed areas.

Men and older boys were steered to large sleeping areas on one side of a central hallway in the lowest passenger level of the ship; Anna was directed to enter the other side—large rooms designated for women, girls and small children. The air in the packed spaces was foul already; small portholes high above bunks were filthy and tightly closed. The few electric lights overhead, which the ticket master had bragged about so much, were dim at best. Anna would find that their brightness fluctuated with the speed of the ship's steam engines throughout the trip. The lights were anchored beneath a ceiling among a tangled mass of pipes of various sizes that snaked every direction.

The fourteen-year-old mimicked what she saw around her and moved in the rush of people as fast as she could to find an empty bunk in the first room she entered. An older Dutch woman, identifying herself as a "Netherlander," noticed the anxiety in the eyes of the lone girl. She motioned toward the empty upper bunk above her own lower space where she had settled with her year-old son. Anna was relieved to claim it. The woman kindly helped Anna lift her small trunk upward.

The two maneuvered it over the wooden rim of the upper bed, meant to keep people from falling out. Finally the trunk perched next to the one soiled wool blanket rationed to each sleeper, a cover which obviously had kept countless travelers warm already. Anna climbed upward on wood rungs at the end of the bunk, testing her new experience in a bed so far above the floor.

Once she was sitting cross-legged on her upper bunk, Anna surveyed the women scurrying around below her to find a nest for their daughters, sisters, mothers and babies. Old women in black shuffled down aisles as they could, confused as to what to do, where to light. Whiffs of garlic and body odors trailed behind them. A pregnant woman nearby tried to settle two toddlers in the berth above the place she had claimed for herself to sleep. The fussing mother reminded Anna of *Maminka* trying to manage her and her brother and sisters in their crowded space at home.

The girl also noticed many women snatching blankets from unclaimed bunks to make their own beds more comfortable. The fourteen-year-old determined that she would carry her blanket with her wherever she went, so as not to have it come up missing.

All bunks were claimed quickly and there remained an overflow crowd of upset, nearly weeping women. In German a steward yelled through the crowd to search another room further down the central hall for more beds. Those who understood his comment rushed anxiously out toward other possibilities, children in tow. Those who hadn't understood followed the moving mass anyway. Many found all sleeping spaces filled, and were destined to camp on deck the entire trip.

Struggling to communicate with the motherly Dutch woman, Anna made arrangements to trade watching each other's possessions while the other left the area. The woman's pink cheeks and her friendly manner with the trunk made the girl feel immediately that she could trust her. Her little boy, *Jan*, smiled at Anna, then shyly nuzzled his mother's neck. His face looked flushed; he coughed spasmodically.

Then, already becoming a wiser traveler, the fourteen-year-old realized that wearing her good suit would only soil it in these surroundings. She quickly changed back into her gingham dress and tucked the linen jacket and skirt carefully into her trunk for safekeeping. As she did so her eyes fell on *Babička Marie's bábuška*. She unfolded it carefully. Inside it lay her pale pink rosary.

The holy beads reminded the girl of Saint Barbara's Cathedral and the comforting shadow of its pinnacles stretching toward Velký Lunec. For a few moments she fingered the crucifix murmuring the Hail Mary of her school days. She repeated each family member's name, asking the Holy Mother to look over them all. And she pleaded that her family not forget her, even though she was miles and miles away among strangers on a very big and confusing S.S. Kronprinz Wilhelm.

Anna then climbed down from her bunk to investigate the third class quarters in which she would sail across the vast Atlantic Ocean. She discovered a limited space set aside for luggage in her sleeping area. Most women kept their things under or near their bunks so they could guard them, however, making aisles cluttered and dangerous to navigate in the dim light.

Putting her blanket over her shoulder, the girl then left the sleeping quarters to enter a maze of busy hallways. As she did so, she tried her best to remember twists and turns of the passageways, so that she could guide herself back to her bunk again. She walked by several large rooms filled with row upon row of packed, identical bunks.

The fourteen-year-old saw signs in German with arrows pointing toward "Deck" and "Dining Hall"; then she turned into a smelly and dirty women's latrine. Already urine puddled across its floor into a sticky drain. A frazzled broom for sweeping the mess stood nearby. Women in *bábuškas* were rapidly tucking the meager supply of slick squares of toilet paper into their pockets to hide it under mattresses for their families.

Anna walked on tiptoe to use the facility, but determined that she would do so as seldom as possible. Even so she tucked a handful of toilet tissue into her bodice for her own future needs. She was learning.

There was a grimy row of metal sinks on one wall of the latrine. The running water heralded by the ticket master was but a trickle of murky liquid from worn faucets. It splattered and rattled against the metal, but the process of having water so readily available on a ship intrigued the peasant girl. Anna turned a faucet handle off and on several times to watch it work, washing her hands and smiling her slanted smile. It was much nicer than having to pump and fetch water from a well. After examining the already-soiled towels for drying hands, hooked to the wall, she opted to walk out of the area tapping her wet fingers on the wool blanket drooping from her shoulder.

Further down the central hall the dimly lit third-class dining room was empty of people, a rope strung across its doorway. Two obviously hungry children stood gripping the rope with tiny fingers as they pondered the area. Odors from the next meal told hungry Anna she could anticipate potatoes of some kind. Her stomach clenched because it was, as usual, empty. She hadn't wanted to exchange her Czech money for more German coins that morning, and she and Joe only had enough to purchase hunks of stale bread before boarding the Kronprinz.

She asked a nearby woman stacking bowls on a table in the dining hall when the midday meal would be served. The worker's surly German mumblings discouraged the girl from asking more. The children, pouting, turned away. Before moving on, Anna noted with some apprehension that the row upon row of crowded wooden tables had rims around their edges to accommodate the rolling seas she had been warned about.

Soon Anna noticed that people in the hallway were walking toward steps leading upward and she felt fresh air coming from above. She quickly blended into the moving crowd and followed it up a stairway to the open steerage deck.

Once there the girl breathed deeply as seagulls cawed and swooped overhead. The sky was a beautiful blue daubed with drifting snow-white clouds. A cool breeze from the water caused Anna to unfurl her blanket to put it around her shoulders and body for warmth, as many of the men and women already on deck had done. The limited space was crowded with those who had fled the packed, stuffy quarters below as quickly as possible.

Wandering among the mass of people and listening to the many different languages being spoken around her, Anna was relieved to hear Czech words coming from a group near a hanging lifeboat. She spoke to a boy about her age who said he was from Slovakia, which she knew was south of her home in Bohemia. A few of his words she did not recognize, but the two managed to talk about the birds scurrying around them and when food might be served. The boy said he was traveling with his parents and two sisters, and was headed for Milwaukee, "up above Chicago," to work with his father in the breweries.

Then Anna spied Godfather Joe seated directly on the deck by a large airshaft. Next to him an old woman slumped, weary and forlorn. The fourteen-year-old wondered how this elderly *babička* would fare on a trip across the ocean to America. No family seemed to be nearby to care for her.

Here and there on the steerage deck, baggage too large to be stored with owners in their sleeping space was stacked in piles. Someone had tied ropes around the mound of assorted luggage to keep pieces from sliding dangerously when the ship was moving. People whose baggage was among the piles stood or sat close by to protect their belongings. They would sleep there, too.

When the girl studied the rows of lifeboats hung from ropes near outer railings, her heart shivered. She didn't want to think of bobbing about in the ocean huddled in one. She wondered how all the people on the Kronprinz could squeeze into the number in her view; there were so many more people than boats.

The steerage deck was filled to its capacity and buzzing with conversations when everyone was startled by the blast of the ship's horn announcing that the hour had arrived for the Kronprinz to sail. Almost immediately Anna and Joe felt the vibration of the ship's screws through the soles of their feet. The huge ship, with the help of tugs guiding its way, eased away from Bremen docks toward America. A few people cheered. Most looked as anxious as the teenager and her godfather. Anna felt a cramping sadness as the old grandmother next to Joe Valenda put her head in her hands and wept.

Once under way, its deep horn blasting, the ship moved around large anchored cargo ships, oil tankers and other passenger liners. The Kronprinz steamed quickly to escape the Weser River as Anna and Joe worked through a directed and brief lifeboat drill, which only managed to remind the two farmers of their fears about surviving the trip.

They then joined the crowd to lean over the side railings, peering with curiosity at the wake the big ship cut in the gray-green water. Salt mist wet their cheeks. Watching the waves splash and ride away, Anna finally grasped why someone had made waves look like inverted V's on Sister *Marie Helena's* classroom map. She smiled at her new understanding of the world.

Everyone soon was dealing with the rocking of the moving ship and the time schedules they were to follow during the trip. Third class passengers learned that there were appropriate shifts and lines in the dining room; nonetheless, many ate their soup and bread standing up. Their first meal, and one varied little thereafter, was potato soup and hard biscuits, tiny grayish rounds of baked dough that were so tasteless they often were fed to gulls on deck or fish in the sea. Passengers began to cope with lines to relieve themselves in the filthy toilets plus lines to climb up and down stairs to the open deck.

Lights were dimmed at ten o'clock, when everyone was expected to be in bed. Anna spent her first night in the strange upper bunk in her gingham dress, only her boots removed and placed at the foot of her mattress. The remaining nights, however, after listening to screeching about shoes stolen in the dark, she slept with her boots clutched to her chest. Steerage passengers went to bed in their clothes because there was no privacy to change, no place to hang garments. Most of the women were embarrassed about their shabby, soiled underclothes anyway, if they owned any at all. They had put their money and energies into their visible clothing, if they even could do that.

Anna at least owned a petticoat. An aunt had cut and stitched one for her niece from discarded garments. The front and back were of different material, different color, and different weight. It caused the underskirt to bunch up at the seams when the girl walked, but she at least had a petticoat to wear beneath her blue gingham dress.

The fourteen-year-old awakened throughout the night to stare at the flicker of the electric lights around her, so different from the nighttime burning coals in her parents' room in Velký Lunec. She listened to the rush of liquids that surged in spasms through the tangle of pipes overhead.

Little *Jan* in the bunk below coughed off and on. His mother tried to hush him, cuddling him within her arms. Other babies cried, as did some women. Mothers talked into the night with their children, their grandmothers and one another; some voices rose in anger, some in anguish. The whole ship seemed to creak and moan. Huge metal screws groaned a level beneath steerage. Anna felt their vibration ripple through her bones as she covered her ears to try to shut out their grinding.

Even the ocean outside bothered the girl as she tried to sleep. Water rushing just beyond the steel walls of her sleeping area made a whooshing sound, strange and unsettling. The fourteen-year-old examined and re-examined the rows of rivets she could see dimly in the hull, praying that they were very strong and would continue to separate her from the deep of the ocean outside.

Lights were brightened slightly at six o'clock in the morning. Long before sunrise men and women were wandering the halls and climbing up to the open air; few slept well. Not surprisingly, when the Kronprinz reached the North Sea, a majority of passengers reacted to the poor food and water, the lack of sleep, and the unaccustomed roll of the ship. Anna joined a large group of voyagers beset with seasickness. It was to cause her distress the entire six days and nights of the trip.

She quickly discovered that the grime and odor of the latrine only upset her stomach more. Mothers dealt with their diaper-changing problem as best they could. They cleaned the soiled rags in the toilets and wash basins, and many learned to tie the cloths to the railings on deck for quick drying. Often, however, they hung the wet material over ends of their bunks in the sleeping area. It made the stale air of the sleeping space more foul every day. And lying in her bunk at night listening to others retching compounded Anna's wooziness.

During the daytime, up on deck, the girl often joined others dashing to a line of miserable people retching over the side of the ship. It didn't help that Godfather Joe just laughed at her through it all. He experienced no stomach problems whatsoever and he ate everything offered in the dining lines. "No needles" worked for him, he constantly reminded her.

Anna took note with concern that the old woman who made her think of *Babička Marie* sat on the deck in the same spot by the air shaft every day, usually with her head in her hands. She saw a young man bring her food from time to time. Their language told her they were Germans. She wondered where they were bound.

But there were a few light moments during the daytime hours on the steerage deck. Anna was happily distracted when music erupted the second afternoon. Some men and boys had pulled out their harmonicas; one had a fiddle. Knots of onlookers grabbed a partner and whirled and hummed to the music as others clapped and spurred them on. Differing languages didn't inhibit strangers who wanted to dance.

With another Czech girl Anna twirled to the rhythm with her quick feet, bumping into others in the crowd as the deck swayed with the waves. Then a boy with huge feet, who yelled he was a *Rusky* (Russian), grabbed her quickly during a circle polka. Even Godfather Joe managed to dance a bit with his goddaughter.

By evening the buzz and snickers on the steerage deck concerned the behavior of a few young couples. They were bundling beneath their grimy wool blankets in shadows under a stairway. The stairs upward from the steerage deck were roped off so that third class passengers would not mingle with those above them. Under those stairs young men and women separated by the night rules of the ship discovered a place for a little privacy to lie together. Older women scoffed and turned their heads; men, including Old Joe, laughed and joked coarsely. Anna hurried by the squirming blankets when she needed to pass them by.

The third day the fourteen-year-old met a girl about her own age named *Jetta*, who stepped beside Anna at the deck's railing. The two swayed with the roll of the ship as they became acquainted. The girl was a German who had lived just outside Prague, so she by necessity spoke both German and Czech well. The two girls were able to communicate easily in Anna's native tongue and they began to seek out one another when they were on the crowded deck.

Jetta was traveling with her uncle and aunt to Chicago, to join her grandparents. The uncle was a butcher who made the best sausage in their village. They planned to work in a packing plant until they could save enough money to open their own family sausage shop.

One morning, as the two girls stood beneath a lifeboat munching their leftover breakfast biscuits, the German girl asked, "What will your life be like in the place called 'Iowa,' *Aničko?*"

The question made Anna realize that she didn't know at all what kind of home she would be staying in with Joe Valenda's son and his family. All she knew from letters is that he farmed on rented land.

But she reasoned that because America was such a rich country, perhaps his house would be like that of cobbler Kopecký with its bright rugs and casement windows. Or it could be like the Scavenisks'.

"It might have a big kitchen with ceramic tiles around its fireplace," she finally answered. "And a separate laundry shed. Maybe there even will be a copper tub for me to bathe in."

As they picked at their hard little biscuits, the topic drifted to the best meal each of them had ever eaten.

Jetta said, "I love my Uncle Willie's *Wiener Schnitzel*, fixed with peas and new potatoes fresh from the garden. And good German beer."

Anna described the wedding feast she had helped prepare at the Scavenisks', the leftovers which she ate in the kitchen afterwards.

"I helped the cook fix roast duck with plum stuffing, potato pancakes with thick gravy, deep red pickled beets and poppy seed cake for dessert. I ate until my belly hurt!"

By the end of their descriptions both young girls were looking with disdain at the grayish baked dough in their hands. In unison they leaned over the railing and dropped the remains of the biscuits to the fish below.

Just then a giggling boy jostled them as he dashed by playing tag. Until "lights out" children ran loose in the ocean air of the deck, freed of the confines of their cramped sleeping quarters. They generally zigzagged crashing into adults on deck, annoying almost everybody.

Older men like Joe Valenda gathered in knots daily to complain and exchange ribald jokes. One dirty man in a frayed cap passed around his deck of pornographic Dutch cards, their message understandable in any language. The roar of gross laughter and comments from the group caused some nearby mothers to shake their heads in disgust and shoo their children out of earshot.

All in the mass of weary and apprehensive peasants from central Europe did their best to find ways to pass the long hours of the voyage, to adjust to cutting through a rolling ocean with no land visible, to not think of what could occur to make them rely on their lifeboat drill.

Anna would forever remember the moment when she suddenly realized that she no longer could see land of any sort. As she spun in a circle, her different eyes swept the horizon. All around her ocean and sky met everywhere. She hurried through the crowd from one side of the ship to the other, squinting to find signs of land, but there were none. The fourteen-year-old gasped, feeling strangely exhilarated, but at the same time anxious and alone. She was living an adventure she never could have imagined.

Once the ship cruised through the North Sea, it steamed west through the narrow Straits of Dover north of Calais, but third-class passengers had no idea where they were. No one bothered to tell them. Sister *Marie Helena* was not there to explain to Anna exactly where she "was," so the girl continued to busy herself within the restricted environment of the ship, where she "was" at the moment.

She learned to deal adeptly with cramped quarters encased by steel walls, the crowds restlessly waiting for food and trying to find a place to sit and eat, the filthy conditions in the latrines, and the long nights that allowed her little sound sleep. Fortunately storms didn't compound problems. Anna and Joe Valenda enjoyed a voyage with relatively good weather.

Occasionally during daylight the ship's captain came out on his deck above and waved at the steerage passengers far below him. Many waved back, feeling privileged at the attention. First- and second-class passengers also looked down from time to time over their upper deck railings at the packed people traveling in third class far below them. They seldom waved. They often just shook their heads at the motley crowd of women in *bábuškas*, the wild children darting through the crowd, the ragged nature of the lot. Some women covered their noses with lace handkerchiefs as the stench of the weary and unwashed in steerage lifted to them with an ocean breeze.

When Anna and *Jetta* peered up to see the well-dressed travelers, they wondered what they were saying and doing in their finery, where their fancy boots carried them each day. Neither girl, wrapped as they were in soiled blankets, could imagine the clean, sometimes spacious quarters those traveling above them enjoyed.

After passing through the English Channel, the Kronprinz turned west toward America to cross the vast Atlantic Ocean. It is nearly four thousand miles from Bremen to New York City. Traveling those miles Anna struggled through her seasickness, but she grew nevertheless to enjoy the salt breezes ruffling her fine brown hair, the sound of ship's bells slicing off time, the caw of a diminishing flock of sea gulls following the wake of the Kronprinz. Her eyes drank in the blue-gray sea and sky blending at the horizon after the breathtaking glow of garnet and gold sunsets.

And the peasant girl quickly learned how to visit with strangers. Conversations usually began with where they had come from and where they were going. They then moved into complaints about the ship's food, the crowding and the challenges of the trip.

Nearly always they led to the general and growing fear of what would happen to them all at Ellis Island once they arrived in America. U.S. Immigration Laws confused and frightened them, and they knew that they had to sort through an English language few understood. Anna's anxiety about the next hurdle of her trip began to grow.

She and people she spoke with already had been put through the emigration processes at Bremen. They knew from information sessions at home and letters from relatives in the new country that more examinations were due them on Ellis Island. Some referred to the Center as the "Isle of Tears." Others scoffed at anyone who called the Island the "Golden Door" or the "Isle of Hope."

Numerous tales circulated about persons known who were processed at the Immigration Center but were not allowed to enter the United States. People who looked ill were placed in the immigrants' hospital for observation or treatment; they also sometimes were sent right back across the ocean to their European lives.

None could bear the idea of not being allowed to stay in America. They had labored too hard, sacrificed too much, to be forced to return home after it all. The fourteen-year-old heard one old German woman from Hamburg mutter, "If I don't make it, I'll jump into the sea. I can't bear to go back."

Anna shuddered at the thought that she or Joe could run into trouble trying to enter the United States. She desperately hoped that her seasickness would subside when she walked ashore onto steady ground. She wanted to prove to authorities that she was strong and would be a good, healthy worker in America.

None of the Kronprinz travelers could know that only about two percent of the thirteen million persons who passed through Ellis Island during its Registry existence was turned away. That's not a large number relatively, but it's large enough for people affected. In 1893 the U.S. Supreme Court had determined that immigrants had no rights in the United States. In March of 1903, just two months before Anna's trip, Congress had passed a bill assessing a $2 head tax on all coming into the country. Additionally, for the first time it excluded classes of people from entering the country: idiots, felons, anarchists, polygamists, the insane, and women of "bad reputation."

In addition to worrying about whether they would make it through the immigration process, steerage passengers discussed their fears about connections with relatives that were to be waiting for them in New

York, or wherever their final destination happened to be. Communication from Europe to America was difficult and letters often were long delayed or lost. Directions and meeting times were sometimes confusing.

Anna and Godfather Joe became more and more concerned about whether the old man's daughter, Anna Zieman, would meet them in New York City as she had written she would. What could they do if she did not come to Ellis Island to find them? So passed the many hours on deck for young Anna Mrkvička as she steamed from her homeland to a new life.

The fourth night out Anna and most sleepers in the crowded steerage bunks were awakened by brief screeching and angry shouting coming from somewhere in the shadows. The noise quickly died away. Anna turned over and hugged her boots, drifting back to fitful sleep. The next day *Jetta* shared rumors about the disturbance with her Czech friend when they met on deck after breakfast.

A story was circulating that an old man had wandered into the women's latrine late in the night, his pants unbuttoned. A woman assisting her small daughter at a toilet screamed when she saw him. She quickly grabbed the urine-soaked broom near the drain and whacked him over the head with it repeatedly, at which the man yelped and turned to flee down the hall.

No one knew whether the interloper had wandered into the wrong latrine in sleepy confusion, or whether he had been up to mischief. The two girls spent the next hour examining each man wandering the deck for bruises, trying to identify the culprit.

Finally, after six long days and nights rolling side to side with Atlantic waves, the voyage on the Kronprinz drew to a close. Ship personnel spread the word at supper that by the next morning the skyline of New York City would be in view. Passengers were to pack their things and prepare for landing. The news catapulted men and women into frantic activity getting their things in order to disembark. Few slept that night.

Anna's mind was whirling as she imagined what was in store for her at Ellis Island, but her attention was pulled in the dark of night to little *Jan* in the bunk below. He was still flushed and coughing, and his mother was frantic with worry that his fever could cause problems at the Immigration Center. The Dutch woman's head popped over the edge of the upper bunk. She motioned with her hands until she made Anna understand she needed help. She gave the girl a clean rag to dampen with water from the latrine.

Once Anna returned with the moist cloth, the mother put it on the little boy's head, hoping to cool him down. The fourteen-year-old felt her concern. Watching the two of them reminded her of *Maminka* and the many hours she had helped her mother nurse her sisters and brother. She had slept cuddling little Mary all night countless times as her younger sister whimpered with an earache, even after *Otec* had blown his warm pipe smoke into the sick child's ears to soothe them. She recalled *Maminka's* arms holding her when she herself was a toddler sick with the croup. A wrenching pain twisted her heart; she missed them all so much.

At dawn the next day Kronprinz steerage passengers were in disarray, shuffling toward the open deck to be ready for America. Little *Jan's* fever seemed to have broken. The red-cheeked Dutch mother smiled at Anna and motioned for her to feel the boy's forehead. The fourteen-year-old smiled back at the child's coolness on her palm.

She then moved to don her good linen suit and pack all else into the small trunk. She was ready to put her best self forward at Ellis Island. Somehow she must make it through the next ordeal, even though she still dealt with a woozy stomach and numbness from lack of sleep.

In the light of morning, landfall was visible long before New York City poked its skyline into view. People cheered to finally see the shadow of land at the edge of the ocean. They had made it after all, and had not had to test their lifeboat drill.

It seemed as though all one thousand of the steerage passengers aboard the Kronprinz crammed themselves shoulder to shoulder on their lower deck, anxious to reach America. Anna tried to search the crowd for *Jetta*, but she was unable to see much over the mass of adults much taller than she. She wished she could share with her this special warm eighth day of June as they both steamed toward New York City.

The fourteen-year-old turned her small round face to the sun, thankful to be readying to leave the constant rocking of the Kronprinz. Billowing white clouds above swam a blue summer sky. The girl tried not to think of the gruel and stale bread served at breakfast, lest her stomach not accept food yet another time. She had noted that her suit was loose on her body; if *Babička Marie* were alive she would admonish her to eat to "plump" herself. Would that she could.

Somewhere on deck a harmonica played as gulls swooped over the crowd. Finally Anna's ears caught the words "The Lady" murmuring through the crowd. The harmonica went silent as excitement grew. The slight girl tried to position herself where she could see the Statue of Liberty she had heard so much about. The Kronprinz had crossed finally through the Hudson River Lower Bay and the Narrows into Upper Bay. The tall white statue grew larger and larger in New York's harbor. Whoops of gratitude welled up from the ship as the Statue's majesty loomed high above the many ships clustering around it.

The fourteen-year-old shivered as she peered upward at the torch held high above the crown on The Grand Lady's head. She joined other passengers as they lifted fists to repeat what someone yelled through the crowd: "*Vive la liberté!*" She and most of those around her were not quite sure what the French words actually meant, but they shouted them anyway, caught up in the exuberance of the moment.

Families around her knelt to thank God for their delivery. Jews in shawls prayed. Many passengers wept. Anna spied the old woman so like *Babička Marie* finally standing up near her spot by the air shaft, a flood of tears running down her wrinkled cheeks. At last the young man and another woman, perhaps her children, had joined her. The girl thought of *Maminka* and her own family. She wished they were swaying on the deck with her in the warm June sunshine, sharing every moment. Even in the mass of people around her little Anna felt suddenly alone.

It soon became obvious that although Kronprinz passengers anticipated quickly leaving the ship when they were in the harbor, a long wait was in store for them before they would be allowed to move on. The liner was but a short distance from Ellis Island when it dropped anchor among many other ships and boats in what was at the time the largest port in the world.

Each liner carrying immigrants had to wait its turn for a cadre of administrative processors from the Island to board their ships and do their work, and for barges and tenders to come afterwards to transport passengers ashore. As the impatient voyagers waited, there was little to do but watch the bustling port activities around them. Large ships, with the help of nudging tugboats, jockeyed for position in the water, blasting their horns.

Eventually immigration officials in small boats scooted to the Kronprinz and boarded the ship through a door opened in the ship's hull near the water line. They immediately climbed to the stateroom and second class areas of the ship to complete required paper work. After brief reviews with the upper class travelers, the administrators allowed those families to disembark below, thirty or so to a barge, bypassing the Island's Registry Hall entry process altogether. It would not be so for steerage passengers.

As Anna and the crowd of impoverished Europeans anxiously waited for someone to pay them attention, they cursed and grumbled among themselves in vexation at the delay. Restlessly waiting, they swept their eyes time after time over the magnificent skyline of Manhattan.

"They look like stone mountains," Anna murmured of the seemingly endless line of buildings spread as far as she could see either direction. Old Joe nodded.

Twentieth-century skyscrapers like the Empire State Building had not yet been built in 1903, but the Flatiron Building in an area soon to be named Times Square had been completed in 1902; with its height of three hundred feet it was said to be the tallest building in the world at the time. Gothic Saint Patrick's Cathedral stood on 5th Avenue and the Byzantine Cathedral Church of Saint John the Divine reached toward the heavens, firmly established.

Passengers waiting to leave the Kronprinz could see Battery Park, bustling docks and warehouses. What the immigrants did glimpse of New York City that day, their first sight of their new country, would forever symbolize "America" to them.

Anna and Joe shifted from foot to foot, rubbernecking from the City to the Statue of Liberty, which continued to overwhelm them with its symbolism and grandeur. It had been completed and put in place not quite twenty years before the two entered New York Harbor. The young Czech peasant felt that the Lady's large eyes searched her out especially in welcome.

Across the water the girl also could see her destination, Ellis Island, so close and yet so far. The main Immigration Registry Hall, referred to by some in the crowd as "The Palace," stood on a twenty-seven acre site. Before it Anna could see a large American flag whipped about with the breezes, its forty-five white stars on a blue background snapping back and forth. Oklahoma was not to become a state until 1907, four years into Anna's life on the prairies of Iowa; Arizona and New Mexico would gain statehood in 1912, at which time at least the "lower forty-eight" United States of north America would be complete.

Those like the fourteen-year-old waiting in 1903 to enter Ellis Island had no idea of its history. Because of the flood of immigrants coming to America the latter part of the nineteenth century, wooden buildings had been completed off New York City in 1892, only to burn down five years later. They had been rebuilt of fireproof materials at the cost of $1.5 million by 1900, a scant three years before Anna and Joe arrived to ponder and wander their halls.

The girl could see why people called the Registry Hall "The Palace." It was handsome and imposing with its corner turrets, its large rounded windows framed in fine white stone. It looked especially fresh and new to the fourteen-year-old, who could only compare it to the centuries-old buildings that crowded the streets of Kutná Hora.

As the time finally arrived for Anna and her godfather to be set on course for processing, they were ordered back down to a lower room on the ship so that agents could provide them with needed landing cards. Old Joe fussed as the two were carried along with the packed, moving mass, complaining that he was being pushed and prodded like the cattle and swine he had herded into pens as a young farmer. Anna explained whatever she understood to him as the two were manipulated into yet more rows of people below deck.

At long last standing before a processing table, the fourteen-year-old was prepared for landing. An immigration agent printed on a card "Anna Mrkvička, Age 14," and shuffled through the ship's manifest to check information gathered from her in Bremen about her origin and final destination. She then was directed in English and gestures to pin the card to her suit so it could be easily seen as she moved on.

It was the first Anna had heard much of this new *anglický* language of America. It sounded strange to her Czech ears. Her anxiety rose. Old Joe huffed and puffed in confusion with the directions until the girl helped him fasten his card on his scruffy suit coat. All steerage passengers were so tagged.

After descending even further to the opening in the hull of the ship, and waiting for their turn on coming and going barges, Anna and Joe finally were directed into a landing craft where they and their baggage were crammed into seating for thirty, and they were transported to the Island dock. Thousands of the steerage passengers from the Kronprinz and other passenger liners were laboriously transferred to Ellis Island in this way; the process took hours to complete.

Water splashed and blew over Anna's good linen suit as she sped thumping in the boat over waves toward Registry Hall. She was annoyed with herself that she had decided to wear her best clothes this day.

Chapter Six

Weeks at Ellis Island

WHEN THE TWO Czechs from Velký Lunec at last stepped onto the soil of their new land, their bodies sagged with relief and weariness. Anna legs were especially responsive to being on solid land and not having to adjust to the roll of the sea. The girl thought her stomach felt better already, even though it was by then empty and grinding.

She watched men and women around her drop down to kiss the American soil they had sought so long. Some stepped out of their places in line to kneel and pray, many with rosaries in their hands. Anna noticed that gruff Old Joe had tears in his eyes, which he quickly wiped away with the sleeve of his dirty jacket.

As soon as the barge was emptied, it turned about to putt back quickly for yet another load of passengers, and Anna and her group were motioned to queue up with their baggage in a large lower foyer of the Registry building. They needed to ready themselves for the series of immigration examinations and the completion of mounds of bureaucratic paperwork ahead. Everyone was suffering from exhaustion and hunger, not having had anything to eat since early morning.

Those with large baggage were directed to leave it in the area set aside for storage. There were arguments and wails when people became concerned that all they owned in the world might come up missing. Attendants tried to assure them that their things would be tagged, watched and protected. Anna and Joe were allowed to keep their small luggage.

Crowded on all sides in the foyer, the fourteen-year-old was shoved along with her barge group until something surprising happened. Volunteers seemed to step from nowhere into the anxious crowd, and smiling women placed large doughnuts in the hands of Anna and other tired travelers. Cups of milk for the children also were distributed. Everyone gulped the snack down quickly; a few asked for more. The different eyes of the fourteen-year-old brightened considerably with the wonderful taste of her first "American doughnut."

The women volunteers were members of one of the many organizations giving their time to the Island. They represented most ethnic groups coming through the Registry, and they could speak various languages to help newcomers sort through the unfamiliar immigration process. Most had been through the entry ordeal themselves.

They quickly informed the newly arrived travelers that bilingual counselors would be available "upstairs" as they wove through registration. They would be given free postcards or letter paper and postage as soon as possible so that they could send word home about their safe arrival. If they could not write, they would be helped by someone who could. And they would be assisted getting word that they had arrived to those who were to meet them at Ellis Island or elsewhere in America. Anna's attention perked up at that news. She and Joe were increasingly concerned as to how Anna Zieman would find them.

The two then were directed to inch up wide stairs toward the large Registration Hall above. As Anna raised her trunk from step to step she noticed that men with blue chalk in their hands stood quietly along the stairway, looking over each immigrant. Such a man reached out and marked the coat of a woman just ahead of her with the chalk. She was relieved when he did not mark her linen suit as she passed him, nor that of Godfather Joe's just behind her. The old man was sweating profusely and puffing up the stairs, his anxiety mounting with all the newness.

What the fourteen-year-old did not understand was that doctors were identifying with the chalk those immigrants who appeared to have some medical problem, so that they could be paid special attention during their physical screening. If they saw someone with difficulty breathing, poor eyesight, scalp disease or a crooked back, the men with chalk stepped forward quickly and placed a blue mark on his or her clothing. Two of every ten people entering the Island were marked with such codes, among them "B" for back problem, "E" for sight or eye concerns, "Pg" for pregnant.

Once Anna and Joe arrived at the large Registry Hall upstairs, they reeled at its size and its mass of people and activity. The space reeked with the smell of long-unwashed bodies, even as two large fans whirred at both ends, vainly trying to circulate the heavy air. A cacophony of different languages flooded the hot and stuffy room. The space was vast, at least as large as a football field. It had arched windows high up under a raised roof.

Thousands of people and their baggage were everywhere in lines cordoned off with metal fencing. Belongings were shoved slowly ahead of those moving forward. Parents clutched the hands of their children, fearing separation. Old Joe's "like cattle and swine" became a recurring mutter, intermingled with his creative Czech cursing.

Soon an attendant directed them to the end of a long line. The Czechs joined hundreds representing all nationalities as they tried to move toward one of the many federal bureaucrats far ahead. The uniformed men sat at small, rough wooden tables cluttered with stacks of papers. The Hall was so jammed that little ones in the crowd could not see daylight unless they looked straight up. With her lack of height, Anna could not see much beyond the taller, bulkier adults around her either.

The girl and her godfather were filled with fear as they crept forward. A pregnant woman near them, a "Pg" marked on her dress, fainted in the heat. She was carried away by attendants, her concerned husband trailing along behind. He anxiously shouted Irish words at the men in uniform carrying his wife, but they did not seem to understand him. Everyone wondered where the woman was being taken. Back to her ship? Apprehension and fright were palpable in the large room. Through the minds of all trudging through the lines ran the thought that the harried men at the tables might not actually admit them to America.

The peasants from Velký Lunec were but two among the thousands whose fate immigration authorities determined daily in 1903. Anna and Joe had arrived during the years of the peak of the European emigrant flow to the United States. Between 1901 and 1910 nearly nine million immigrants swelled the U.S. population by over ten per cent. It was not unusual for twenty thousand foreigners to be seeking entrance to the United States at several borders daily. Ellis Island, where Anna groped her way through immigration, was the main port of entry from Europe. It processed seventy-five percent of people seeking to enter America, while Philadelphia, Boston, Baltimore, Charleston and New Orleans handled the rest.

At Ellis Island authorities sometimes dealt with five thousand persons each day, seven days a week, in shifts of twelve to fourteen hours. June 8, 1903, it took Anna and Joe nearly five hours to reach the front of their first line. By then they were weak with hunger, and it was dark outside and near time to close down processing; electric lights had been lit.

Once again a man behind a desk yelled "*česky!*" and an interpreter came to help the two Bohemians answer twenty-nine questions. Their replies were compared with the Kronprinz manifest and what they had told authorities in Bremen. The same questions were asked of all entrants, and they did not concern just name, age, origin and destination.

Interpreters peppered Anna with "Do you gamble? How much money do you have? Are you married? What kinds of work can you do in America? Have you ever been arrested?"

At that question the fourteen-year-old winced, remembering the fine *Maminka* had paid the village police when she was six and had let the family geese wander to feed in a neighbor's field. She decided not to mention it, but her small body tensed fearing that somehow the no-nonsense man in uniform already knew of her transgression.

Suddenly, however, the girl was startled from her anxiety as the man ended his inquiry and thumped a black-inked "Registered" stamp down with flourish on her papers. She now had evidence that "Anna Mrkvička, age 14," had passed her first immigration hurdle. After the long five-hour wait, five minutes had put her papers in satisfactory order. Joe passed his first test as well, and he and his goddaughter were motioned on.

In one corner of the vast Hall social workers stood behind a counter under a sign reading "Questions?" written in several languages. There Anna learned that a limited number of bunks was up another flight of stairs, and available to anyone on a first come, first served basis. She and her godfather would need to stay days and nights at Ellis Island until they completed all their registration requirements and Anna Zieman came to pick them up.

The helpful counselors also explained the schedules of the dining hall, which they noted was still open; it served meals without charge. A woman gave Anna postage and post cards with a sketch of the Statue of Liberty on them, and she advised the fourteen-year-old to write to her aunt, Mrs. Zieman, right away. Joe's daughter needed to make arrangements to come for them.

Standing at a crowded writing table with a provided pencil, Anna began to compose with great care a message home to her family. She smiled thinking of their delight when the postman delivered the card with its picture of The Grand Lady. She knew *Maminka* would put it on the lone window ledge next to the row of holy cards so that neighbors and family could read and re-read it many times.

She wrote with knitted brow, her face contorted, struggling to get the Czech words just right, as Sister *Marie Helena* would have wanted. She squeezed into the small pace provided on the card . . .

> We are in America.
> The ship and ocean were big.
> I caught the seasickness.
> Godfather did not.
> Love, Anička.

Then she wrestled with what to say to Joe's daughter, her stepaunt, in New York City.

Finally . . .

Dear *Teta* Anna-
Your father is at Ellis Island.
He did not get the seasickness.
Please come.

Anna Mrkvička

She carefully wrote on the first card the address of Building #36 in Velký Lunec. Then she copied on the other that of *Teta* Anna, gathering it from a crumpled letter Old Joe carried in his pocket.

Smiling her slanted smile, she then carefully slipped the cards into the slot of a U.S. mailbox nearby, her fingers hesitantly letting them go. It was the first mail she had ever written and posted herself. And it was from America. Many other immigrants were standing at the table struggling with cards and letters. A young German girl was muttering with confusion about what side of the writing area on the post card the address was to be placed.

Anna proudly stepped over to point and explain, "Where it goes . . . put here. Your words . . . put there," as though she had written such cards many times. Grinning, she walked quickly away toward the dining hall.

Even though it was late, servers behind a food line gave all comers hot bean soup, bread and butter and a new treat for most in attendance–a banana. Anna and Joe were nearly faint with hunger. They wolfed down the food eagerly, sitting at a long varnished table filled with tired men, women and children from all corners of Europe.

As for the welcome food, they especially enjoyed butter for their bread. They watched how others ate the strange "banana," and after peeling the yellow skin down carefully on all its sides, they were pleasantly surprised at the fruit's sweet, mushy taste and texture.

Of course by the time the two reached the men's and women's dormitories upstairs, the triple-tiered bunks were already filled with people sleeping almost shoulder to shoulder. There were thousands wandering the Hall; in 1903 the sleeping dormitories accommodated only a few hundred. Anna looked in just long enough to notice that the space was far cleaner than the ship's quarters had been.

The bunks were three-tiered pieces of rectangular canvas attached to steel frames with springs, and they were designed to be pushed up overhead during the day and pulled down for sleeping at night. Crisp gray sheets and pillowcases stretched over flat mattresses and pillows. The fourteen-year-old never had slept on sheets, but she had washed and ironed many at the Kopeckýs' and Scavinisks'. She was determined to sleep on one of those clean sheets the next night, if she could get in line early enough. She and Joe wearily headed back down to the Registry Hall to find a spot somewhere, to try to get some sleep after their long and eventful day.

There was little rest in the strange surroundings. Anna sat on the crowded floor and dosed with her head on her arms over the lid of her trunk. Dawn filtered through the windows of the Hall at last. By then people were wandering to the latrines and lining up for breakfast in the dining room. The fourteen-year-old and her godfather rushed for food before starting their next immigration task. In fact, getting in line to eat became a top priority each one of the many days they were to be wards of Ellis Island. They ate everything offered, although meals continued to consist of many foods unknown to them. Oranges were a new treat.

The cooks in the dining hall tried to satisfy the vast ethnicity of diners swarming to them for food. Italians wouldn't eat oatmeal; people from Holland, like the Dutch mother on the Kronprinz, wouldn't eat spaghetti. This day's breakfast included prunes, Anna's favorite from Bohemia. And more of the tasty bread with butter was served, which the girl sprinkled with sugar, copying others at her table. She had not eaten so well since working for Mrs. Scavenisk. Her stomach felt much better.

After breakfast social workers steered the two toward their next trials; they were to complete their physical and mental screenings. Before they left the Island, they needed an Immigrant's Health Certificate in hand.

Men and women were separated on benches provided in the medical examination areas. Attendants collected immigrants' identity cards, and then Anna and Joe waited to be called after their names made their way to the top of the piles from which doctors worked. Anna was led to a shower area where she and the other women shrieked from the shock of icy cold water. The girl was then given a blanket to wrap around herself as she was examined.

Once before a doctor, the fourteen-year-old was asked to open the blanket so that her chest and breathing could be checked for tuberculosis. The stethoscope maneuvered by the man in white was cold. Anna's different eyes grew wide. She wondered what the strange thing told about her insides. The doctor's hands quickly checked the girl's back for straightness, her skin and scalp for disease. Standing in a crowd of strangers she was embarrassed, but she was not as humiliated as was her godfather.

In the men's area each man was required to shower also, but they were given their clothes afterwards. Standing in line, Joe Valenda was directed by the examining doctor to lower his pants to have his penis checked for venereal disease. He became hot and bothered about it, cursing beneath his breath, but he didn't refuse to cooperate with the authorities, as he had in Bremen.

The next trial for both the girl and her godfather was an examination for trachoma, a frequent eye illness in the immigrant population. Anna's eyelids were rolled back with a buttonhook to check for disease. It hurt, and it terrified her. Joe's physician used a matchstick as a tool. The old man was huffing and muttering by the time his screening was complete. When both their Health Cards were thumped with another stamp, the two Czechs were shooed on their way.

After a soup lunch they stood in line hours once more to complete their mental screening. When finally before the examiner, the two were required to put puzzles together, and they were asked numerous questions. Anna felt queries as a whole were simple. Finally she was asked whether she could count in Czech backwards from one hundred to zero. She had played that game many times at home, showing off to *Babička Marie's* delight. She rattled the correct reverse sequence off so quickly, the attendant laughed halfway through and stamped her Health Certificate "Approved" with gusto.

Joe was more frustrated with his questions. The final one "How many feet does a horse have?" confused him greatly.

What did these people mean? He had feet; horses had hooves. If he said "Four" would they think he did not know the difference between feet and hooves? If he said "None," would they think he was a stupid old man? He finally decided to say in Czech, "I have two legs. Horses have four," which seemed to satisfy the people behind the desk. An "Approved" stamp banged down on his Health Certificate as well.

Anna Mrkvička and Joe Valenda were among the ninety percent of immigrants at Ellis Island who passed their mental exams the first time. Those remaining were given three chances to find the right answers before they were denied entry to America because of mental deficiency.

Those who did not pass their physical screenings due to illness were sent to the Ellis Island Hospital. The fainting pregnant Irish woman had been taken to a very busy maternity ward there. At one point in the Island's existence it is said that 355 babies lay in the hospital nursery at one time.

How ill were the people rubbing elbows with Anna Mrkvička at the Registry Hall? Records state that between 1900 and 1954 nearly 3500 people died at the Ellis Island hospital, 1400 of whom were children. When medical teams could not help sick boys and girls, they were sent back to their country of origin; one parent was required to accompany them.

Anna watched with sympathy during her stay at the Hall as many people wailed with despair because a member of their family had not been approved for admittance to America. It tore mothers and fathers from children, young adults from elderly parents. Couples sometimes were separated, vowing to reunite later. Those sent back carried papers stamped "LPC," which meant they were not acceptable to the United States because they were "Likely to become a public charge."

By the time the very thankful Anna and Joe received their properly stamped Health Certificates in 1903, it was mid-afternoon June 10, a Wednesday. Counselors told the two that they might as well quit for the day and line up the next morning to exchange money and pay their immigrant Head Tax. The tax was their last Registry requirement.

The two hurried to grab bunks, and were successful this time. They arranged with sensible-looking neighbors in the dormitories to watch each other's things while they ate. Anna managed to claim a third tier bunk in a stuffy corner.

When she finally stripped to her patchwork petticoat and lay down on clean sheets early that evening, she gripped her pink rosary, praying to the Virgin . . . "Holy Mary, Mother of God, please don't let *Maminka* and Antonia and Mary and Frank forget me. Thank you for helping me count backwards, and for The Grand Lady, and for stopping the seasickness . . . and for clean sheets . . . and a pillowcase . . ." at which the fourteen-year-old at last drifted into a well-deserved sleep; it was the best rest she would have since leaving her poverty-stricken home thousands of miles ago.

After exchanging their Czech coins for American money the following day, and paying the two dollar Head Tax newly required of all immigrants, Joe and Anna studied their remaining U.S. money. Both worried whether they had enough left to pay for the ferry ride to New York City and eventually the train ride to Iowa.

Anna would spend the next days becoming familiar with the new coins knotted in *Babička's bábuška*. Once she learned the English words "What is?" from a volunteer, she peppered him with questions until she understood that five copper pennies equaled a nickel, two nickels a shiny dime, and ten dimes a "dollar," which sounded like the Czech "*tolar.*" The girl examined each coin carefully, both sides–its texture, color and images, date minted.

Four Indian head pennies especially interested her, with their engraved carved feather headdresses curving from forehead to neck. She was gleeful to find one of her pennies stamped "1889," the year of her birth. She knew it was her "lucky American penny" and she would keep it always. The fourteen-year-old bit it to see how hard it was, just as she'd seen her elders do with coins many times, although she never understood why they did so. Money always tasted metallic and bad.

The two Czechs began to face each day at the Island finding ways to fill the long hours. They wandered the grounds and corridors of Ellis Island, often asking counselors about word from Anna Zieman. They enviously watched others who had passed their tests as they united with their loved ones at the "Kissing Post" downstairs and boarded the ferry for Manhattan. "When will she come?" Joe and Anna exchanged several times a day, impatient to see their daughter and aunt. And more grimly, "What if she doesn't?"

Social workers had arranged activities for the many immigrants stranded at the Island days and even weeks after their Registry experience. Sadness surrounded those suspended in time in a system foreign and confusing to them. They were trapped in limbo without recourse on a strange island, floating without anchor between their old world and the new one they had sought so desperately.

Communication between those in Registry Hall and those in New York City was a problem. Mail to people supposed to claim those waiting at Ellis Island was sometimes misdirected; hand-written addresses often were incorrect or illegible. None but a few of the wealthy had telephones at that time, or could afford message couriers.

And transportation to and from the Island was not easy for laborers of limited means like Anna Zieman. The city of nearly 3.5 million people was widely spread out. It was difficult to travel through its crowded dirt streets, the clog of traffic, and horses and buggies vying for space with pedestrians and horse-drawn trolleys. Few automobiles were in existence. Some commuter railroads were in operation and noisy elevated trains had operated since 1870, but getting places usually required many transfers and interim waiting. It also was difficult for workers to get time off from their jobs to take care of family responsibilities. They were at the mercy of autocratic business owners with little empathy for their workers' problems.

Daily Anna checked at the Information Desk for any word from Anna Zieman. If her aunt had received the post card she so carefully had written to her, why didn't she come? Joe paced here and there, cap in hand, irritated and impatient.

The girl and her godfather spent time each day outside under June sun or clouds, strolling the grass with other immigrants temporarily displaced. Authorities organized games for children. The fourteen-year-old watched ragged boys and girls giggle and bounce red balls around a circle, and joined them from time to time. Not knowing each other's language didn't bother them a bit. The peasant girl had never seen marbles, or a football, or the games involving them, which volunteers led.

The girl was most happy to discover that a dance was arranged outdoors at Ellis Island for Sunday afternoon. There still was no word from Joe's daughter. Anna's quick feet whirled over the grass with stranger partners as a small band played. Everyone tried to enjoy the distraction. It at least helped to pass dragging time.

The following Tuesday Anna unexpectedly stumbled upon *Jetta* coming out of the dining room after the midday meal; the two girls grinned with surprise to have found one another again in the mass of people, and immediately caught up on their status at the Island. *Jetta* and her aunt and uncle had been slightly delayed due to flu-like symptoms that had sent her aunt to the hospital. But the illness had cleared up with rest and time, and the three were headed for the ferry within the hour; they were going directly to a New York City train station to head toward their final destination in Chicago. The girls awkwardly exchanged good-byes and good luck as the German girl dashed on to catch up with her family.

Anna sadly watched her disappear into the crowd. When would Joe's daughter come so that she, too, could be on her way? She went again to the social workers, who said that because it had been a week since the girl's arrival, and she had received no answer from her aunt, they would send a telegram to Mrs. Zieman for her. That stood a better chance than the post card of finding the woman in the crowded maze of ethnic enclaves on the Lower East Side, where Joe's daughter lived.

The fourteen-year-old watched a helpful volunteer write in English ten words to Anna Zieman from the U.S. Immigration Authority: "Your father and niece wait for you at Ellis Island." Young Anna thought that surely that would bring the woman to them.

The counselors suggested then that the young Czech attend "serving" lessons, which taught helpful maid skills for women and girls. The girl attended a few sessions, where effort also was made to teach useful English words.

Anna puckered her thin lips and worked her mouth to form everyday phrases in the new *anglický* language, words like "Hello, Good-bye, Please, Thank you," and "Police." Volunteers showed the group common signs and explained their meanings in several languages. The young Czech tried to lock in her memory the meaning of printed words like "Trolley, Open, Closed, Stop!" and once more "Police." But she had to translate them into her native language to grasp meaning. Her mind had to tumble from "open" to *otevřeno*. This somersault of translation would hinder her for years to come as she struggled with the English of America.

As for the serving lessons, she discovered that she already knew much of what was taught about serving at table, where to place dishes and knives and forks. The young Czech realized that because of her experiences with the Scavenisks she knew more about being a proper serving girl than most young women in the classes.

To help Joe fill his time, volunteers suggested he join other men outdoors for morning calisthenics. The bulky Czech wandered to watch those lying face down on the grass, pushing themselves up and down with their arms, but he stood aloof on the sidelines with other older men. They grumpily shook their heads at what they saw as useless effort. Instead they shuffled down to the water's edge to sit and watch the busy ships bringing more and more thousands to the Island. Godfather Joe continued to mutter "swine and cattle," adding, "When will I leave this goddam place?"

There also were group sessions to explain to waiting immigrants what they would be facing in New York City. Counselors described as best they could that there were factions in the Lower East Side, where many steerage passengers were bound, which might try to take unfair advantage of newcomers. They should beware of strangers and keep their money close at all times. They should try not to walk the streets alone.

They did not explain in depth other factions within the United States, those which had an impact on how unwelcome newcomers sometimes would be in this different culture. Wealthy Bostonians in 1894 had begun an Immigrant Restriction League to petition officials to slow what they saw as an onslaught of foreign people in their midst. The Ku Klux Klan, dormant since the Civil War, had revived, objecting to people of color entering the country. Even educated Americans like Senator Henry Cabot Lodge had said for the record, "Slavic immigrants threaten to contaminate the land." The president of Colgate University had stated publicly, "The melting pot is breeding out the higher divisions of the white race."

Forces in America were both pulling immigrants like young Anna and her godfather to join the work force in the country, and pushing their different cultures and ethnicity away. The two Czechs would have to learn by experience to differentiate between those willing to help and those determined to take advantage of them in their adopted society.

One day Anna discovered first-hand that lone women were treated differently at the Registry Hall. A tattered-looking Czech girl a few years older than the fourteen-year-old approached when she heard Anna speaking Czech to Old Joe. She said her name was *Růyena*, and that she was from Prague. She seemed eager to find another Czech person to relate to in the mass of people around her, most accompanied by members of their families.

Růyena had been given money by her elderly grandmother to go as far as New York City to start a new life. The granddaughter had no other relatives, so she had set out alone. She had passed all her immigrant tests, but she told Anna anxiously that the authorities would not release her because she was a lone young woman with no "protector." Anna's shoulders drooped when she was told that it had been three weeks since the girl had arrived at the Island. She envisioned her own stay stretching forever into the future.

Social workers were trying to find someone to sponsor *Růyena*, but the lone girl was frightened. She kept asking Anna over and over whether she thought the authorities would send her back to Prague if they couldn't find someone to help her soon. The fourteen-year-old didn't know what to say, considering her own problem of not having been claimed as yet.

There were reasons behind a reluctance to let lone women immigrants into America. White slavery and prostitution flourished in the seamy, crowded neighborhoods of New York City, most immigrants' first taste of the United States. Some volunteers took women alone under their wing for a time, trying to help them find honest work and a safe place to live. Some such volunteer had to be found to escort *Růyena* off the island. Only then could she leave.

Because of these rules for women immigrating by themselves, curious liaisons often were arranged in steerage on the ships steaming toward America. Marriage between strangers seemed a logical way for some women to avoid immigration problems and possible rejection at

Ellis Island. Ships' captains sometimes made such unions official before The Grand Lady loomed into view.

So the days slowly came and went for Anna and her godfather. The two continued to wander every nook and cranny of the Hall and to pace the grounds outside when it was not raining. They spent hours watching crowds of immigrants work their way down lines to the formidable men in uniforms. And they looked on as most walked out of the Hall toward the ferry, leaving them behind to wait . . . and wait.

A week after the telegram was sent, volunteers did have news for the girl when she checked at the Question Desk. A postcard had arrived from Anna Zieman addressed to Joe Valenda.

> *Otce.* It is July 1 or 2 before
> I can get from work. Look for me then.
> Daughter Anna

By this time it was June 22, still nine or ten days from the dates Anna Zieman mentioned. Joe swore; Anna was overwhelmed with disappointment. The counselors told them that it was all right; many had problems connecting with relatives at Ellis Island. The two-dollar Head Tax helped pay for their food. At least they now knew when Anna Zieman was coming. Nevertheless, the fourteen-year-old and her godfather both began to wonder if they really ever were going to leave the halls of Immigration.

She and Joe continued to wander through days divided by trips to the dining room and seeing others pass through the process and out toward Manhattan. Volunteers did steer Anna to a room where picture books from the Public Libraries of New York City were brought regularly for the use of waiting immigrants.

Anna had never seen so many books. Her school rooms had but few, and the nuns had guarded them closely. While she couldn't read the English texts, she spent hours turning pages, looking at pictures and drawings of her new land. When a volunteer discovered that she was bound for Iowa, she found for her a book about the Midwest with nineteenth-century images of its prairies. Anna's different eyes looked intently at buffalo, Plains Indians, forts, sod houses, as well as crews working on the flat land to build the transcontinental railroad west. It all looked strange to the girl, particularly the drawings of dark-eyed Indians wrapped in blankets. They didn't look like the one on the penny. They had no feathers sprouting like flower petals from their heads. The prairie looked big and bleak, almost like the ocean she had just crossed; it had no mountains like her homeland. "What is?" she said pointing to another picture of a homestead. "A windmill," was a volunteer's answer, "bringing water up from a well for animals to drink." Anna tried to understand, puzzled. It didn't look like Velký Lunec at all, this "Iowa."

Other picture books of America illustrated jagged high mountains and barren deserts, gold rush camps, cowboys on galloping horses chasing steers. And there were images of people with black skin, which Anna had never seen, working in cotton fields. Prints of New York City showed railroads high up on what looked like wooden bridges, tall buildings towering over crowded streets, the amazing lace-like wires fastened to the Brooklyn Bridge, which was completed in 1883. Anna wondered how she would ever find her place in this big new country.

That night she lay on yet another strange bunk, stuck on an island set apart from both Bohemia and America. In a fitful dream she was a little girl again, running as fast as her legs would carry her through the woods of Velký Lunec toward *Babička Marie*, trying to escape the spirits of the woods. Frantic and out of breath she looked with her different eyes over her shoulder again and again to find the comforting spires of Saint Barbara's Cathedral, but shadows enveloped it like a cloak until it faded and disappeared from her view entirely. She woke with a start, her heart shivering.

The first of July came and went without Anna Zieman's arrival, even though both her niece and father waited all day with their baggage, parked on a bench near the Question Desk. Joe Valenda sat angrily with cap in hand through the hours, his jaw clamped tight, swearing in frustration at the July heat. Little Anna optimistically had once more donned her brown linen suit.

Clouds outside threatened bad weather, so it was even more muggy and stifling in the Hall than usual. Perspiration trickled down the girl's face and neck until she loosened her jacket in discomfort, her thin lips puckered to a pout.

Finally, late Thursday morning the second of July, as the two once more sat despondently waiting on a bench, a message was delivered to the Desk that Mrs. Zieman was downstairs at the Kissing Post, waiting to collect "Joe Valenda and Anna Mrkvička." Authorities noted the Czechs' departure date on their records and the two almost ran down the stairs among swarms of other people also leaving Registry Hall. When they neared the Kissing Post they heard crying, laughing and a cacophony of excited voices as immigrants met loved ones after their exhausting journeys.

Joe and his daughter began to weep the minute their eyes met. Anna stood aside until her aunt, whose belly revealed an early stage of pregnancy, stopped hugging her father. Then the woman turned to address little Anna, who had been only a small child the last time the two had seen one another in Velký Lunec.

She scanned the daughter of her stepbrother, *Karel.* The girl stood before her in a rumpled, ill-fitting linen suit, her best boots on her feet. She was barely as tall as her aunt's chin, her fine brown hair drawn back in one long braid limp from the heat. Perspiration trickled down her forehead. *Teta* Anna was immediately moved by the weary anxiety in the young Czech's eyes. She remembered how her own son, Walter, now twelve, had felt leaving his homeland and arriving frightened in a strange country.

"*Aničko, Aničko!*" the older woman exclaimed as she folded the girl in her arms. At that maternal kindness young Anna's eyes flooded with tears. It had been a long journey filled with anxious days and nights struggling with seasickness and grieving for her homeland. The peasant girl from the beet fields of Bohemia had shouldered tremendous responsibilities. Relief at seeing someone from home, and of having warm family arms around her once again, allowed the fourteen-year-old to let go and have a good cry. It had been five weeks and well over three thousand miles since she had left her mother's side.

Chapter Seven

Six Weeks in New York City

AFTER PURCHASING FERRY tickets, Anna Zieman pinned her address, written in English, onto the clothing of her niece and father. She didn't want them to become lost in the confusion of New York City. She instructed them to stay close to her on their trip to her rented rooms, but to find a policeman and show him her address if they somehow became separated. Young Anna determined not to let her aunt out of her sight until they were safely at the Ziemans'.

A brief ride over the water carried the three to the busy Battery docks of south Manhattan. Even though winds began to whip storm clouds overhead, splashing water spray over them all, a tumble of words continued among the reunited three.

Anna Zieman was able to speak Czech to Joe and her niece, German and beginner's English to her husband, son and merchants in the mixed Manhattan culture within which she lived. She apologized for being delayed meeting the two at Ellis Island. She hurried on to say that she had never received the post card her niece said she had sent, news that disappointed the girl. Even though young Anna continued to listen to her stepaunt, she mulled at the same time whether her written message with the Grand Lady on it ever would reach *Maminka* and her sisters across the ocean.

When a delivery boy late one evening finally had wandered up three flights of stairs to the Zieman rooms with the telegram from Ellis Island, Joe's daughter had just arrived home from another twelve-hour workday at the sewing rooms where she finished sleeves at a shirtwaist factory. A very large order recently had been received by the Dutch Jew who owned the business, and he'd announced that thousands of shirts had to be completed before any workers would be allowed a day off. If she had left she would have lost her job.

The order finally had been completed the previous afternoon; *Teta* Anna had a few days of respite before she had to report to work again. She was happy to have some precious time to spend with her visitors and get them settled.

The woman's husband, Adolf, worked the night shift on the overhead electric railroad, the "el" that clattered above the streets of downtown Manhattan. As the ferry pulled next to its dock, Anna Zieman told her niece and father that her husband would manage to get them free passes on the el so that she could show them the city. That news lifted the spirit of the fourteen-year-old greatly. She began to feel excited, smiling because she already had seen pictures of the high-up trains in the Ellis Island picture books.

Once on the dock, Anna and Joe were told to stay close to their guide, lest they become lost in the mob that rushed around them. Some scurrying people were beginning to protect their heads from spitting rain with crumpled sheets of *The New York Times* grabbed from overflowing trash bins. The fourteen-year-old stepped lively to keep up, clutching her trunk tightly.

The three had several trolley transfers to make to travel northward to the Zieman rooms. They made their way to a crowded trolley stop and soon scrambled to board a horse-drawn car as *Teta* Anna urged "Quickly! Quickly!" All seats were taken nonetheless, and they stood with others in the aisles holding onto hanging straps to keep from falling as the car jerked forward.

The conductor clanged his bell at horses and buggies racing across his path and bicycles weaving too close, as well as pedestrians dodging through the heavy traffic. The car was so full that riders hung from its doors and steps in the rain. Joe mumbled and cursed about being stacked like a wet fish in a basket. Anna grinned, wondering how many more animals he would liken them to before they made their way to Iowa.

The girl looked as best she could through the windows opened in the muggy heat. She saw warehouses, factories, storage tanks, coal dumps, sugar mills and breweries crowded on acres around the docks. Black men like those in the picture books, their skin glistening in the rain, worked beside white men pushing wheelbarrows heavy with goods and sacks.

Anna would see many black men and women among New York City crowds during her stay there. The Dutch had originally brought black Africans to Manhattan, usually as slaves. After the completion of the Erie Canal in 1825, the city had mushroomed into a busy port helping to carry trade to the canal, the Great Lakes and routes west. When the end of the Civil War lured former slaves north for jobs and a better life in the bustling place, the city already was a vibrant commercial center with a commodity exchange, a banking industry and manufacturing districts.

Long before young Anna arrived in the city, ethnic and racial clashes in crowded living conditions had encouraged citizens who could afford to move to do so. They left the crowded streets of Manhattan to relocate in the more segregated Bronx, Brooklyn, Queens and Staten Island boroughs.

When the three stopped to transfer to other streetcars, men tried to push fliers advertising patent medicines or restaurants into their hands. Anna stared at walking bill boards, panels slung over the shoulders of men front and back, again advertising markets, products and services.

The Czechs gradually wove their way though the immigrant enclave of the Lower East Side, a densely populated section of the city packed between the Hudson and East Rivers. Nearly half of the population of all the wards of New York City was jammed into these neighborhoods. The fourteen-year-old caught her first glimpse of what she would be living among the next six weeks.

She saw block upon block of crowded shops and markets at street level, their signs in many languages she could not read. Above them stretched walk-up apartments and tenements with washings strung near windows on pulleys and rope from building to building. Faded and patched shirts, dresses and trousers billowed overhead. The Czech girl, who had fussed about how to dry washings as long as she could remember, was fascinated. She thought drying them over the street to be a clever solution in this crowded place.

The trolley rumbled on tracks laid down on dirt and brick streets through Chinatown, where Anna watched in awe the activities of the first Orientals she had ever seen. In felt shoes and boxy Chinese jackets, men, women and innumerable children frantically scooted in the wind and rain from shop to shop. Men in square hats, pigtails down their backs, gathered beneath awnings. Strange printing was brushed up and down on signs over laundries and markets. Smells of rice and fish and pungent spices mixed with that of dusty dampness wafted through the trolley windows. Anna suddenly realized how hungry she was; she hadn't eaten since early morning.

Soon they were stopping in Little Italy, where even in the rain dark-haired people wandered markets filled with rows of fruits and vegetables. Overflowing ash barrels dotted sidewalks. Awnings on shops read "*La Bella*" and "*Pasquale's Ristorante.*" Odors of cooked tomatoes and garlic floated in the air. And the ever-present loaded clotheslines furled their faded garments overhead like ships' flags, even as the hefty arms of wives poked out of open windows to reel in shirts and pants from the rain. Rickety tenement buildings covered every inch along the streets; here and there stable lanes for horses were wedged among them.

Teta Anna explained as they stopped and started that certain neighborhoods in "The Lower East" housed groups from different motherlands–Russians, Chinese, Irish, Italians. There was a smaller Czech area she said they would visit; her son, Walter, was working there for the summer, rolling cigars with a Czech family. And there was a little Germany, *Kleindeutschland*, in which her husband's cousin, Oscar, lived. That group numbered nearly 800,000. Mostly Lutherans, she explained.

Anna noticed many churches squeezed among other buildings, and they often were not Catholic like her grand Saint Barbara's, standing on its own hill above the woods of Velký Lunec. Then she suddenly realized what was missing from these street scenes. Trees. She saw none among the crowded buildings until the trolley passed Mulberry Bend Park, after which it rattled through blocks of the Jewish community.

In that segment of the Lower East Side nearly 300,000 German, Polish, Hungarian and Russian Jews segmented themselves into neighborhoods. They followed Conservative, Orthodox, Reform and Hasidic traditions. Bearded men in black hurried by synagogues and kosher shops, their black umbrellas floating above them in the rain.

When the three finally arrived at the Ziemans' trolley stop north of Hester Street, Anna and Joe followed their guide to dodge through wet and crowded streets. They rubbed elbows with women with market baskets on their arms having to do the daily shopping for supper no matter the weather. Boys pushed wheelbarrows full of wet potatoes. Men argued in a number of languages about prices for goods in stalls pushed under awnings to be kept dry, their used clothing and trinkets laid out on boards.

Finally *Teta* Anna ducked into a market, as she, too, needed to shop for their supper. She had purposely walked by a stale bread vendor; only fresh food would do for her company.

Anna, close behind her, breathed in the pungent odors of fruit, vegetables and raw meat in the market as she intently watched Joe's daughter roam from bin to bin to find the best of the lot spread before her. The pregnant woman negotiated with a German butcher for the best *Weißwurst* (white sausage) prepared that day. He addressed her familiarly as "Mrs. Zieman", the "S" and "Z" blurring together on his tongue.

The aunt pressed the man in the bloody white apron for a suitable free soup bone. The first one the butcher retrieved from under his counter had little meat left on it, and she urged him to search for another. Then when he found one suitable she said he might as well wrap the first one up, too. No one else would want it. She winked at her niece as the man wearily sighed and rolled the sausage and the bones in butcher paper.

Then *Teta* Anna carefully picked out two-dozen large quahog clams, food strange to the fourteen-year-old. The older woman explained to her niece that each clamshell must be tight to be safe to eat, and she set back two that didn't meet her standards. Young Anna stared at the clams, wondering how she was supposed to bite and chew the gray stone-like shells.

After selecting ripe apricots, potatoes and a round of fresh rye bread, *Teta* Anna paid the shop owner, counting out coins carefully from a small purse she had fastened for safety to the inside of her skirt pocket. Her niece intently watched her, taking note of what coins were used to buy the food. She was anxious to learn how to properly spend her own money, tied now in *Babička's bábuška*.

Then Joe's daughter steered them all to a nearby crowded saloon where she purchased a small pail of warm beer. It was the first time her father perked up and left off his grumping about his hunger, the crowds and the weather. He actually smiled in anticipation of a bit of beer. Only then were the three weary Bohemians finally able to walk the final block of their Manhattan journey to the entrance of the apartment house that held the Zieman rooms.

The brownstone row house was the tired remains of what once had been a handsome home for a single Dutch family. While it was located some distance from the most dangerous and unpleasant areas of the Lower East's tenement district—the Bowery and the infamous Fourth Ward—its crowded neighborhood nevertheless was over-populated with a work-weary mixture of many nationalities. Most families there were saving as they could to move elsewhere as soon as possible.

As immigrants by the hundreds of thousands had swarmed to New York City during the nineteenth century, a steady transition in the Lower East Side had taken place because of its location. What had been a fashionable setting near the East River for respectable, upper class homes and brownstone flats, by 1857 had become a run down area over-developed by real estate agents and boarding-house keepers.

Businessmen had bought once spacious houses to slice them up into tiny collections of rental spaces, into rooms often with no windows to allow light or fresh air. They had converted the old homes to hold as many immigrants as possible, those poor laborers who needed to live close to their daily work in factories and the nearby dock and shipping area.

Additionally, in what once had been back-yard gardens of the former homes—fenced-in areas filled with flowers and crushed seashell paths—

they had erected a jumble of wooden tenements. Behind rows of usually three-storied old houses in the most-crowded sections of the Lower East Side, loomed taller, rickety wooden structures, their doors opening to stairways descending to grim back alleys.

In the alleys of the least-cared-for real estate in the city, garbage and communal pumps stood side-by-side with latrines. Manure from horse stalls and trash were home to colonies of rats roaming indiscriminately to spread disease. Basement tenants sometimes entered their damp rooms down a ladder through a window. Stale beer dives, frequented by the most downtrodden citizenry of the city, were tucked into any available nooks and crannies among it all.

The profit for landlords of these cheaply structured lodgings was high, fifteen to forty percent, which provided incentive to create even more. Some owners even rented stables to immigrants who could afford no other shelter, for a few dollars a year. Numbers of hapless workers were reduced to sleeping in run-down hotel lobbies on ragged chairs or sofas, paying fifty cents a week for the privilege.

In 1890, thirteen years before young immigrant Anna's visit, a book by New York *Tribune* reporter, Jacob A. Riis, *How the Other Half Lives,* revealed the alarming statistics of tenement living in the Lower East Side. He documented that the cost per square foot to rent there was higher than anywhere else in New York City. Death rates were higher, especially for children. Murder rates were larger, as were numbers of the insane taken from tenements to asylums. Public schools were so crowded that the few poor children who were able to attend classes could do so only part of a day.

By the time Anna Mrkvička arrived in the area in 1903, at least the dangerous Mulberry Bend tenements had been demolished. Its lawless "Bandits' Roost" and "Thieves' Alley" had been replaced by the tree-lined Mulberry Bend Park the young Czech saw on her trolley ride to the Ziemans'. Builders of conscience and a City Tenant House Commission were studying ways to change the sordid conditions immigrant New Yorkers endured. They had begun demanding daylight in all the rooms rented to the poor in the problematic areas, and they were trying to guarantee more space per family.

With her arrival at the northern fringe of the Lower East Side of Manhattan, little Anna became immersed in many of the growing problems of the robust youngster of American democracy. Its society at the beginning of the twentieth century was struggling in its own unique way with industrialization and its impact on a rapidly expanding, diverse population. Unfortunately, connected to that industrialization were the often ill-gotten prizes of capitalism.

The fourteen-year-old was to find out gradually that the United States, as well as her homeland, had its history of political, religious, and class problems for her to deal with, albeit ones with shorter shadows than those in Europe. As she arrived in New York City the summer of 1903, Turks were readying once more to massacre Christians in the Balkans south of Bohemia. Serbian King Alexander and Queen Draga had recently been murdered in their bedchambers. Friction in Europe was building to World War I.

At the same time, Anna's new country still was nursing wounds from the Civil War between the North and South, bitterly fought in the 1860s. The *Times* reported mob rule and lynchings taking place the day the girl left Ellis Island. In Evanston, Indiana, a crowd defied soldiers and lynched a "Negro." A race war began in Topeka, Kansas, over black and white participants in a crap game.

Trade unions were confronting management in New York City, acting out their anger about working conditions. Bricklayers were engaging in slowdowns. Stonecutters, house smiths, carpenters and joiners were in arbitration with the Building Trades Employers' Association. Elsewhere in the United States miners had struck in Arizona, hotel workers in Chicago.

National union unrest revealed the social distrust and hatred in the country among racial and ethnic groups seeking the same jobs. It highlighted ideological arguments about socialism vs. capitalism. All these elements of dissension were exploding in the Lower East Side when the young Czech arrived to spend busy days and nights in New York City, her first real taste of America.

The original fine facade of the three-story Zieman brownstone was still somewhat evident as young Anna approached it. The girl compared the chipped gargoyles atop worn columns around its entrance to those she'd admired on the old patricians' homes in Kutná Hora. Worn double front doors opened to a blue and white mosaic vestibule floor, random tiles missing, but still grand to a fourteen-year-old born to a dirt floor under a thatched roof.

Once inside, Joe and his goddaughter lugged their baggage behind pregnant Anna up three flights of stairs through a sometimes-grimy central hallway. Nonetheless young Anna enjoyed the once grand wallpaper along the way; its pattern of faded leaves spun around her like a tree. Some long-ago woodcarvers had decorated the corners of banisters with leaves and flowers. Now the old oak designs were worn and chipped by the wear and tear of hundreds of tenants through the decades.

The rooms of the original spacious house had been partitioned into twelve "apartments," four to a floor. They housed fifty-eight people of various nationalities, twenty-nine of them children under twelve. Voices and the cries of babies came from hall doors opened in the heat for circulation. In the first floor hallway flies swarmed around garbage stacked in corners. A mouse alarmed by footsteps scooted from a pile to slip and slide pell-mell down the hall. It brought frustrated reaction from Joe's daughter.

"Damn Irish O'Haras! Too lazy to carry their rubbish out back like they should!" she complained, explaining that the city picked up garbage from a back area fenced to hold it. *Teta* Anna continued to chatter along the way about living arrangements in the house, even as dirty children played near the second landing, running and whooping at one another.

She said that residents all gathered their water from the communal basement kitchen. The original inside pump at the sink stood unused, having been replaced recently with a faucet connected to city water; sewage lines were sometimes a problem, however. Young Anna quickly said that she would begin fetching water for the family up the three flights of stairs each day. *Maminka* had taught her well.

Teta Anna explained that behind the house was a pump and trough where women of the house washed their clothes during warm weather. The drying of garments was accomplished with the help of pulleys and fire escapes attached to the building near apartment windows. There also was the old latrine in the back yard, helpful when the overused water closet off the kitchen was not working, which was often.

The basement "Tub Room" for bathing stood next to the toilet stall and was used by tenants on a rotating basis, one-half day for each household. Anna Zieman said they were lucky with their arrangements. Some apartment houses provided no way to bathe and tenants had to frequent public bathhouses.

When she arrived at the brownstone, young Anna had noticed a sign with an arrow pointing down crumbling steps to a shop below street level, and she asked her aunt about it. She was told that space in the front part of the basement had been rented to a Hungarian used clothing storeowner who also acted as "Superintendent" for the building.

He collected rent and tried to maintain order, although women at the laundry trough complained that he was always too busy within his shop to do much good. Occasionally he had to get a policeman to settle tenant arguments, mediate wife beatings, or clear out intoxicated drifters who wandered through to sleep in the hallways. The Hungarian slept in a storage room and used the communal kitchen behind his shop for his own cooking, which forced everyone in the building to share the aroma of his garlic and onion stews.

"But we don't shop in his store, *Aničko*. I get better prices at Mrs. Kinkel's down the street. I'll take you there. Some things of mine are too tight for me now. We'll tuck them smaller for you to wear." The fourteen-year-old smiled, warmed by her aunt's kindness. The two garments she had brought from home were soiled and messy from the trip and her sickness. And her ears had perked up at the mention of a tub. She still longed for a bath like those available to the Scavenisks.

The three were perspiring heavily as they climbed higher upward. The building became hotter at each floor. Finally, on the third landing, which had been cleaned that morning by *Teta* Anna, Joe's daughter pulled a key on a string around her neck from under her blouse and unlocked the door to her two rooms. One was not much bigger than a closet; a bed was shoved into it and was surrounded by worn clothing hung on hooks. Bedding overflowed overhead shelving.

The larger room originally had been a spacious bedroom. It had two east windows facing the street, which Anna Zieman had dressed with pea vines planted in small wooden cheese boxes on the sills. The plants coiled upward in the light among simple muslin curtains to a frayed, green window shade. A door that originally opened to a small metal balcony now led to a narrow, rusted metal fire escape. Rimming the walls were a wooden table and four mix-matched chairs, an oak cupboard with glass door, the trunk the Ziemans had carried from Bohemia and a gas cook stove.

A decrepit fireplace yawned its sooty opening in the center of one wall. A covered slop jar stood in one corner to avoid trips to the basement water closet at night. A tight metal-lined food box stood in the other.

Joe's daughter grabbed a box of matches and proudly lit the gas jet under a lamp globe by the door to the hall. It hissed, glowing softly in the room made dim by heavy clouds outside. Anna Zieman knew her father and niece had not seen gas in Velký Lunec.

"See!" she said. "Gas." Then pointing to her small stove, "And it cooks, too. No wood or coal for ash barrels. More clean!" Young Anna and Joe collapsed in exhaustion on the chairs, eyes wide with pleasure at the gaslight.

"And we face east, the morning sun, not back over the latrine." She wrinkled her nose with disgust at the smell from the latrine and alley garbage in the rear rooms.

Joe's daughter looked for approval of her home from her father, who years ago had not blessed her marriage to a "goddam pushy German," a Lutheran on top of it. While Adolf had submitted to a Catholic marriage in Bohemia, when he'd moved to America he forbid his wife and son to attend mass, unbeknownst to his father-in-law.

The old man nodded his head at his daughter's housekeeping; a smile almost flickered in his whiskered face. The rooms were very clean. The bare wood floor had been swept with a broom now propped by the stove. The fourteen-year-old noticed that the bed, covered with worn sheets and blankets, was tightly made the way Mrs. Kopecký liked.

Teta Anna removed a clean cloth on the table. It had covered salt and pepper shakers and day-old bread under an upside-down bowl to protect it from roaches. She pointed to dishes of different sizes and patterns carefully placed on a yellowed lace runner behind the glass of the cupboard, quickly explaining that a platter was a wedding gift from Adolf's mother. They had carefully brought it to America in their trunk.

The woman said that her husband had already left for his night work on the elevated trains, and that her son, Walter, would be home shortly. Her father was to sleep in the bed nights with his grandson, and Adolf would sleep there during the day. She and her niece would curl up on blankets on the floor with extra used pillows she had bought in Mrs. Kinkel's shop. They could sleep on the roof nights "under the stars" when it wasn't raining, to escape the terrible summer heat. She was an efficient wife, very satisfied with her careful arrangements.

As the severe storm that had threatened all day finally let loose with thunder and lightning, rattling the room's windows, the fourteen-year-old felt great relief to be resting in a chair, to be finished with Immigration authorities, and to be in the safe care of *Teta* Anna.

But when her aunt said with a smile, "*Aničko*, let's fix us some supper," the hungry girl jumped up eagerly. That first meal in New York City at the Ziemans' would be etched in the young Czech's memory forever.

She would learn to cook for the first time on a gas stove; she would sit down to eat savoring that she had survived the Kronprinz trip and Ellis Island; she would enjoy with gusto the wonderful new taste of American steamed clams; and she would be very glad to find that she didn't have to chew the shells.

Twelve-year-old Walter, reeking from the cigar tobacco he'd worked and handled all day, arrived home just in time to claim his share of supper. He was a tall boy whose too-short sleeves and pants revealed his rapid growth. His light Germanic hair made him handsome, young Anna thought. The boy was distant with the new girl in his space at first, but as the warm beer loosened everyone at table after a hard day, he began to laugh at and with his Czech cousin as she and Joe fumbled to attack the strange new clams.

Anna Mrkvička's first night at the Ziemans' was spent beside her aunt on floor bedding: a winter coat of Adolf's and a frayed blanket. The girl listened to rain drop from eaves outside the door ajar to the balcony, and thump loudly on the metal damper of the aged fireplace.

A wet, sooty smell filled the rooms. Nonetheless, the tired fourteen-year-old quickly drifted to sleep wondering if it was raining on the thatched roofs of Velký Lunec.

The next morning Anna Zieman had her son off to work, her two guests up and breakfast ready when her husband climbed the steps and entered the apartment. His uniform and hat were wet with perspiration, and he carried his empty syrup lunch pail and an armload of newspapers left on his train car.

Both he and his wife were trying to learn to read English from *The New York Times,* with their son's help. Walter attended a public school and his parents were proud that he was learning the language of America well. Finally the much-read newspapers would wrap potato peelings and garbage for collection. The Ziemans wasted nothing.

Adolf was tired and grumpy, but he pumped his father-in-law's hand in greeting to keep family peace, setting aside their old hostilities about religion. And he smiled kindly at his wife's niece, playfully calling her "little Annie." The girl watched him closely as they all ate a morning meal—coffee, bread and gruel. She was fascinated with his gray mustache, curled up at the ends with wax. His head was balding above bright blue eyes. After eating he carefully rolled a cigarette and lit it with a sigh. Young Anna was able to decipher most of the German breakfast conversation that followed.

The el had been busy in the rain until two to three o'clock in the morning. Adolf was a conductor, taking money and tickets, dispensing transfers and shooing passengers to the back of the electric cars. All night he traded conversations with his work mate, a young Hungarian motorman, *Tibor* Szabo, the driver of the car.

The younger man had shown Adolf how to mix cinnamon with his cigarette tobacco for good taste and smell. The girl had wondered about the sweet odor of her uncle's cigarette. It was not like that of her father's pipe at all.

The weary conductor complained about the crowded cars on the runs he and *Tibor* managed, and two outages that stopped the elevated for a time, delaying their schedules. Union members were fussing about having to work too long hours and needing more money, while the "goddam bigwigs up town" said their dollars needed to be invested in transformer repairs and more trains. He shrugged at the unending problems of moving rushing millions around New York City, a place that never seemed to sleep. Then the man yawned and crawled into the bed vacated by Old Joe. His wife had switched worn bedding; keeping piles separate for the sleepers.

Teta Anna spent the remaining day helping her company clean up after their long trip. She had exchanged her half-day access to the tub room with an Austrian woman on the floor below; they all could take baths and wash hair that afternoon. In the morning her expert sewing fingers adjusted two of her blouses for her stepniece. Her father discovered the rusty fire escape to be an interesting place to sit on a weather-beaten wooden box and watch activity on the street around him. Everywhere opened windows were filled with mostly old women and children, their elbows on sills, seeking relief from heat and boredom.

Because both her stepniece and her father needed clothes to wear while they were washing all they owned, *Teta* Anna guided the Czechs the few blocks to Mrs. Kinkel's shop. The two new immigrants followed the pregnant woman as different languages spun around them. They made their way along crowded sidewalks lined with markets and shops, and jammed additionally with pushcarts of food and wares. Uniformed policemen with nightsticks walked among it all to monitor theft. Horse-drawn wagons and an ambulance clopped by.

Scales hung handily on sidewalks to weigh apples, oranges, bananas, or tomatoes picked from wooden crates. Anna was amazed at all the varieties of food. Raw beef and fresh fish were stacked on ice flecked with sawdust, which melted in the heat, dribbled onto streets, ran into puddles. The smell of fresh baked bread mixed with that of rotting garbage, horse manure, dust and sweating bodies.

Pyramids of canned goods behind storefront glass were stacked high. Young Anna noticed the many signs propped in windows at the second level, even though she couldn't read their English; "Dentist: Teeth pulled 50 cents" was hand-printed over a large drawing of a white molar. "Attorney at Law" filled a window near another with "Dressmaker" pinned to a curtain.

At one corner a fire hydrant had been opened in the heat. Children squealed through cold water as lookouts scanned the streets for the police. Adults skirted the spray shaking their heads. In one store window the fourteen-year-old saw a pastel poster showing a delicate woman with beautiful hair holding a bar of Pear's Soap in her hand. *Teta* Anna noticed her pause, and said she had a sweet-smelling Pear's bar her niece could use in her bath that afternoon. Old Joe loped along behind the two chattering females, muttering "like cattle and swine" and complaining about the how hot he was with no shade trees in sight.

The group finally entered a door under a sign reading "Kinkel's Used Clothes." The shop inside was confusing to young Anna. Her aunt and Mrs. Kinkel knew each other and spoke in German. Heaps of clothing sorted by size and style were crowded into crooked, narrow aisles of wooden bins. The girl was glad that her aunt knew exactly how to proceed in the muddle of piles surrounding them.

Teta Anna moved quickly to fish through a box of girls' blouses and she scooped out two in the best condition, holding them up to her niece to check their size. They were wrinkled and needed a button or two, but they could be salvaged with mending and a good ironing. One blouse had embroidered blue flowers on its collar, which pleased the fourteen-year-old. Smiling, she touched the stitchery in appreciation of someone's needlework. Two cotton skirts that were short enough for little Anna soon were found, as was another petticoat and assorted underwear, not too stained.

Joe's daughter then turned to search out pants and shirts for her father, whose clothing even when his trip began smelled sour. She had in mind to get rid of the hopeless suit her father wore. It reeked. She had a little extra money from the long hours of piecework she had just completed; she had earned $6.72 for her previous seven-day week. She wanted to help her family get started in America as best she could.

The old man grumpily fussed as his daughter outfitted him with a couple changes of clothing, kerchiefs for blowing his nose, and worn under drawers. Then the negotiating began.

Anna Zieman and Mrs. Kinkel stepped carefully through a verbal dance to price the goods selected. *Teta* Anna pointed out the missing buttons, a loose hem, a pale scorch mark from an errant sad iron on a shirttail. Young Anna was impressed with her aunt's skill at getting the cost for her skirts and blouses down to seventeen cents, and for Old

Joe's things, a quarter. The pregnant woman even talked the shop owner into throwing in an old blue ribbon for her niece's hair at no extra cost, considering that the girl was brand new to the city. She winked at her niece when Mrs. Kinkel turned to put her coins in the cash box.

Then the two older women began to discuss something that interested the girl a great deal. The young Czech didn't comprehend all the German phrases whipping between *Teta* Anna and the shop owner, but she understood that her aunt asked Mrs. Kinkel if she might know of a job for her young niece.

After queries back and forth, the shopkeeper said that her husband's sister-in-law, Gertrude, a dressmaker, worked all but Sundays in her husband's tailor shop. Now that school was out of session, she needed someone reliable to care for her young twins. It was getting too hot to keep them shut up in the store all day, and they were under foot.

Suddenly the shopkeeper's serious eyes looked down on young Anna. "Are you a good worker?" she asked.

"Oh, yes," the girl struggled to say correctly in German. "I take care of my brother and sisters at home. I worked out for *Maminka* two years. I cook and iron." And she added quickly. "I can make good *koláče* and liver dumplings."

The last remark piqued Mrs. Kinkel's interest. "Well! Come back in a couple of days. I will have answers for you," she said. The three Czechs walked out of the shop smiling, with somewhat faded but serviceable clothing, and the amazing chance of a job for Anna Mrkvička. The girl's heart was pounding with excitement at a prospect for work in America. She was eager to earn wages all her own.

Now that the fourteen-year-old had clean clothes to wear while she laundered her others, she and her aunt trudged down from their third-floor rooms to the back yard pump of the apartment building to scrub and rinse a basket overflowing with soiled clothing. Adolf was snoring in his bed when the two returned to lay some things out to dry on the fire escape railings, putting rags between them and the rust.

Remaining garments were fastened with wooden clothespins to rope and pulley stretched over the narrow street. Young Anna took note that her aunt was careful to hide under garments beneath outer clothing, so she did the same with her patchwork petticoat. The girl then jerked her wet gingham dress and her brown linen suit out over a horse pulling a milk wagon on the street far below.

She grinned to see her clothes hanging there, her special announcement that Anna Mrkvička from Bohemia had arrived in New York City. Sleeves and skirts fluttered in breezes from the East River. Yesterday's storm had cleared out the mugginess, if not the heat.

Teta Anna said that they would have a picnic up on the roof later and sleep there in cooler air that night. The next day, July fourth, they would pack a lunch and go to the East River to watch special Independence Day celebrations "with firecrackers." The young Czech's eyes grew wide with anticipation. If only her sisters could be here with her to see it all. Life in Velký Lunec was so different, so quiet, so very far away.

When it came time for the family's baths, Adolf had awakened, and he and Joe were given first turns; the two Annas heated water on the gas stove in the basement kitchen and filled the large tub in the bathroom after they scrubbed rings from it with a worn brush and harsh soap. As Adolf washed himself, water was heated for Joe's bath. As a guest, young Anna was given the next turn.

The men had used rough soap on their sweaty bodies, but *Teta* Anna handed her niece her own used bar of prized Pear's soap, kept carefully after each use in a Mason jar. The girl held it like a treasure, sniffing its sweet perfume. She finally was to enjoy a tub bath just like the Scavenisks'.

The water was pleasantly warm. The soap smelled like plum trees near Velký Lunec, or spring flowers spread in the meadows below Saint Barbara's. As she stepped into the tub, young Anna felt the anxieties from the long trip begin to wash away. She carefully lowered herself into the clean water, smiling at the delicious feel of it on her skin, and then she lay back with a long sigh of relief.

She scrubbed her long brown hair. With a worn rag she made suds with the precious soap and started at her neck to rub methodically down her arms and over her small breasts to her thighs and finally to her feet and each toe. She rinsed away the trains and the Kronprinz and Ellis Island, all the while thinking, *What a country, this America!*

Late in the afternoon, before Adolf left for his work, the two Annas packed a market basket with a picnic lunch of bread, cheese and apples. Walter, home from work, fetched another pail of beer from a saloon. Young Anna followed her aunt's family to the end of the back hall where rickety steps led up to open air under a blue sky. Slats of wood had been laid over the tar mixture of the flat roof to protect it from footprint damage. The seven stair-step O'Hara children were playing around a chimney near the front of the building in the blazing heat, which seemed unbearable to young Anna.

But her aunt headed for a cool spot to spread their ragged blanket. The sun was setting in the west, so the shadow of a large round wooden water storage vat provided shade and coolness on its east side. Rainwater from yesterday's storm seeped through and dampened slats of the vat, providing a pleasant enough place in the shade for a picnic on the otherwise sweltering roof.

The vat was an example of the city's primary fire defense system for most buildings. Large canvas hoses spread from the vats downward inside the building to hang in the halls of each floor. Unfortunately, building owners did not follow rules for checking the system regularly. The nozzles of the hoses corroded over time and the canvas material grew old and stiff and mostly unusable after a few years.

The problem was to come into focus eight years after young Anna left the city, in 1911. The great Triangle Shirtwaist Factory fire in the Lower East Side killed 145 women sewing-machine workers like Anna Zieman in twenty minutes. They burned to death or jumped from windows ten floors to die on sidewalks below. Workroom canvas hoses proved rotten and useless; many women plunged to their death when they crowded onto a decrepit fire escape and it crumbled beneath them. "Required" fire drills in the workrooms had not been practiced for years.

But July 3 of 1903, the Ziemans showed their guests a good time perched on their roof in the shade of the big water storage vat. Young Anna had never been so high up in her life. She looked out over the crowded outline of neighboring roofs and again felt the absence of trees and their shade. At home the woods of Velký Lunec helped cool her from summer's heat. Here a forest of brick and concrete buildings surrounded her, waves of their pent-up heat shimmering upward. To make up for that harshness, however, a beautiful blue sky sparkled overhead, bereft of clouds following the night's storm.

After eating, Walter led his cousin to the small brick wall framing the edge of the roof, urging her to lean over and peek down on the scene below. The yap of barking dogs, the whinny of horses, the hum of pedestrians' voices drifted up to the young Czech. The height made her woozy, reminding her of her seasickness on the Kronprinz, and she backed away from the edge quickly. The boy laughed, mocking her as "a scaredy girl."

Notwithstanding Walter's teasing, young Anna thought the picnic on the roof delightful. She hungrily ate every crumb offered to her as she leaned against the cool damp water vat and scanned the eastern deepening blue of New York sky. Adolf soon left for his el night shift.

That night young Anna and her aunt carried frayed blankets and pillows to the roof to sleep, along with a lantern. Walter had taken a late bath, his turn in the tub room, and he followed them up the rickety steps, a butcher knife tucked under his shirt. *Teta* Anna explained to her niece that all the building roofs on the block were connected, allowing people to wander from rooftop to rooftop. Sometimes strangers up to no good meandered among sleepers. But the fourteen-year-old was not to worry. Walter would be nearby to protect them.

Old Joe preferred the mattress in the Ziemans' rooms, so he slept perspiring on the third floor behind a locked door. Each apartment had only one key. The Ziemans' usually was in Joe's daughter's possession. When schedules were confusing, the precious key was left with the Hungarian superintendent in the basement. This night the pregnant wife didn't want to leave her door unlocked with her father asleep, so she instructed Old Joe to lock himself in until her return at dawn. He had the slop jar; the roof sleepers would make their way to the basement toilet if necessary.

Once settled on a blanket that was little relief from the sharpness of slats under her back, young Anna tried to find a comfortable position in the open air. She had been placed safely between her aunt and cousin. The girl scanned adjoining roofs.

As her aunt had predicted, they were spread with sleepers from all tenements on the block, and heads were bobbing on roofs across the street as well. Hundreds of perspiring neighbors had bedded down here and there under a darkened sky, exhausted from work and heat. Many men removed their shirts to relish any cool breeze coming from the East River. The fourteen-year-old lay staring at a creamy moon long after even crying babies and children had quieted down. Bodies on the roofs stirred and moved about all through the night, many heading for a water closet or latrine down flights of stairs.

The girl's heart was racing with the excitement of this New York City under the stars. Even in the darkness she heard horses clopping by below, imagined them slipping in and out of the magic circles of gas light from street lamps. A tinny piano played Joplin's "Maple Street Rag" in a nearby saloon. From somewhere faint voices sang "Peg O My Heart." The music was different from any the young Czech had ever heard.

The young girl prayed to the Virgin and Saint Barbara, asking that *Maminka* and her family not forget her as she lay high up on a roof far away in America. She wondered if they had received her Grand Lady post card, and whether Antonia and Mary were looking at the same pale luminescent moon that she was. Velký Lunec seemed further away each day of her new life.

Anna was awakened once in the dead of night when three of the O'Hara boys stumbled by her, but she noticed that they headed for the rear, west edge of the roof. With curiosity she watched them in the night light as they made their way to pee over the edge of the roof into the alley far below. She felt for the little ones, too sleepy or scared to trudge down the four flights of dark stairs to the water closet in a shadowed basement, but she understood why Teta Anna preferred her rooms on the east end, the front of the building, away from the odors of the back yard.

The O'Hara boys reminded her of her little brother, Frank, and the many times she'd helped him through the night. Homesickness for her family brought tears before sleep overtook her once again.

The Fourth of July dawned clear and hot. Scampering early from the roof to her many wifely chores, Anna Zieman led her son and niece down to prepare breakfast for Adolf, who arrived home weary from crowds already carousing for the holiday. He quickly went to bed after eating, as his son and wife and her two guests headed out the door to board packed trolleys headed for the East River. The two Annas carried a blanket and a basket of bread and fruit.

Walter stayed by his grandfather Joe, who shuffled along behind trying to keep up with his fast-stepping daughter. Both newcomers had the Zieman address pinned inside their clothing again, which would be the practice each time they left their Lower East Side home the remainder of their stay.

Even though many laborers had to work this day, by the time the four arrived at the river large crowds filled a grassy parkway under rows of pleasant shade trees. A brass band was playing, its tuba blaring.

The wealthy of New York had fled the city early in the summer to escape the heat, traveling to the Adirondacks, Chautauqua Lake, the seashore. Those gathered at the East River were laborers not working, women with their children and aging parents, or small merchants who let hired help do the work of the day.

Firecrackers popped here and there as hooting boys scooted among the crowd, scaring everyone with unexpected bangs near their feet. Young Anna jumped at the noise and explosions at first, then laughed with the excitement of it. She had never seen fireworks nor smelled their strong burnt sulfur.

The fourteen-year-old saw for the first time women on the beach in the fantastic two dollar bathing fashion of the day–bloomers to above the knee and frilly hats covering pulled-up, bouffant hair styles. She giggled in amazement, wishing Antonia and Mary could see these women and girls of America. Walter mimicked a fat woman's mincing barefooted steps across the hot sand of the beach. The cousins collapsed in laughter.

Boats and ships on the river were decorated with bunting and flags to honor the day. They blasted their horns as passengers yelled and waved at the crowds on the riverbanks. On shore, various types of revolvers were fired into the air, bringing swarms of policemen to escort shooters to the nearest precinct station. Those with guns were fined two dollars if they were shooting blanks, five dollars if they had loaded their weapons with real bullets.

The political Tammany Society had been careful to provide "short talkers" as speakers for the Independence Day celebration. Perspiring men in shirtsleeves hushed the band and shouted their pride in America from stages draped with red, white and blue. They received in turn a smattering of applause, an occasional catcall and raised fist. A few brawls erupted around pails of beer bought from nearby saloons.

Hawkers roamed the increasingly drunken crowds. Stands on wheels offered hot dogs, which *Teta* Anna described as "hot dachshund sausages." Roving men touted miniature cloth flags, two for a penny, and little plaster casts of the Statue of Liberty. *Teta* Anna spent a penny for flags for her niece and son.

After gulping their plain basket lunch, the two cousins jumped up from their blanket to chase each other through the mob with other racing children, giggling and waving their tiny patriotic flags grandly. Even Old Joe, seated by his daughter, chuckled at their giddiness.

As evening approached, the fourteen-year-old reluctantly followed her hosts home gripping her little flag tightly in a sweaty hand. She was sunburned and satiated with her first Independence Day in America. The day also represented her own new independence from Velký Lunec, her parents and her country. Her different eyes would for years to come struggle to focus from her former life to her countless new beginnings in America.

As packed trolleys wove the quartet through steaming neighborhoods, a fire wagon sped by them to answer an alarm. As its bell clanged, its horses charged through scampering crowds of people frantically trying to get out of the way. *Teta* Anna shook her head, her eyes filled with fright at the horror of blazing tenements.

She had watched many crowded row houses go up in flames, unknown numbers of tenants trapped inside. Once the old structures started burning, water from the pumper wagons had little luck getting fires under control, and often hydrants were too far away to help. To complicate matters, gas pipes sometimes exploded. Many of New York City's poorest died in the Lower East Side when fires swirled out of control.

As the tired four finally neared home on foot and passed the saloon near the Ziemans' apartment house, they encountered more drunken crowds on the sidewalk. Men were angry and swearing about who had tossed firecrackers into the tavern. Mr. O'Hara was nose to nose with a stout Pole, shouting slurred insults as one of his young sons cried and tried to pull him toward home. Anna and her son steered their niece and Old Joe by their elbows into the street to skirt the ruckus, to move them quickly to their building for safety. *Teta* Anna and her father both mumbled this time about the "goddam Irish."

The travelers all were glad finally to reach home. Anna Zieman looked upward at the position of the window shades in her rooms and knew that Adolf already had left the apartment for his work on the elevated trains. The key would be in the basement with the superintendent.

The woman explained to her niece and father the special signal the family used for the location of the key. If the shades were pulled down completely, the key was with the building superintendent. If one was raised, someone was in the rooms. The signal saved family members coming and going at different times from climbing the steps only to find the door locked, and having to go down and back up three flights of stairs to be able to enter their rooms.

That night it was noisy sleeping on the roof as guns and firecrackers exploded in the neighborhood at all hours. *Teta* Anna and Walter both placed knives in their clothing before they climbed the stairs upward, anticipating unruliness. Within an hour a fight broke out on an adjacent roof. Aroused sleepers cursed at those involved, adding that if they didn't settle down the police would be fetched to throw them in jail. One gruff man yelled he would knock a few teeth out if they didn't shut up. Young Anna noticed during a fitful sleep that the pops and bangs diminished only as the sky showed a faint light in the east, introducing her next busy day in New York City.

That Friday morning Adolf came home with transit passes for his wife and her guests, explaining that it would be best for them to travel uptown before the Saturday and Sunday crowds. *Teta* Anna had to return to work the following Monday. She agreed that today was the day to do some sightseeing, saying with excitement to her niece, "Today you see an amazing museum, *Aničko*." The girl had no idea what a "museum" was, but the gleefulness of her aunt's voice told her something special was in store for her this day. As Walter was sent off to roll cigars with the Czechs, and Adolf went wearily to bed, the three sightseers left the Zieman rooms.

Traveling the Broadway trolleys uptown, and ogling everything she saw, young Anna asked her aunt about the many sailors strolling the streets as they neared the heart of Manhattan. They changed trolleys at Longacre Square at the intersections of 42nd Street and Seventh Avenue, where the Flatiron Building stretched toward the sky. The area would be renamed "Times Square" in 1904 when the Times Building was completed.

Teta Anna explained to her niece that the uniformed men wandering the Square were from various countries and navies, and were on shore leave from the hundreds of ships anchored in the largest port city in the world. The sailors always seemed to head for the white lights of the theater district and its dancing girls, and they entered long lines for tickets to see "The Wizard of Oz" at the Majestic Theater.

Here and there religious societies had built chapels and settlement houses to try to bring some God-fearing order into the "sinful" chaos the transient traffic caused in the city, the drunkenness and roving prostitutes. They had little success. "Stay away from the sailors while you are here, *Aničko*," the experienced woman warned her niece. "Go inside a shop or cross the street if you see them coming."

At one intersection the trolley stopped next to a huge hole in the ground, workers crawling around its walls like ants. Anna peppered her aunt with questions. The building of a subway system had begun in the city in 1891, and its first sections were due to open the following year, 1904. Contractors were working around the clock to finish the project on time.

The fourteen-year-old watched the swarming workers with fascination, but she couldn't imagine traveling on a train with dirt all around her; it would be like being buried, like *Babička Marie* in her grave. But her aunt said the *Times* wrote that subways were supposed to be a faster way to travel than horse-drawn trolleys or even the elevated trains. She was sure that if the newspaper with "all the news fit to print" said subways were a good thing, it must be so.

The three rumbled past Central Park, its Great Lawn, Sheep

Meadow and Belvedere Castle. Young Anna's different eyes looked longingly at the trees and the shade as she wiped perspiration from her face and arms in the packed trolley. It was difficult to escape the glaring July sun and discomfort from its heat.

Then they arrived at 77th Street and the trolley came to a halt at the American Museum of Natural History. *Teta* Anna said "Quickly. Quickly," and they climbed down to the walkway to stand before a large, impressive stone building. Broad steps led upward to its entrance, hundreds of visitors ascending and descending them. Once young Anna climbed to the shaded, cooler space of the building, her mouth dropped open.

The bone reconstruction of a huge dinosaur skeleton loomed above her. She stood for a time just staring upward. The good nuns had spent no time describing prehistoric history to the peasant children rowed before them in the basic Catholic classes of Kutná Hora, even though paleontologists had been busy finding such fossils throughout the nineteenth century. The women probably had little knowledge of it.

Teta Anna could read some of the English descriptions tacked near displays. As the three circled the bones she tried to explain as best she could to her niece and father that brilliant men of science said such an animal, with flesh on its bones, had trod the earth millions of years before.

The young girl's mind could not grasp the idea, even as the three wandered throughout the echoing rooms of the museum. Young Anna saw displays of animals from all over the world, some still living and some long extinct. A stuffed buffalo from the Midwest prairies especially caught her attention; she recognized it from the picture books of Ellis Island. It was huge, bulky, and its horns were intimidating

Teta Anna said that while her brother in Iowa had never mentioned buffalo in his few letters, Adolf said that they still roamed Iowa and beyond, along with Indians. Perhaps the girl would see them when she was settled on the farm. Many of the questions young Anna asked about the museum were answered by her aunt; many were not. The older woman, herself an immigrant, was confused about much that she saw. Her answers were a combination of fact and East Coast myth and speculation.

After hours wandering the displays, when the three Czechs joined others to descend the wide front steps of the museum to the trolley stop, unrest swirled in the mind and heart of the fourteen-year-old. It was a vast jump from a dirt-floored room in Bohemia and her basic Catholic education to the sophisticated realities contained in the series of displays at the American Museum of Natural History.

The bones of the dinosaurs especially troubled the girl. When did God make them, and how did such big animals get on the ark Sister *Marie Helena* described so reverently? The peasant girl was exhausted with the unanswered questions whirling in her head, and she was uneasy after the strange newness of the huge museum, its dusty smells and the echo of voices in its halls. Nevertheless, she would remember the day of the museum with amazement the rest of her life.

Old Joe was dragging, weary and mumbling about being hungry, completely confused about what he had seen that day. He longed for the giant trees and the familiarity of his quiet life in Velký Lunec, and a cool pail of beer.

A short ride on a trolley took the three to an elevated train station where Anna Zieman wanted to show off how her husband made his living. Climbing wooden stairs to the height of the electric tracks, young Anna looked down and around as she went. It was then that she excitedly spied a shiny Oldsmobile, the first horseless carriage she had ever seen. Her aunt joined her staring, eyes wide, as such cars did not travel the Lower East Side. Others near them stopped to ogle the beautiful machine.

"Some millionaire," Anna Zieman whispered to her niece. The Curved Dash Runabout looked like a fancy buggy with its large wheels and high body. It was made of wood painted black, and had a toboggan-like front. Two beautiful people, very much like the first class passengers young Anna had seen on the Kronprinz, sat in the one double leather seat behind two shiny headlight lanterns.

The woman wore a broad Victorian hat. Her butter-colored voile dress had airy, puffy sleeves. The man driving beside her sported a curled mustache and a beautiful blue suit. He glanced haughtily back at the people around him who looked with envy at the impressive polished style of his automobile.

When the fourteen-year-old and her aunt related the sighting to

Adolf that evening, he said they could have seen one of the swells written about in the *Times*, like John D. Rockefeller or J.P. Morgan. Over a thousand "robber baron" capitalists lived in New York City, and union workers ranted and raved about them constantly. "Only bigwigs like that could afford a new Oldsmobile," Adolf declared.

Henry Ford, however, soon would send automobiles to New York City that a few workers eventually would be able to afford as the economy grew. Within a couple of weeks from Anna's horseless carriage sighting, the first two-seat, two-cylinder Ford Model A was driven off Detroit production lines.

Once on the high platform, the three sightseers waited just a few minutes until a train came rumbling into view and shrieked to a stop, disgorging swarms of pushing passengers. *Teta* Anna urged "Quickly, quickly," yet again as the three pressed their way into a car.

When the girl entered the train, she watched with interest the duties of the uniformed conductor as he took their passes and shooed them to seats so that aisles would be clear for standing passengers. She imagined her stepuncle moving people about each night and felt proud to know him. After but a brief stop the train hummed loudly and took off on its creaky bridge above the street as young Anna peered out opened windows eye-level with the tops of many buildings. Below her, trolleys and buggies and pedestrians moved about streets often crisscrossed with telegraph and electric lines.

While the three Czechs whirred over the electric rails, Anna Zieman passed out bread and boiled eggs from her string bag for their lunch. They could eat and rest on a long elevated train ride through the city, provided by Adolf's free passes.

As if the day had not given enough for the new immigrants to think about, once finished with the el ride and on their way back south toward the Lower East Side, Anna Zieman pointed out a cinema and its marquis to her niece. "The Great Train Robbery" was playing. It was an eight-minute film with no captions or sound, cut from still scene to still scene at breakneck speed. *Teta* Anna said that she and Adolf had seen it on one of her husband's nights off. "It's so exciting, *Aničko*! My heart stopped," she exclaimed, going on to say that perhaps Walter would take his cousin to see it one evening after the fourteen-year-old was earning her own money.

Both Annas hoped that the job of caring for the dressmaker's twins would materialize. Anna Zieman said they would check the following day, Saturday, to see if it had been arranged.

When the three finally wove their way southward to the Zieman neighborhood, afternoon heat was radiating from streets and tenements. They stopped at a market for supper makings and climbed the stairs into the stuffiness of their third floor rooms. Adolf had awakened, and quickly the Annas prepared another picnic for the roof.

The next day, the sixth of July 1903, was to be another important time for both Czech travelers. Not only did Anna Zieman pin down the childcare job for her niece, Adolf came home in the morning with a tip from *Tibor* about a job for Joe Valenda. A fire station within walking distance needed a man to clean its horse stalls. Because Saturday night was to be Adolf's night off, he would accompany his father-in-law to the station to look into it after breakfast. His day sleeping routine was always thrown off during his break from night work.

Teta Anna and her niece walked to Mrs. Kinkel's shop as the pregnant woman talked to the fourteen-year-old about how to present herself for an American job. Once there, the girl sighed with relief when Mrs. Kinkel relayed that her sister-in-law, Gertrude, was interested in meeting Mrs. Zieman's niece, and gave them the address to Kinkel's Tailor Shop, several blocks away.

As they walked on, Anna Zieman instilled in young Anna how to remember directions in the big city. The girl always had the Zieman address tucked on her person, but she needed to start remembering the paths she took. The older woman had her niece pay special attention to buildings and shops on corners where they turned right or left.

She pulled a stub of pencil and a piece of butcher paper from her pocket to make a map for the girl showing English names of streets. While the fourteen-year-old could not read English, she could match the markings on the paper with street signs. And of course there were always policemen circulating their beats in the neighborhood. Young Anna did her best to remember it all, but the frantic bustle of the streets made her uneasy.

The tailor shop was busy. It stood at street level in a block of grimy white brick buildings, but the store inside was clean. A dress and suit draped on shapely mannequins stood in the window. Anna thought they looked beautiful.

Gertrude Kinkel looked young Anna over carefully when she was presented to her by Anna Zieman. The girl had worn her new/used blouse with the blue flowers embroidered on its color, now ironed and neat. Her hair was carefully combed and pulled back, the worn blue ribbon tied around it in a bow. The girl smiled her best tilted smile, hoping the woman would like her. She especially was eager to make her own money so that she could go with Walter to see "The Great Train Robbery."

The three quickly moved through a curtain to a back room, the Kinkel parlor, where the dressmaker's eight-year-old twins, Sophie and Stephan, were playing on the floor with wooden blocks, alphabet letters painted on their sides. A stuffed teddy bear was propped up between the children as though it were playing with the blocks, too. The shop owners had indulged their children with the toy craze of the day, a fuzzy bear inspired by President Teddy Roosevelt's rescue of a young cub on one of his many hunting trips. The fourteen-year-old smiled at the twins, her different eyes twinkling; they smiled back.

The children's mother explained that she wanted to hire someone who could take Sophie and Stephan out of their hot rooms daily for walks to a small park near her church a few blocks away. The job included making lunch for the children and keeping them occupied in the Kinkel living quarters until suppertime. A devout Catholic, the dressmaker did not work Sundays, "especially with dear Pope Leo's life failing away," she said, crossing herself.

So the job would be for six days weekly for a month. In August Mrs. Kinkel was to accompany the twins for a week with members of the Down Town Relief Bureau on their fresh air jaunt to the seashore. She had helped organize other neighborhood mothers to go on the trip funded by the charitable wealthy of upper Manhattan. It had been designed to give mothers and children in the Lower East Side a brief rest from the terrible heat of New York City in August.

The dressmaker said that she was prepared to pay a good worker fifty cents a day, or $3.00 a week. Whomever she hired would be expected to prepare lunch for the children and could eat with them. The woman was satisfied, after talking to the fourteen-year-old in German, that she could communicate well enough with the Czech girl. Young Anna seemed experienced with children from her own family and her two years of work.

The mother was pleased when young Anna spoke up to say that she was eager to learn to speak the English of America, which the Kinkel children already had conquered from their schooling. The Kinkels spoke both their native German and English. "Americanization" was stressed in public school classes and by most immigrant parents. The dressmaker began to nod her head, indicating her acceptance of the girl.

Then Anna Zieman stepped in. "Besides fixing lunch, *Anička* can help with supper, too, before she leaves evenings." She paused to study Bessie Kinkel's positive reaction before she continued. "And she can make *koláče* and liver dumplings." That idea seemed to please Gertrude greatly, so the pregnant woman quickly went on, "Preparing the evening food, the added work of it, might be worth a bit more. For six days . . . perhaps four dollars?" She stopped. An awkward silence fell over the conversation, but the pregnant woman just smiled pleasantly at the dressmaker.

Young Anna's heart froze. She was afraid her aunt had turned Mrs. Kinkel away from giving her the job. The dressmaker finally sighed and said to the girl, "You can make poppy seed *koláče?*" The girl nodded vigorously. There was an uncomfortable pause before the dressmaker went on. "Then I will pay $3.50, if you will fix supper and *koláče* from time to time. The poppy seed ones are Mr. Kinkel's favorite." Then she crossed her arms and gazed at Anna Zieman with stern finality.

Anna's aunt nodded in agreement. It was settled. Anna Mrkvička was hired for her very first job in America. She would earn money that she herself could spend. She could go to "The Great Train Robbery" with Walter.

The delighted Annas laughed and chattered arm in arm all the way back to the Ziemans'. And when Adolf and Joe Valenda climbed the stairs to find them fixing supper and tidying the apartment, they, too, had good news. Old Joe would clean manure from the Fire House horse stalls just a forty minute walk away, giving relief to a worker Joe's age who had hurt his leg. The job should last until it was time for the old man to board a train for Iowa.

The Fire Chief had been surprised that the two men knew of the opening so quickly, but Adolf explained that the man who had hurt his leg was the friend of a great uncle of his work mate, *Tibor* Szabo. Word of mouth was the usual way most jobs were located in the neighborhood, along with hand-printed signs propped in windows: "Man Wanted, Heavy Work" or "Opening for Woman Clerk." Often "No Irish need apply!" also was fastened nearby.

To celebrate the good fortune in the Zieman household that night, Adolf and his father-in-law had stopped at a tavern to buy a bottle of Wolfe's Schnapps, and after supper he and Old Joe both drank ample glasses of the liqueur as they smoked five-cent Cremo cigars. The mistress of the household pursed her lips at her husband's extravagance.

The pregnant woman deposited Walter's pay along with every extra cent she could spare in a neighborhood bank, to save for her dream of moving across the great bridge to Brooklyn. With the baby coming she longed for more room in a safer neighborhood, one that offered better schools. But it was a good evening in spite of her husband's spending; everyone in the cramped household now had paying jobs.

That night Adolf and his wife shared the one bed in their rooms. Old Joe trudged to the roof with Walter and his cousin, and even though the wooden strips beneath the blanket were uncomfortable, the warm schnapps had the old man snoring quickly.

Anna Mrkvička's first workweek in America was a milestone in her life. She and the twins soon were walking hand in hand to a small park near the tailor's shop, where they romped in green grass under tall shade trees. Sophie, a quiet girl, clutched her teddy bear; Stephan skipped and hopped and talked constantly, pointing to things to teach English to "Annie." It made the eight-year-old boy feel important.

Gertrude Kinkel showed the new hire the way to the church and park her first day, admonishing her not to talk to strangers. She must hold onto the children's hands crossing streets. She was not to let the twins out of her sight. She must be careful of fire wagons galloping to fires; the wagons sometimes ran down children in the rush and confusion. The mother showed the girl the Precinct police station, and added her shop's written address to the Ziemans' address and the map already tucked inside young Anna's clothing.

The dressmaker soon was very happy with the way the girl handled the twins, as well as the game the three played with English words. It was good review for her out-of-school children. To Annie's "What is?" they would reply "street light" or "park bench" carefully in English, giggling when the fourteen-year-old clumsily tried to copy their pronunciations. But the young Czech laughed good-naturedly with Sophie and Stephan, just as she had with her younger sisters and brother. The children soon squealed "Annie, Annie," with excitement when she arrived mornings.

And Mr. Kinkel devoured the poppy seed *koláče* the girl baked one rainy afternoon. Her cooking skills learned at the Scavenisks' did not go unnoticed. Gertrude Kinkel was very pleased with her fast-stepping hired girl.

At the end of the first week the dressmaker counted into young Anna's palm two silver dollars, two fifty cent pieces and two quarters, much to the girl's delight. On the way home the fourteen-year-old nearly skipped down the street. She had looked at little purses in a store window each day to and from work, and she proudly walked through the shop door to buy a purse like *Teta* Anna's, a purse of her own to hold her new American money.

The girl spent delicious time examining each small pouch a clerk put before her, clicking metal clasps to see that they were tight and safe. Finally she decided on a black leather one with a ring fastened to one of its sides. A string or safety pin could be put through the ring to keep it safe in her pocket. "This one," she said, paying one precious nickel for her first ever purchase of something new and all her own.

The fourteen-year-old was so engrossed with checking her pocket and the money in her purse when she left the shop, that she suddenly realized she recognized nothing on the street around her. Panicking, she quickly referred to the map and backtracked to where she had not made a required turn to the left. "Stupid girl!" she said aloud in Czech. She never made that mistake again.

At the market near the Ziemans', young Anna stopped to buy apples for the household, the biggest and best she could find in the bin. She was grateful for how her aunt had welcomed her, and she wanted to help with the cost of food now that she was earning her own money.

Each time the fourteen-year-old entered a bountiful market she wandered in wonder at the goods on shelves and in barrels and crates. She was tempted to sample every new thing before her—tin cans full of peas and beans and peaches, crackers shaped like little animals, tooth paste, Coca Cola, Shredded Wheat, Hershey bars and Cracker Jacks. The abundance always overwhelmed her, but she thought prices were much too high.

Five pounds of coffee sold for thirty-five cents, a cloth bag of sugar twenty-eight. Potatoes cost fifteen cents a peck, eggs twenty-three cents a dozen. Anna eventually would weaken to spend her hard-earned coins for a bit of chocolate and her very own bar of Pear's soap, but not with her first American earnings.

She and *Teta* Anna had discussed how she must save her money for the trip to Iowa and her new life there, so each purchase had to be approached with care. She would learn to negotiate with the butcher for not one, but two soup bones, just as *Teta* Anna did, and she would spar with Mrs. Kinkel at the used clothing store for another skirt and blouse to take to Iowa. Earning her own money opened wonderful opportunities to the fourteen-year-old peasant girl, but new clothing was beyond her budget; unused stockings were twenty cents a pair, under drawers fifteen cents.

In the meantime that week, Old Joe had his special directions about how to arrive home safely from the Fire House. While he couldn't read or write, he could count. Adolf had given him a formula to follow. He was to walk six blocks to the left at the corner saloon near the Ziemans', eight blocks to the left again, then right seven more. The pattern was reversed when he headed home.

Joe Valenda memorized the directions and found his way to and from his work concentrating hard and counting under his breath. For reassurance he often patted the written address of the Ziemans in his pocket. He knew that if he became lost in the confusion of the overbearing city, some stranger would have to read to him the English words written on the rumpled paper.

So began the six weeks in New York City Anna Mrkvička would describe as "wonderful" the rest of her long life. Days and nights soon settled into a pattern. All five living in the Ziemans' two rooms went to work at different times, in different directions. The one bed was never unused for long. Sometimes night rain chased roof sleepers down into the stuffy two rooms, but as time passed, young Anna and her aunt grew to laugh together over the complications of their crowded living.

It was up to the woman and girl to work outside of the home and also take care of the many chores of the household. Even though they labored long hours, there still was marketing and meal preparation to manage. They shared the washing of piles of dirty clothes and hanging them to dry, carrying them up and down the long flights of stairs. Ironing was burdensome and especially unpleasant in the heat. There were clothes to mend, socks to darn.

Anna Mrkvička, her mother's eldest child, had been trained early in her life to shoulder more than her share of caring for her household in Velký Lunec. She rose with her aunt at first light to take the slop jar down to the latrine if need be, and to fetch two full pails of water from the basement faucet for cooking, drinking, washing hands and faces. Then, with *Teta* Anna she prepared food for breakfast and packed lunches, swept and tidied the rooms.

Keeping the crowded space and five bodies clean was no small task, but young Anna decided to take time to water the curling pea vines growing in the cheese boxes in the Ziemans' window. She checked carefully daily to see if new tendrils were sprouting toward the sun. Her aunt often asked her with a smile, "Will we have peas for supper, *Aničko?*" at which the girl would grin and answer, "Not yet tonight."

The Annas together soon solved the problem of the smelly manure-caked shoes Old Joe wore home from his work in the Fire Station horse stalls. The pregnant woman didn't want the filthy boots in her rooms. She quickly bought another used pair for her father from the Kinkel shop, and Joe Valenda's dirty shoes were tied by their laces to the rope and pulley and reeled far out away from the building.

The first time the two Annas yanked the reeking boots over the busy traffic below, the girl and her aunt broke into uproarious laughter about the "shit over the street" people were walking under. Pedestrians would need to watch not only where they stepped, but what they were stepping beneath.

The regularly scheduled Zieman "bath time" mornings meant that everyone had to rise before dawn to bathe before traveling to work that day. Only Adolf, who worked nights, was able to relax in the tub after breakfast. His wife or niece still heated water and filled his tub for him before they left to work at the shirt factory and the dressmaker's.

Young Anna did all she could to help her aunt, whom she noticed often stroking her back due to the weight and growing discomfort of her pregnancy. The girl had seen her mother also stretch and rub her aching body when her belly was swollen with new life. As days passed the bond between the two Annas grew.

A couple of weeks later, one evening when the others were out working, Teta Anna seemed especially tired as she kneaded her cramped shoulders. When she and her niece finished hanging washed clothes on the pulley over the street, she winked at the fourteen-year-old and moved to lift her husband's tobacco and cigarette papers from the glass-front cupboard. "Don't tell your uncle," she cautioned the girl as she sat at the table to carefully place the cinnamon-laced tobacco in the paper. She expertly rolled and licked it closed, revealing her experience. In Velký Lunec many women smoked their husband's pipes, and even their own, but young Anna had never seen a woman smoke a cigarette.

Then Anna Zieman tucked the cigarette and matches carefully in her pocket, motioning for her niece to follow her up to the roof. They would find some relief for their tired bodies as they rested their aching backs against the coolness of the water vat.

Once settled on the roof, Teta Anna lit her secret prize and inhaled deeply, offering a puff to her niece. The fourteen-year-old took the cigarette carefully between her thumb and forefinger and sucked the smoke in deeply as her aunt had done, at which point she hacked and sputtered, immediately feeling her stomach rebel. As she handed the cigarette back to her aunt, they both laughed and settled down to relax together after a hot and hard day's work.

As talk eventually turned to their lives back in Kutná Hora, young Anna discovered that her aunt had been as terrified of Sister *Marie Helena* as she had been, that both of them had sat fearfully on the same hard, splintered seats in the regimented Catholic School. They shared their memories of the beauty of Saint Barbara's Cathedral on the hill, at which point the girl asked her aunt why she did not go to mass Sundays when she didn't have to sew at the workroom. The girl mentioned her own pale rosary still tucked in her trunk in *Babička Marie*'s *bábuška*. It lay now next to her treasures from America– the miniature Fourth of July flag and the 1889 Indian head penny.

The older Anna paused, inhaling the stolen cigarette deeply. Then she admitted that she greatly missed going to mass and confession, but that her husband angrily opposed her religion. She said she would try to take her niece to a service if possible during her stay, when Adolf was working or not at home, but that he would be furious if he found out.

Adolf Zieman had been reared a Lutheran, and even though he didn't attend church regularly, he had forbidden his wife to continue the Catholic litany once they were in America. No children of his would be "under the thumb of any Roman Pope," he had declared. That shocked fourteen-year-old Anna. In the hamlet of Velký Lunec everyone was Catholic.

The pregnant wife said with a sigh, looking into her niece's different eyes, "Marry a nice 'Bohemie' boy, *Anička*. It will make life much easier for you." Even though Anna Zieman usually was in efficient but pleasant good humor, the talk about her religion made her eyes sad. The fourteen-year-old wished she had not broached the subject.

One Sunday when Walter had to work with the Czechs making cigars on lower Tenth Street, *Teta* Anna also had to work. She suggested that her niece accompany her son to visit the Czech neighborhood, to see how Walter made cigars. The boy would show his cousin the route and draw a map so that she could come home safely.

With the twelve-year-old leading the way, Anna ventured southward many blocks into factory areas in the Lower East Side, buildings with workrooms like those where Anna Zieman helped manufacture shirtwaists. The two entered neighborhoods where tenements were even more crowded than the Ziemans'. Small children sat peering out of upstairs factory windows where their parents worked, sewing machines roaring behind them. The street heat was stifling. It was muggy. Rain threatened.

When Anna and Walter entered the cigar-making enclaves, a stench from overflowing ash barrels enveloped them. Tobacco stems stripped of their leaves spilled out of rusty containers onto the walkway. Anna noticed with some relief that the names on shops around her were overwhelmingly Czech, and that most people scurrying by were speaking her native tongue.

Finally, at a crumbling red brick row building, the two walked up three flights of worn stairs scattered with trash and reeking of urine and garbage. Opened doors on each floor revealed rows of Czech men, women and children cutting and rolling cigars as fast as they could. Walter and Anna entered the sweltering rooms of the Matějíček family, which included an ill father, a nearly toothless mother, and three barefooted children ranging in age from two to nine years. The man of the house sat in the corner on a bed wheezing for breath, the youngest child in his lap. His color was gray.

The wife of the household was pleased to meet Walter's cousin, to visit with someone just recently from her own Bohemia. She bid the girl to sit near her workbench, and asked about Anna's family and home near Kutná Hora, the girl's trip over in steerage. Then, as her brown-stained fingers returned to work the strong-smelling tobacco, she began to share her own family's story.

In the frigid winter, when Mr. Matějíček had become sick and unable to work any longer at cigar making, the family was in crisis. He had been a blacksmith in Bohemia, but had not been able to find work with his trade in Manhattan the seven years since their arrival.

Only one of the children was old enough to be of much help working the tobacco, and Mrs. Matějíček knew of no other way to make a living. When Anna Zieman heard of the family's situation through another worker at the shirt factory, she suggested that her son, Walter, could help out during the summer, until school was back in session.

Strikes by union-led Czech tobacco workers had brought the pay for finished cigars up to $4.50 per thousand, which amounted to about six and a half cents per hour per worker, if they worked rapidly. The Matějíčeks' landlord/employer furnished the tobacco and charged the impoverished family $12.50 rent a month for two crowded rooms, one to sleep and cook in, one to work in. The space had neither running water nor a fireplace to keep the rooms warm in the winter. A latrine was in a back alley. The ceiling was collapsing from water damage in the family's living area. The harried wife cursed the landlord, saying he never repaired anything.

The worn mother and her nine-year-old had to work from sunrise to sunset seven days a week to survive, but could do so only when their employer made tobacco leaves available. They had some respite when supply shipments were late, but down times brought them no money with which to live. When summer worker Walter Zieman went back to classes in September, they would have to find someone else to take his place, and again share their earnings.

There was no talk of sending the children to school, so no one in the household had learned English, even after their seven years in America. The father's health was growing worse; Mrs. Matějíček feared that he would have to be sent to hospital one day soon. When young Anna studied the man fighting for breath on the worn mattress, she was reminded of how *Babička Marie* had looked the months before she died. She thought sadly that Mr. Matějíček probably would not survive much longer.

Mrs. Matějíček continued to chatter as she, her daughter and Walter sat at the workbench cutting tobacco leaves with stumpy knives. The eldest child was too young to work the razor sharp blades, so she did her best to roll tobacco already cut into cones, then Walter firmed them more tightly into finished cigars. A pouch of worn brown and greasy bed–tick, fastened in front of the whole length of the bench, caught scraps of waste. The stench and the heat and the unhealthy fumes in the workroom gradually made young Anna feel nauseated.

Then the two-year-old climbed down whimpering from her father's lap and toddled to the stranger, wrapping her arms around Anna's legs. She was about the age of foster child *Anton* Procházka, at home in *Maminka's* care, and she was soiled and soaked within a dirty diaper.

Anna offered to change the child, and the mother waved her to the other room to a pile of rough rags near a stack of soiled diapers swarming with flies. The girl reluctantly added another dirty wad to the pile. Once somewhat cleaner, the pale child didn't want to let the helpful visitor go, but the fourteen-year-old felt the need to leave the sadness of the rooms and bid good-bye to the Matějíčeks and their disheartening life.

She explained to them that she had a long walk home and washing and ironing to do while her uncle slept. There was supper to prepare later. The woman waved over the mess in her living quarters and nodded with understanding as Anna extricated herself from the arms of the small child and bid the family and Walter good-bye. The little one began to cry as the visitor walked out the door and down the stairs.

Once she reached the crowded street, Anna noticed a Bellevue Hospital horse-drawn ambulance parked nearby. A small crowd was stopped to watch a dead-still woman on a stretcher being put inside its doors.

That scene and the Matějíčeks' sad situation bothered the fourteen-year-old all her way home. The smelly cigar workrooms were worse than even her parents' crowded conditions in Bohemia. At least in Velký Lunec children could work and play outside where the air was fresh.

She thought it not good that the Matějíček children were not attending school. She didn't know that at that time one fifth of all boys and girls in the United States between the ages of ten and sixteen were often employed and not in school. No consistent child labor and school attendance laws protected them as yet, although the socially minded were trying to rectify the situation.

In Bohemia, Anna Mrkvička had had the advantage of some schooling. The determination of the Catholic Church and the Habsburg dynasty saw to it that Austrian peasants try to learn to read and write. The girl had been the first of her parents' children to be literate, which had made the family proud, but when she stepped onto American soil, she became just one more in the mass of immigrants who could not speak, read nor write the language of their new country.

But young Anna walked back toward the Ziemans' feeling grateful to have her job with the Kinkel twins. She was glad that her aunt's family did not have to make their living rolling tobacco, and that Walter would be returning to school at summer's end. Her heart ached as she remembered the tugging at her skirt of the sad little two-year-old.

As she walked north through blocks and blocks of textile factories, the young Czech looked with more scrutiny at the buzzing sewing activity beyond windows above the streets. *Teta* Anna had told her of the hardships she dealt with on her job at only one of the over three hundred such sewing factories in the Lower East Side.

Workers were fined for going to the toilet or talking to another worker, for anything that left their sewing machines idle. When work was scheduled Sunday, a sign was posted, "If you don't come in Sunday, you need not come in Monday." That caution had kept Anna Zieman from picking up her stepniece and father from Ellis Island earlier than she had. Unions were trying to organize garment workers, but most laborers were afraid of losing their jobs if they cooperated with them. Adolf and Anna Zieman argued often about what was best, to support collective bargaining or not.

As the young immigrant walked toward the Ziemans', it started to drizzle and the dense crowd on the sidewalks began to break apart, to dash here and there to find shelter. When ninety-pound Anna stopped to check her map, the crowd jostled her as though she were invisible. A burley man stepped on her toe, which brought from her a string of swear words often sputtered by her father. It helped the pain.

Once, when she paused under a damp awning, she was nearly surrounded by three drunken sailors. She realized that they were talking about her in a language she didn't understand, and in a tone that made her stomach clench. The quick-thinking girl slithered around them and crossed the wet street with hurried steps as *Teta* Anna had regularly advised her to do.

Suddenly the fourteen-year-old was overcome with heat and the crowded stress of the big city, and she realized what a relief it would be to live and work on open farmland once again. She walked among the pack of bustling people getting wetter by the minute, but her mind was remembering birds singing in old shade trees as she awoke in her parents' small room. She could feel the cool relief of dipping her bare toes in the nearby village pond, and hear the gentle low of cattle, the nearby murmur of neighbors.

The books she had spent days leafing through on Ellis Island had shown pictures of Iowa prairie grasses and sweeping vistas framed with groves of forest. Would the Valenda farm in Iowa have cool shade trees nearby, a pond like that near Velký Lunec? From that point on young Anna pondered more and more what her life would be on the vast plains in the middle of America, where even more miles would separate her from her homeland and her family.

One night when Walter arrived home early from work, he and young Anna finally were able to go to the cinema. After a trolley ride, the two cousins sat on wooden benches in a dark theater, eyes wide with expectation. The smell of sweating bodies filled the hot and stuffy room. People all around them fussed in various languages, impatient for the show to begin. Then suddenly a title page flashed upon the screen: "The Great Train Robbery, produced by The Edison Manufacturing Company."

Immediately, pale hand-colored pictures rapidly whizzed before them, showing images of a plot based on the tales and myths of the countless outlaws of the Wild West, bandits the likes of Jesse James and Billy the Kid. There were neither captions nor sound; exaggerated action told the story.

The fourteen-year-old watched as jerking photographs of robbers on horseback zoomed by before her surprised eyes. Bandits with bandannas tied around their necks jumped from their horses, and, after wild fisticuffs, hog-tied a telegraph operator before rushing to stop a train. Terrified passengers were forced from railroad cars and robbed. In the meantime, the wily operator freed himself and rushed to a nearby music hall where dancers in reddish, yellow, and green costumes were captured mid-step. A posse was gathered to pursue the outlaws.

Gunplay ensued. Through the remaining moving pictures, as the posse on horseback chased the villains, the heart of the fourteen-year-old pounded her ribs. She tightly gripped her cousin's clammy hand. At the end of the tableaus, the chief outlaw pointed his gun at the camera and shot directly at the audience. The next screen showed only a square of bloody red.

Gasps and screams exploded from Anna and everyone around her. The terrified girl clutched her breast and looked down aghast, expecting to see blood flowing from a gaping wound. Then the lights came on and excited patrons exited as they exclaimed and compared their fright with everyone within earshot. All the way home on the trolley the cousins chattered and giggled about their amazing experience.

The next morning at breakfast, when the two regaled Adolf with their exciting tale of "The Great Train Robbery," Anna's uncle warned the girl that she would have to watch out for such robbers on her long trip to Iowa. Bandits often stopped and boarded trains, he said. Sometimes they blew up the tracks with dynamite. The girl's eyes grew wide, the "moving" pictures racing through her mind.

Her uncle said that driver *Tibor*, long fascinated with trains and their lore, had told him stories about robbers and engineers many nights as they steered their elevated cars through the dark in the wee hours of the morning. *Tibor* had talked about Butch Cassidy, the Sundance Kid, and their robberies in Utah. The Union Pacific Railroad had finally hired armed Pinkerton detectives to protect their trains. Adolf said of the two bandits, "Killed in a shoot-out in Bolivia, they were!"

And as far as the Midwest, right where Anna was headed, bandits the likes of Jesse James still roamed the area. Then the uncle added with disgust, "James was outsmarted finally. Killed for a $10,000 reward by a goddam treacherous member of his own gang."

Young Anna, of course, would wonder thereafter whether she would be held up on her train ride to Iowa. Would she be forced by a villain with evil eyes and a big gun to give up her savings from her new little purse and *Babička Marie's bábuška*?

Adolf continued to spin train yarns for his "little Annie," the only one in the household who had not heard his stories many, many times. He told how *Tibor* sometimes sang "The Ballad of Casey Jones," for the benefit of a smattering of early morning passengers. He'd warble in his baritone how Engineer Casey rammed his Cannonball Express into a freight train trying to make up time. He'd been killed in the crash, quilling his six-tone whistle in his own special way. At that point *Tibor* always blasted the elevated car's horn for good measure. The *Times* had printed the story of the Cannonball in 1900, and being a fellow trainman, Conductor Adolf had struggled through its English to learn the story.

Near the end of July, special headlines splashed across the newspaper.

Pope Leo XIII died and lay in state in the Basilica of Saint Peter in Rome. The two Annas sneaked to a special mass for the Holy Father while Adolf was sleeping, and knelt side by side at a neighborhood parish church. It would be young Anna's last visit to a church for a long time.

And Adolf came home spouting about two events of July 23: electrical problems with his elevated train, and "that busybody, Mother Jones." There had been an explosion at the main powerhouse providing electricity for the trains, halting them all. Neither he nor *Tibor* had any idea what had happened, or when the trains would move again, stuck as they were high over the streets without any means of communication. Adolf had orders under such circumstances to keep people in the train due to the danger of the third electric rail; when current came back on, anybody touching the rail could be electrocuted.

While he had tried to keep his passengers safe in the darkened cars, a few belligerent men charged around him cursing, and took off groping along the tracks toward the nearest station. "I yelled at the damned fools to come back," Adolf said, "but they ignored me." Fortunately his passengers made it safely to a station long before the electricity finally came back on, but it had been a stressful night. Anna's uncle was in a bad mood all through breakfast, his sculpted mustache twitching.

The second news item he had read in the *Times* made him rant and rave further. Seventy-three-year-old Mother Jones, "that goddam socialist", was in town stirring up people about child labor laws. "None of her business," said Adolf. "I will decide when my son works, and for how long."

Jones, the aggressive union activist, had arrived in the city with her "army of boys," and had attained a permit to march through the streets to Theodore Roosevelt's Manhattan mansion. She wanted to confront the 26th American President about the terrible factory conditions young children, often orphans, endured. They were maimed and sickened from overworking dawn to dusk, and their pay was usually twenty-five cents a day or less. The army of boys, accompanied by two fifes and drums on their march, had carried placards through Manhattan streets which read "55 hours or Nothing" and "Prosperity, Where is Our Share?"

Anna Zieman spoke up to Adolf about this issue. She said that she believed children should not be working such long hours, and should be attending school; some boys and girls seven and eight years old were employed with their mothers in her sewing room, and she had seen terrible accidents when machine needles went through their little fingernails. One girl had lost a thumb entirely when such a wound became infected.

Adolf cut her down, saying in anger, "The goddam Socialist should stay out of a father's business." He didn't want anyone telling him how Walter was to be raised. He had worked from dawn to dusk himself as a child, and it had taught him the realities of life. His pregnant wife pursed her lips and went silent.

Young Anna didn't know what to make of it all. *Maminka* had decided when and where she worked in Velký Lunec. It was hard for her to grasp why some old "Mother" would be marching in the streets to try to help boys and girls not her own. But when she thought of the Matějíček children, she wished that someone would look out for them.

Adolf wasn't the only person upset with Mother Jones and her cause. In fact, railroad magnate Cornelius Vanderbilt was so bold to bellow his capitalistic attitudes publicly during this era of focus on questionable labor practices. About the impact of company owners' decisions on American workers and consumers he proclaimed, "The public interest be damned!"

Nevertheless, by 1913 the likes of Mother Jones and the Women's Trade Union League would force Congress to pass thirty-three new labor laws to protect American workers. School attendance laws slowly would be implemented. Enforcing them in the crowded Lower East Side would come too late to save children like the Matějíčeks', however.

The three Ziemans often discussed at mealtimes how strikes sometimes were succeeding to bring about fewer work hours and higher pay. Workers kept up a drumbeat of complaints about indifferent owners and monopolies that profited richly from their labor. They strongly objected to seven-day weeks of ten to fourteen hours each day. Coal miners were striking in Pennsylvania; the Board of Building Trades was always in arbitration in New York City. Adolf and his wife and son agreed how wrong some of the work practices were, but they didn't know how far they dared go to bring about change.

Anna Mrkvička's time in New York City introduced her to the many forces of industrialization and class distinction in America, and the young Czech peasant began her struggle to understand how she was to fit into this new democracy. She would have to learn to do it within a money-driven capitalistic framework about which she had no education. It was all so different from the dictates of her difficult but relatively simple life under the Austrian monarchy in Velký Lunec.

The President of the newly adopted country of the fourteen-year-old also was struggling with the industrial problems of the gilded Victorian Age. He had succeeded the assassinated William McKinley in the White House in 1901, at a time already disrupted by problems between capitalism and worker/consumers. Teddy Roosevelt found that it had been easier to lead his Rough Riders up San Juan Hill in the war with Spain in Cuba in 1898, than it was to deal with the excesses of big business during an era of tremendous social change.

He would develop into a "trustbuster," taking on the railroad, steel and coal capitalists who sometimes held the public captive with their monopolistic pricing of wages and goods. Strikes and marches were accelerating as workers became angrier each day about the grinding realities of their labor and their lives.

The different Czech and American eyes of young Anna absorbed as much as they could her six weeks in New York City. She couldn't grasp the complex social issues of America, and at only fourteen she most certainly couldn't understand the market problems tied to the country's food producing plains where she was headed. She would find that making a living on the rich prairies of Iowa was to be a challenge quite different from how her family had survived for generations working the land in Bohemia.

The four weeks with the Kinkel twins passed quickly. The dressmaker counted final pay into Anna's hand, and with a smile gave her an extra nickel because she liked the girl. The fourteen-year-old walked the hot streets home very proud of herself. She had earned $14 in America, much more than the fifty cents a week at her last job with the Scavenisks. A good portion of her earnings was tucked in *Babička Marie's bábuška* and her new little purse. She now had a few dollars besides money for her ticket to Iowa.

Teta Anna had received a letter from her brother, *Petr* Valenda, in Iowa. It answered her notice to him that his father and stepneice had been claimed from Ellis Island in July. *Petr* said that he would pick up the two from the late afternoon train at Center Point August 20. He and his boys would pause from their threshing schedule with crews in neighbors' fields. *Otec* and *Anička* could assist with that work, and it would soon be corn-picking time. Four extra hands would be helpful.

Young Anna was filled with hope and apprehension as she faced another long rail trip, this time complicated, she was convinced, by the possibility of bandits robbing her train. Her mind filled more each day with the pictures she had seen of Iowa, its Indians, its tall grass, its buffalo. Her aunt assured her that she would be fine in Iowa, that *Petr* would watch out for her, but she added that she knew little about her brother's wife. She had never met the woman.

August 18, 1903, Anna Mrkvička rose early and packed her small trunk, this time with a few new/used clothes. She wrapped her keepsakes carefully in *Babička Marie's bábuška*, smiling at the miniature flag and memories of her first American Independence Day. She safety-pinned her small purse of money on a string in her pocket. One last time she watered the east window pea vine after bringing pails of water for the family from the basement faucet. The plant's tendrils had grown since the girl's arrival, twisting higher around the muslin curtains.

"The vines will miss you, *Aničko*," her aunt said softly.

Because Anna Zieman had to work the day of the immigrants' departure, it was arranged that young Walter would guide the two travelers by trolley to the train station. Both Annas shed tears as the older woman said good-bye to her father and his goddaughter in her crowded rooms. She carefully pinned their names and destination in English on the girl's blouse with the blue flowers on its collar, and her father's used suit from the Kinkel shop.

At last the pregnant woman, now six weeks larger with child, hugged her stepniece and said, "Make a good life in Iowa, *Aničko*." She added as she turned to leave for work, " . . . and find a nice 'Bohemie' boy to marry!" a twinkle in her teary eyes. The group would never be together again.

New York's Penn Station, built in 1871, was being grandly renovated in 1903, but trains still departed there. The two Czechs wound their way behind Walter by trolley to the station and the ticket window, only to have to pick through confusing construction to find the proper tracks leading toward Chicago and eventually Iowa.

After awkward good-byes to her twelve-year-old cousin, Anna stepped once again past a smartly uniformed train conductor. She entered a wooden car hitched behind a large black engine of the day, white steam puffing from its sides. Steel train cars would not be introduced until 1904. The girl and Joe Valenda had more than another thousand miles to travel. They would do so on arteries of steel tracks laid down through several of the United States, before they could settle at last on the tough prairies of Iowa.

The two found seats near other immigrants moving westward in America, some also with their destinations printed in English on tags attached to their clothing. They all were weary from their travels. Sadness from their past etched their faces, but they were pushing through anxiety into unknown futures nonetheless.

As Anna settled her small trunk near her for the trip, images of her already long journey filled her mind—her first steps onto a train in Kutná Hora and the swaying of the ocean beneath the Kronprinz. She thought of little *Jan* and his red-cheeked "Netherlander" mother in steerage, wondering where they were now. Was *Jetta*, who nibbled at the terrible biscuits with her on the lurching deck of the big ship, this day working with her uncle in a packing plant in Chicago? Or had they already made enough money in amazing America to start their own sausage shop? And Anna hoped that lone traveler *Růyena* had been able to leave the crowded confines of Ellis Island, that she hadn't been forced to bear another sickening ocean trip carrying her back to Europe.

Thinking of her own agonizingly long journey and delay at Ellis Island, memories of the warm and welcoming arms of *Teta* Anna momentarily brought tears. Images of what her aunt had shown her of Manhattan mixed with the city scenes passing away from her outside the train window.

The huge, looming dinosaur bones in the museum sometimes troubled her dreams, as did the feel of the dark, hot cinema and her fear of the evil eyes of the moving picture outlaws. She recalled the elevated train ride carrying her through Manhattan, revealing tall buildings all around her that seemed to touch the sky. Her mind still crackled with the jolting pop of firecrackers at her feet the magical Fourth of July on the banks of the East River.

She thought of her first American job, the giggles of the Kinkel twins, the money she'd earned to purchase her first little purse. Especially she thought fondly of *Teta* Anna's many acts of kindness. She hoped her aunt's childbirth would be easy and that her baby would be born healthy. *Maminka* had told her often of the many difficult births she assisted as a midwife.

And again she felt the tug at her skirt of the little Matějíček girl. She shook her head at the hopeless state of the Czech cigar-makers in their unsafe surroundings. There seemed to be little hope for a future for the frail children and their overworked parents.

Locked in such musings as her train chugged away from New York City, the fourteen-year-old suddenly felt overwhelmed with longing for her own family. As the train surged forward, the space between Anna and her work-worn mother, her sisters and brother, opened behind her like a fathomless black hole. Her heart ached with the question: "Will I ever see them again?"

But as the girl was carried through the tenements and warehouses of the largest urban area in America, crowded buildings gradually became less evident. Green, leafy trees, small towns and farmlands come into view. The girl finally began to see first hand the rolling fields the picture books at Ellis Island had promised, and she slowly started to feel better.

It is estimated that over time ten million immigrants like Anna Mrkvička and Joe Valenda chugged away from the most populous east coast region of the United States. Many cut through and around the beautiful Appalachian Mountains to middle America and beyond, swaying side to side with the rhythm of railroads, among planted fields and wild woodlands. The fourteen-year-old and her godfather would travel by rail from New York City to Center Point, Iowa, passing through two of the four time zones established in the United States in 1883. She and Joe did not grasp the time changes, of course. They owned no watches.

Chapter Eight

Into the Heartland

THE DIFFERENT EYES of the young immigrant watched intently the scenes unfolding outside her railcar windows, a panorama of late 1903 summer. She saw thick white pine trees and juniper clutching at hills and eastern mountains, as well as feathery honey locust with their curved and twisted pods. She watched shadows crawl across pastures and colorful wildflower meadows sprouting black-eyed susans, hillsides of purple and fuchsia. Butterflies, birds and August gnats flitted everywhere through the heat.

And of course she kept her eyes alert for train robbers galloping on horseback outside her window. None materialized.

Anna didn't know the romance of Walt Whitman's words about early railroad travel in America, "I hear locomotives rushing and roaring. I hear echoes reverberated through the greatest scenery in the world," but she felt the excitement of new discovery as the train charged forward. She couldn't help but join the early American love affair with railroads during her long trip west.

Trains were welding the far reaches of the United States' countryside together, sprinkling ethnic diversity here and there along their routes.

Anna and Old Joe sat side-by-side with nationalities including those of Germany, Sweden, England, Ireland and Norway, all adding their special blend to America's melting pot.

The two Czechs fortunately were able to take timely advantage of the "iron horses" that were well in place by 1903. They didn't have to travel laboriously to Iowa by horse and wagon or stage, steamboats and barges, and even on foot, as earlier settlers had to do. And they saw along their route many rough and dirty railroad section hands in grimy work clothes fastening still more steel rails in place. The young girl was fascinated by the rhythms of "gandy dancers" as they laid down more long miles of track.

At the end of the Civil War there were limited railroads traveling the immigrants' route from the east coast west; rail lines in general had stopped at the Missouri River, barely beyond Anna's Iowa destination. That changed in May of 1869, in Promontory, Utah. In that Wild West town a golden spike was hammered into the last piece of track on the first transcontinental rail bed running from New York City to San Francisco. The Union Pacific heading west and the Central Pacific heading east had raced to see which line could lay the most track before their milestone meeting.

By 1916 nearly 250,000 miles of railroads would be laid in America east to west and north to south, to move goods and people like the two Czechs all over the continent. At the time of Anna's trip, cowboys regularly were herding cattle to railheads where stock was loaded to be transported to distant markets.

The girl's train accommodations for her trip to Iowa were meager, but she found her car a bit cleaner than she would have years earlier. Windows had to be thrown open in stifling August, and soot from engine smokestacks still drifted inside cars onto her clothes and into her eyes, but by 1900 Northern Pacific's North Coast Limited had made some improvement to cleanliness. They advertised cleaner burning anthracite coal stoking their Lackawanna Road engines.

The fourteen-year-old had noticed a poster tacked near the ticket window in New York City, showing two smartly coifed and white-gloved women having tea in an elegant rail dining car. Their beauty had reminded Anna of the pretty girl advertising her precious Pear's soap on the shop window near her aunt's apartment. The immigrant couldn't read the poem in English printed beneath the crisp, clean sketch:

> Yes, Phoebe, I can now see why
> The praises of this road you cry.
> My gloves are white as when last night
> We took the Road of Anthracite.

Anna caught glimpses of passengers like those two well-dressed poster women as she rambled west, even though they traveled in a much different class of train from hers.

The eyes of the fourteen-year-old grew wide with what they saw at one point. Her own train sat still, sidetracked, as a fancy Pullman "hotel train" moved by her window, receiving track priority. Late 1800 posters distributed by both the Rock Island and the Chicago, Milwaukee and Saint Paul Railroads bragged of "Palace Dining Cars" and "Palace Reclining Chairs." Anna saw well-to-do Victorian-era train travelers move about in cars grandly furnished with wine and game rooms, barbershops and ice chests for cool drinks. Visually, decorations were sumptuous, sporting elaborately carved walnut and cherry wood paneling, guilt mirrors, drapes, organs, and even libraries.

Anna and her godfather, on the other hand, traveled without splendor. Even though Pullman "Sleeping Cars" were part of their train, the two could not afford a berth on one of them. The fourteen-year-old felt lucky to sit on a padded train seat rather than a European train car wooden bench. Instead of the dining car service of the wealthy, newsboys sauntered through her car from time to time selling fruit lollipops, cigars, soap, and "tinned edibles." They also hawked newspapers, which most immigrant passengers could not read.

Once as she waited in line to use the latrine, a nervous young woman behind her murmured to her the German word for water, obviously wondering whether the line led to where she could quench her thirst. Anna pointed to where she could get a drink, but she made a face when she added apologetically in her halting German that it tasted bad.

The two then managed a choppy conversation accompanied with many gestures. Gabriele Schmidt was eager to talk; she had traveled a long way by herself. She was headed for a small town in Ohio to take care of a widower's home and five children. Her uncle in Münster had made the arrangements. She was very nervous about what the man would be like. Her parents were dead, and she choked back tears when she spoke of the younger sister she had had to leave in Münster.

Anna shared the story of her trip from Bohemia as best she could. She told of her own concerns about making a life on the prairie of Iowa, and about buffalo and Indians. From then on, during the brief remainder of the time they sat near one another on the train, the two kindred immigrants exchanged glances and shy smiles.

In the Blue Ridge Mountains Anna and Gabriele both stared in awe at the steep, carved cliffs veering over them on one side, snake-like rivers curving below on the other. Anna saw for the first time evidence of coal, iron ore and zinc mining. She was learning much about the world beyond what Sister *Marie Helena's* rigid classroom had been able to teach her; the long trip was an education all its own.

At dusk Anna's car was illuminated. Train lighting had progressed from candles to compressed coal gas to electricity during the 1800s. By the time night lights began to glow, the young Czech had long left New York, and she scrunched into her seat to try to rest among the incessant sways and lurches of the train. The engine's whistle blew at crossings and to announce arrival at stations. Fellow travelers constantly careened up and down the aisles to the latrine; fussy children cried.

The experienced young traveler had learned to tolerate train activity from her trip through Germany, but her nagging worry about train robbers kept her vigilant. She finally decided after dark that outlaws also would be seeking sleep. At least at night they would not be trying to rob her of her purse.

The two Czechs figured out the meaning of conductors "All aboARD!" after they repeatedly heard the booming voices rise at the end of announcements in special pattern each time. The English calls echoed through the cars along with periodic station alerts: "Pittsburgh, NEXT stop. PittsBURGH!" or "FORT Wayne." When new passengers joined the train, the conductors also circulated up and down aisles crying, "TICkets, please. TICkets!" Anna and Joe's sleep was disturbed often. Old Joe was in his usual ill humor, grumbling rhythmically once more, "Like cattle and swine."

The miles from New York to Chicago took over twenty hours, due to changes of trains, the switching of tracks, and multiple stops for water and coal for steam engines. Frequently passengers were picked up from and delivered to a series of worn wooden platforms. At one of them, somewhere in Ohio, Anna was pulled from restless sleep to see Gabriele Schmidt gather her canvas valise and warily move to depart the train into the darkness.

The fourteen-year-old watched through her window as the young woman cautiously walked to the middle of the platform and stood anxiously peering here and there for someone to come from the night to claim her. A single kerosene lantern swung gently from a wooden peg, lighting the immigrant's worried eyes. The only other light in the darkness spilled through a lone, dirty station window, a telegraph operator on duty inside. Another passenger from the train was greeted by family and the group quickly disappeared into the night. Anna searched the shadows, too, hoping to see someone come forward for Gabriele, but no one materialized.

As the engine hissed billows of steam the train lurched away. Cars clanked to those before and behind them as they adjusted to being in sync with the pull forward, gathering speed. Anna leaned from her opened window to look back, to watch the lone figure near spots of light disappear from view. The young Czech would add the image of Gabriele Schmidt on that wooden platform to the other brief connections she had made with travelers throughout her journey. As she settled back and tried once more to sleep, she hoped that the widower would come for Gabriele soon, and that he would be a nice man with good children like the Kinkel twins.

As light came the next morning, the fourteen-year-old awakened to mist floating through her window. Other windows were slamming, but the girl kept hers open, enjoying the feel of cool rain on her arms, the sight of glistening, green early morning leaves on thirsty trees. Willows by a river dropped to the ground. As the train passed through the showers, and sunlight poked from clouds, mugginess returned; a steamy heat again enveloped Anna and other passengers.

Trains of the day averaged 50-60 miles per hour wide open, but stops, and being side-tracked while other trains passed by them on the same set of tracks, cost hours in travel time. Anna's route west was not a straight one, but it provided a wonderful winding path that introduced her with sight and sound to more of America.

She watched miles of shining track stretch before and behind her, especially around long curves curled through the eastern mountains. In daylight she had been amazed on those curves to see the engine of her train and its last car at the same time; passengers had crowded windows to crane their necks to look. In the ink black of night the sweeping arc of the engine's lamp searched and scanned the eerie darkness ahead as a warning whistle bellowed.

The engine often had to slow for errant livestock standing on or crossing tracks in front of its pointed, scooping cow-catcher, or for elk or deer surprised at night by the rumble of the train and its sharp light piercing shadowy stands of trees.

Rumbling through larger urban areas, Anna saw again the day and night belching of smoke from steel mills and factories still trying to catch up after the business slow-down of the 1870s. Clusters of flimsy workers' housing stood grimly near factory complexes. Soot and smoke fouled the air.

Crossing wooden mazes of tall trestles put fear into the fourteen-year-old as well as into most passengers. Old Joe tightened his jaw and looked away, staring stoically at the ceiling during his slow passage over chasms. Timbers squealed and creaked as the long, heavy train moved cautiously over them. There was always the danger that underpinnings had been weakened during rainstorms.

As Joe and Anna stopped at small town depots, they found them the center of community activity in daylight, quite different from their abandonment at night. Often stations displayed multiple signs saying "Depot," Post Office" and "Eating House" or "Refreshments." Train passengers watched with interest the emotional reunions of relatives and friends on a multitude of wooden platforms, thinking of their own families and loved ones.

Women at the stations were dressed variously in muslin or fine linen. Mustached men often were clad in bowler hats, vests sporting gold pocket watches draped on chains across their stomachs. Working men wore bib overalls. Clustered near depot activity, horse drawn flatbed wagons waited to load freight. Barefoot boys in straw hats watched everything with curiosity.

Occasionally Anna and Joe were allowed to leave their train to buy food or stretch cramped legs, as their engine lingered to be serviced with water and coal. Sometimes they struck up conversations with other Czech- or German-speaking travelers, sharing information about their trips, their destinations. They wandered small depots near town squares, perfect places for traveling politicians to stop and speak on whistle stop tours. One nearby gazebo held a small band, its tuba player red and sweating with his puffing and the heat. A smattering of people had gathered to listen.

Stationmasters, often in green visors and white shirts covered to the elbow with sleeve guards to keep them clean, manned their teletypes and sometimes a primitive wooden telephone switchboard. They also sold tickets and printed with chalk the times of train arrivals and departures on small blackboards hung near pot-bellied stoves, changing times as the teletype clicked out delays. Anna wondered if any of the operators had been hog-tied by outlaws, like the one she had seen in "The Great Train Robbery."

Wooden benches and spittoons usually outfitted waiting rooms. The girl joined passengers to seek out pumps and outhouses nearby when the conductor indicated there was time, rushing back to her car when she heard the now familiar "All aBOARD!" Larger cities had grander depots, usually made of brick. The girl was surprised to find that occasionally they even had separate waiting areas for men and women.

Anna watched, when trains did not stop at small stations, how rail-hands hooked mailbags on the fly when no passenger activity was scheduled. Most people all along the way, small children and adults alike, waved at passengers and engineers as the noisy train zoomed through their fields, pastureland and hamlets. The fourteen-year-old always waved back. People seemed friendly; nevertheless, the girl kept her lookout for marauding outlaws.

In open spaces, when dirt roads and paths ran parallel with tracks, she saw an occasional boy or man on a horse trying to race the train, just to see if he could keep up with it. Her heart stopped with her fear of outlaws each time one came into view, until she could make out grins on the faces of the riders. They were enjoying putting on a show for train passengers, waving to them until they lost the contest and were left behind in the dust.

Horses and buggies also joined in the chase sometimes, bumping over roads of sun-baked dirt and gooey mud ruts left from showers. Anna smiled remembering the tales her uncle, Adolf, had told her about the trains. She didn't grasp that most of what she had been told was part of a growing mythology about the American railroad. People watched from their fields and towns as the iron horses heroically battled weather and terrain to connect small and huge byways alike to the rest of the world.

The trains carried freight and people in and out of relatively isolated areas. Locals set their watches by an engineer's peculiar wailing blast of whistle as his train neared. They searched horizons for puffs of smoke from coal-stoked engines. The engineers took on bigger-than-life stature as their life-saving feats and accidents were chronicled in newspapers and railroad ballads of the day.

In 1889, the year of Anna Mrkvička's birth, engineer John Hess saved countless people in the Little Conemaugh River Valley, warning them of a dam breakage above Johnson, Pennsylvania. He tied his whistle down and ran his engine fast through the valley ahead of rushing water, jumping with his fireman from his cab just two minutes before the roaring flood overtook the train.

The young Czech later would hear in Iowa "The Wreck of the Old '97," a folk ballad written about a mail train that dove off the Stillhouse trestle near Danville, Virginia. It told of an incident that occurred just days after Anna's rail journey west. The engineer and twelve crewmen plunged to their death. While the fourteen-year-old worried about unlikely outlaws taking her money in a train robbery, she had no idea that railroad travel in general was not especially safe for her and Old Joe at that time. Bridges collapsed. There were derailments. There were fires.

The first reliable statistics on the dangers on the railroad were pulled together in 1888. More than three hundred passengers were killed that year, over two thousand injured. Employees were more in danger—over two thousand killed, more than twenty thousand injured. Brakemen often were crushed or maimed uncoupling moving cars; they had to turn iron cranks by hand when engineers signaled them to do so. Automatic couplers were invented in 1897. Anna rode a train with that improvement, along with safer air brakes, relatively new in 1903.

And the danger of the train robbers the young girl worried so much about was waning at the time of her trip. Gun-toting guards protected the mail car of her train in case anybody had any ideas of theft. At the time the railroad was the only way for money and payrolls to be transported bank to bank.

Anna and Joe traveled with the motion of their train over the continent's Interior Low Plateaus, enjoying clusters of hardwood trees like oak, hickory and ash. They saw people fishing for pike or catfish, and spotted hoboes and tramps trudging near train tracks and rivers. The men looked dirty and frightening to the younger Czech.

As the two moved west, farms gradually began to reflect some characteristics that they would find in Iowa: the raising of hogs and cattle, crops like corn, hay, wheat and oats. Trees hung heavy with apples, pears, peaches and cherries. The girl noted that there were no cathedrals like Saint Barbara's, no stone-walled farm spreads like the Scavenisks'.

Their second day of travel Anna and Joe entered northern Illinois and made their way into the huge railroad hub of Chicago. "Refrigerated" cars of beef from Swift's packing plants in Chicago passed Anna's train moving east as she moved west. With windows opened to the heat the two immigrants smelled the stench of the sprawling midwestern stockyards. Dust and a sickly yellow haze hovered over the city built up from marsh land. Factories coughed smoke into the sweltering days of August.

Sometimes they heard cattle, hogs and sheep lowing and snorting in boxcars as they were prodded to unload. The slaughterhouses spread out near the yards were the animals' destination. Most hogs and cattle had been carted by railroad from states south and west to the meat-packing hub of Chicago. Daily meat packers on Armour's production line were butchering thousands of hogs, their squeals evaporating into the muggy, foul air of the city. Farm hand Joe Valenda's "cattle and swine" litany finally was appropriate.

As Anna's train slowly moved into Chicago proper, what she saw seemed much like the New York City she had left. Tenements crowded near the railroad tracks; tired-looking people bustled about in the heat and dust. Warehouses and packing plants spewed smoke into the sky. The city itself stank. The girl and her godfather would have understood Carl Sandburg's poem "Chicago" and its description of the city they entered, had they known of it:

> Hog Butcher for the World,
> Tool Maker, Stacker of Wheat,
> Player with Railroads and the Nation's Freight Handler;
> Stormy, husky, brawling,
> City of the Big Shoulders.

Anna thought of *Jetta* and her uncle working among the flow of animals headed for the packing plants. The "husky, brawling" workers laboring in the stench were largely immigrant Czechs, Poles, Jews, Russians, Lithuanians, Greeks, and Italians. They worked under terrible and dangerous conditions. Throughout the nation socially conscious Americans had already recognized the particular plight of immigrant families in the United States, and the dangerous workplaces they entered to survive in a country so foreign to them.

Jane Addams had established Hull House in Chicago in 1889. There the foreign born like Anna and Joe were taught English and were helped to adjust to American society. Unfortunately, the fourteen-year-old would not have the advantage of such help on the isolated, rented farm in eastern Iowa where she was bound.

Chicago had developed some big city sophistication by the end of the nineteenth century. It had risen with the Industrial Revolution from its soggy location, and had recovered from its devastating fire of 1871, which had left ninety thousand homeless and one third of the city in ashes. It had by 1903 its own socialites. The city's wealthy families, rich from publishing, the meat packing business and railroads, were building American "castles" equal in splendor to those in New York City, but away from the dirty streets of downtown. They had moved to Chicago's Gold Coast along Northshore Drive. Anna and Joe had not the time, money, nor acquaintances to allow them to see much of the lakeside city and its sprawling wonders.

The Czechs' train wound its way to downtown Chicago and to Union Station south of the famous marketing Loop and its skyscrapers. By 1881 the station served five railroad lines. A conductor explained as best he could to the ethnic mix of travelers that they needed to change trains at this stop. After Anna stepped from her car, trunk in hand, she asked questions of people in uniform, pointing to the tag on her blouse and her ticket showing her destination.

She soon discovered that she and her godfather had time to leave the station, to wander nearby to look for something cheap to eat. As they moved along the crowded sidewalks of the "windy city" they glimpsed Lake Michigan, smelled its fresh air, heard its squawking gulls and welcomed the feel of its breezes. They ogled the sawtooth height of buildings along the lakeshore.

Old Joe fussed at the girl that they would be lost in the strange place and would miss their train to Iowa, but the girl's experience in Manhattan helped her deal with the traffic of Chicago streets. She moved them on. The two roamed among horses and wagons, trolleys and bicycles with tinkling bells. Women on the two-wheeled wonders wove among bustling traffic as well as men, but Anna saw one catch her long shirt in wheel spokes and the bicycle's chain, forced to a clumsy stop.

Finally the girl found a market to her liking and went inside to muddle through communication about her purchases. Anna by this time was confident in her ability to locate the best food in market bins, and she did just that, sniffing fruit and pinching bread for freshness. She and her godfather walked out shortly with a quarter of a loaf of bread and two firm red apples.

Unfortunately, the fourteen-year-old soon realized that she had lost her direction in the unknown surroundings, foolishly not paying special attention to the turns and twists of her route. The girl tried to calm an upset Joe as she followed *Teta* Anna's advice by heading for two nearby men clad in blue uniforms and wearing shiny badges.

Before she could inquire about the way back toward the lake and Union Station, Old Joe began waving his arms and spouting in Czech to the Irish policemen that he was lost. One of the men glanced at the nametags and winked at his companion, saying with a smile "Sure, Grandpa, I'll be leadin' you back to the train station." And he did. Anna managed to smile at her grandfather's gruffness and they followed the policeman as they all headed in the right direction once more, lake breezes again caressing their faces.

When departure time arrived, the two climbed aboard a branch railroad line heading toward their final destination. They still had to negotiate train changes in Moline and Cedar Rapids. They needed to cover over two hundred more miles from northern Illinois to Center Point, a small Iowa town west of the Mississippi.

During this last leg of her trip, a weary Anna began to struggle with anxiety mixed with hopeful expectations. She wondered what this place she had struggled so hard to reach would be like. Would she be living in rooms like *Teta* Anna's or as nice as the Kopeckýs'? Or would she be living once again in a cramped room with a dirt floor like that of her poor parents? She would have to adjust once more to strangers she knew little about, in a foreign land whose language frustrated her at every turn. Would she again find it cumbersome to communicate about even simple daily acts?

Once the girl's train left Chicago and moved on west, the type of prairie that was to be home to the fourteen-year-old spread out around her. Her different eyes stared steadily at the scenes passing by. Cirrus clouds swiped the sky. It was still hot and steamy. Browned and drying late summer grasses blanketed the ground; bur oak savanna, their tangled branches sometimes bent by hot winds, clung to dry creek beds. There were few high hills like the soaring promontory in Bohemia from which Saint Barbara's Cathedral peered down on Velký Lunec.

The train passed through acres of small farms, sometimes bordered by barbed wire fences, sometimes still hemmed in by twisting hand-hewn timber worm fences three or more wooden rails high. Often no fences whatsoever charted direction; only rutted wagon lanes surrounded by oats and corn led through fields to clusters of buildings.

There was in addition much untouched tall grass prairie the closer Anna came to Iowa, yellow-green-brown with wild dill, milkweed, sweet clover and cornflowers. Monarch butterflies, bumble bees and goldfinches flew sluggishly in the heat. An occasional hawk overhead circled its prey. The girl particularly studied the homesteads and the simple wooden churches, their narrow spires spiking toward the sky. No centuries old stone buttresses like those of Europe were seen anywhere, nor were stone-walled farmsteads or stucco compounds like the Mrkvičkas'. The girl looked but found no groups of *bábuška*-clad women like *Maminka* bending and working in the fields.

Clapboard farm homes often were little more than unpainted shacks, but a few prosperous white-painted houses stood out in the countryside. Shady porches wrapped around them. Chickens strutted and scratched near red barns.

Washings hung to dry near most houses. Overalls, calico dresses, gray-white towels and bed linens were pinned with wooden clothespins to rope clotheslines. Sometimes clothing simply was laid over fences and bushes to dry, just as it had been by *Maminka* and Anna in Bohemia. A few log cabins were visible, often used as corn bins or abandoned, but sometimes children scampered around them, full of life. Anna took it all in, trying to picture her future.

The girl also saw more golden wheat and rows of browned and drying stalks of field corn, a crop new to her. Sometimes sheep wandered cornrows nibbling and somewhat cleaning weeds from around the stalks. Sun-browned men in the fields worked with horses and occasionally steam driven farm machinery.

Often collie dogs barked at the train; farm tabby cats slithered through tough, tall goldenrod, hunting field mice or pouncing on grasshoppers. Black and white Holstein cattle and fawn-colored Guernseys grazed in pastures or formed lines toward barns. Windmills here and there pumped water for livestock. No outlaws were in evidence anywhere; instead friendly people continued to wave as Anna passed them by.

As the train neared the mighty Mississippi, sandstone began to jut out from rich black glacier dirt. Hills and bluffs rose sometimes three to four hundred feet. When Anna saw the "Big River" ("misisipi" in Indian

Sioux language) it took her breath away. She had never seen any river like it, even though in August its water flow was low and sand bars surfaced here and there.

Old Joe stiffened and stared at the ceiling again as the train crossed a high railroad bridge, its engine creeping along, white steam puffing from its sides. Barges below, full of goods or empty, floated south with the current. A sidewheel steamboat was docked nearby. Anna watched the loading and unloading of freight and people still depending on the long waterway for their travel. She also glimpsed fresh-water pearl button factories along the shore and "clammers" gathering shells for the buttons from the shallows of the river bottom.

Once across the railroad bridge, Anna Mrkvička and Joe Valenda entered the state between two rivers that was to be their home until they died. It was bordered on the east by the great Mississippi and on the west by the Missouri River. Its history couldn't have been more different from that of their homeland in Bohemia.

No hereditary monarchy ruled its people; its past involved the battles of indigenous Native Americans, not tribes of Romans, Goths and Germans. Frenchmen Jacques Marquette and Louis Joliet had floated into the area on the Mississippi in 1673 as they mapped the snaking waterway. Illinois and Iowa Indians of Siouan linguistic stock, dressed in animal skins, greeted them on the shores of the Big Muddy. The land gradually had been claimed by France and pulled away from the Native Americans tribes who had hunted thundering herds of bison on it for generations.

In 1781 France ceded the area to Spain; it was about the time the Habsburgs abolished feudal serfdom for those in their realm like Anna Mrkvička's ancestors. In 1803 the United States had acquired a large section of the plains, including Iowa, in the Louisiana Purchase.

Just forty-three years before Anna's birth, in 1846, the state in its present boundaries had been admitted as the 29th state of the Union– its motto "Our liberties we prize and our rights we will maintain." The young immigrant was joining a proud, basically farming people well grounded in the hard work of making fields from the tough prairies that dominated the heartland.

Those farmers, immigrants from all over Europe, had begun in earnest their taming of the land after the defeat of Sac chieftain Black

Hawk in 1832. Railroads soon arrived to assist the towns springing up on traveled routes and waterways like the Cedar, Wapsipinican and Des Moines Rivers. Determined settlers like Anna and her godfather, from eastern states and nations like Sweden, Norway, Denmark, Holland and Czechoslovakia, built farmsteads and wrestled the plains to food production. By 1890, just thirteen years before the girl entered the state, nearly one in five of the two million Iowans was foreign born.

Joe Valenda's son, like thousands of other immigrants, found his work on the land produced ample agricultural products because it was the most fertile soil on the North American continent. Valuable combinations of crushed rock and soil had been left in the area by receding, melting glaciers thousands of years before nineteenth century development. An ideal climate provided abundant rainfall and long growing seasons.

Added to the availability of fertile soil was the lure of cheap land for immigrants. The Homestead Act of 1862 gave 160 acres to those who lived on and developed them for Iowa farming, if they stayed on their claim for five years. The alternative for farmers was to purchase sections for $1.50 an acre. Five hundred thousand families obtained land in the Midwest by these methods, including the parents of Anna's future husband.

The girl was entering a relatively new rural civilization on her odyssey, but one that had developed rapidly as the number of settlers grew. It had in place a statewide public school system by 1834. The jail in Marion, a town near Cedar Rapids, and then the county seat of Linn County, housed its first inmate in 1846. He was a convicted horse thief. That happened to be the same year that the state capital was moved from Iowa City to Des Moines.

Four universities and colleges had been opened to scholars between 1846 and 1881, centuries after the establishment of Charles University in Prague, but they were already well established by 1903, when Anna arrived. The Iowa Normal School (later to be named Iowa State Teachers' College, and even later the University of Northern Iowa) already boasted of a women students' basketball team, a library with over seventeen thousand books, and the first indoor swimming pool west of the Mississippi.

The Czech girl would discover later that world-renowned Czechoslovakian composer *Antonín* Dvořák had worked on compositions in Spillville, Iowa, just a few years earlier.

When Anna arrived in Iowa, her rights as a woman were progressing. By 1869 the "Northern Woman Suffrage Association" was operating in Dubuque. In 1880 the Iowa General Assembly had passed an act to extend to women the right to hold offices in the state, even though as yet they could not vote in elections.

That same year temperance forces had nearly outlawed beer and liquor in Iowa; some in the society objected to German and Czechs "swigging lager" on Sunday. Because beer was a part of the daily culture of Anna's people in Bohemia, she would be confused for years by the teetotaling aspect of her adopted country.

The girl entered a state with land divided in a linear, planned way not evident in what she had seen of old Europe. In 1858 the entire state had been surveyed and laid out according to federal grids of sections and townships.

And slavery, an element not unlike the serfdom in the Mrkvička clan history, had become an issue in those townships. While royalty had put an end to serfdom in Bohemia, in Anna's adopted America such bondage for people of color was eliminated only after a bitter and bloody North and South clash of democratic principles in 1865.

The Civil War had clarified most Iowans' beliefs about master and slave; the state was clearly abolitionist. Iowa's Quaker families farming near the border of Missouri, a slave state, systematically helped slaves who ran away from their masters. They spearheaded the Underground Railroad network that spread through Iowa, assisting black African Americans in their flight north from southern bondage. The movement was based on Mosaic Law: "Thou shall not deliver unto its master the servant which has escaped from his master unto thee."

Iowa citizens answered President Lincoln's call for volunteers to fight in the bloody battles of the Civil War. The youngest soldier in the entire Union Army was Iowa's Manny Root; at age nine he played a drum at the Battle of Wilderness. Anna later would see in cemeteries rows of markers for those many Iowa citizens who gave their lives for the great struggle for freedom for all Americans.

She also would see elderly veterans living in communities near the Valenda farm, would watch them in their ragged uniforms as they shuffled by in local parades and gathered at general stores and saloons to play dominoes and reminisce about the war.

At only fourteen, Anna did not understand the freedom of choices she entered when she crossed that creaking trestle over the Mississippi River. All the history and common sense values of her new life in Iowa would only gradually begin to pull her away from the childhood beliefs she had formed in the old world of Saint Barbara's Cathedral in Austria.

At last the two immigrants arrived at Cedar Rapids. They only needed then to board an interurban train to Center Point, where *Petr* Valenda was to meet and take them to his rented farm. The girl had no idea that years later she would be living in Cedar Rapids, a manufacturing town on the Cedar River. It was an established urban community with stores, mills, hotels, machine shops, schools and churches on paved streets.

She was impressed with what she briefly saw there. An occasional brand new electric car or Model T whirred and putted besides clomping horses and wagons. They all jerked and bumped over trolley and train tracks cut through the middle of town.

At Moline a talkative Czech woman had boarded the train and had sat across from the two travelers all the way to Cedar Rapids. She quickly pulled Anna's story from her and commenced to chatter to the girl and her godfather in their native tongue.

She told them of the sizable Czech population in the city of over thirty thousand. Many immigrants from Bohemia and Slovakia were settled in "Czech Village" in Cedar Rapids on its southwest side. There Kosek's Bakery was selling the sweet fruity *koláče* which had helped Anna gain her job with Mrs. Kinkel. It baked and sold Bohemian rye bread and *bábovka,* poppy seed coffee rings.

The woman told Old Joe and his goddaughter about Czech fraternal organizations like the Bohemian Savings and Loan, which helped its members purchase their own homes. A network of Czechs already had established a lively Bohemian Dance Hall that held dances Saturday nights, open to any of the three thousand Czechs in Linn County. Saint Wencaslaus Church was twenty years old, and was served by a Czech-speaking priest. Anna's hopes about this new Iowa brightened before she had to bid the older woman good-bye at the Cedar Rapids station.

Shortly the interurban train to Center Point arrived. The last twenty miles of *Anička's* trip seemed to take forever. Both she and Joe Valenda were preoccupied with anticipation as they wound through farmland and the parched cottonwood and elm trees of a waning Linn County summer. When the conductor finally yelled "Center PoINT" and the town's depot came into view, Joe Valenda searched anxiously through windows for the face of his son among the people waiting near the small station. He spied *Petr* there with his wife and three boys, the look on their faces as anxious as that of Joe's.

Before the train lurched to a stop for the last time, Anna and her godfather were up collecting their things, eager to file out. The slight fourteen-year-old patted her hair and straightened her blouse and skirt as she followed her godfather, wanting to make a good impression. In her best high-topped boots she stepped down on the stool placed to assist those leaving the train. At long last the fourteen-year-old had arrived in Iowa to stay, a few dollars in her pocket, scant clothing in her trunk, but hope in her different Czech eyes.

It was an awkward moment when son and father reunited and embraced. Tears flowed down Joe's cheeks, and Anna hovered in the background as the two rejoined. Her father's stepbrother was much taller than her own father, and thin. Where *Petr* had shaved, his cheeks were bleached compared to the rest of his weathered skin. He had a high forehead.

His wife, Georgina, was nearly as tall as he was, and she was heavy the way many women become after pregnancies. She made two of little Anna. Over her fleshy body hung a loose, faded cotton dress; men's shoes encased her feet. *Petr's* hair was gray and thinning; Georgina's, a dull brown, was pulled back in a bun.

The children were introduced to their grandfather, who was amazed at their size. John, fifteen, Clarence, twelve, and five-year-old Charlie, all stared at the new arrivals who had come to them from far across the ocean. The wife, Georgina, smiled faintly, said little. All words spoken were Czech.

When the Valendas finally turned to Anna, the adults exchanged stiff handshakes with her as the boys stood by shuffling foot to foot. *Petr* said to his stepneice, "Well, well! So this is *Karel's* oldest. I expected a bigger girl at fourteen. We'll lose you in the corn rows." The boys snickered. The girl quickly stretched as tall as she could and took notice that twelve-year-old Clarence already was a head taller than she was.

With feelings of discomfort the girl gathered her trunk and followed the family to their horse and wagon for the remainder of the trip; the entourage headed off. Before leaving Center Point they passed the town's new, two-story brick schoolhouse, which Anna thought looked grand. They then lumbered off over miles of dirt roads toward the farmstead that was to set the stage for the first years of Anna's new life.

Petr and Georgina spoke mostly to Old Joe, asking him about the trip and sister Anna in New York. They told him about the farm and *Petr's* busy work schedule in the fields. Joe's son rented eighty acres and had an agreement to help on the landowner's larger holdings as well. Son John helped in the fields, as did Clarence when school was not in session.

Little was said to the younger Czech sitting in back with her trunk and the sons. The boys often glanced at their "cousin," curious. The girl smiled her crooked smile at them hopefully; only Charlie, the five-year-old, smiled back.

Anna Mrkvička's time with the Valendas on their isolated rented farm would be like nothing in the girl's previous life. She would have no members of a caring blood family to support her; she would find that the expectations of her stay with her stepgrandfather's son and daughter-in-law were unclear to everyone involved; she would have no access to the anchor of familiar church liturgy to help her; she would end up having to deal with hunger again under circumstances sadly different from those she had experienced growing up in Velký Lunec.

The young Czech immigrant had guided herself and Old Joe successfully over thousands of miles of ocean and land by that day in August of 1903, and at the tender age of only fourteen. She would have to dip into the courage she had found in herself during that accomplishment many times to help her through the next few difficult and lonely years of her life on the isolated plains of Iowa.

PART THREE

IN AMERICA

Chapter Nine

The First Hard Years

ANNA JIGGLED ALONG in the wagon behind the trotting work horses, traveling over dusty and rutted country roads that squared off every few miles. August sun bore down. The girl shaded her eyes with her hand to take notice of the tough landscape around her. Not a buffalo was in sight, nor Indians wrapped in blankets. Instead Anna saw pastures, harvested wheat and oat fields, drying hay, standing brown corn rows. Meadowlarks, catbirds and red-winged blackbirds perched on a few fence posts, but flitted away from the noise of the wagon. Butterflies skittered among weeds near the road.

There was little breeze. Flies buzzed around them all, torturing the horses as they twitched their rumps and switched their tails in defense. Occasionally the group passed farm houses tucked back from the road. Dogs harshly barking briefly rushed forth to chase the intruders on their territory. Men in fields waved at *Petr*; he waved back, telling his father the names of those he knew who shared with him the stewardship of the land.

At one turn of the road a small white church and graveyard claimed one corner. "*Katolický?*" Anna asked of the boys. They shook their heads,

"Methodist." Nearby a quiet one-room schoolhouse huddled among pine trees, its lessons abandoned during summer work in the fields. "My school," Clarence muttered.

The wagon finally passed over a rough wooden bridge nearing property that *Petr* explained was the farmstead of his landlord. It stood out from the other worn structures Anna had seen along the route. Late day shadows spread before a neat, white-painted farmhouse surrounded by the buildings necessary to its keep: a chicken coup, barn, shed, outhouse. The girl noticed especially the pretty orange marigolds carefully planted to border a sprawling front porch.

A windmill creaked in the barnyard over a water trough for livestock. Behind the barn a haystack stood grandly. Nearby pastures, bordered by barbed wire fences, were filled with cattle that turned their heads at the noise of the wagon on the road. Would she be living with her uncle on such a neat and tidy spread, Anna wondered. "Just a few miles now," *Petr* murmured.

The young Czech was growing very hungry. The apples and bread from Chicago were but a distant memory. She anticipated that surely her aunt had planned a meal for their return from the depot.

At long last the Valendas' rented farm crept into view from behind a line of scrub oak along a dry creek. No other houses were visible in any direction, which seemed strange to Anna, who had lived where clusters of people were always within a walk away. She eagerly looked over the farmstead as they neared it. There were no such clusters of wooden buildings at home in Velký Lunec.

The house the girl was to live in her first years in America was a simple five-room structure, its floor frame lifted a few inches off the ground by heavy lumber and stones from surrounding fields and creek beds. The clapboards were bleached, paint long ago faded away. Their weathered gray framed dirty windows with tattered green shades pulled down to sills inside them, barriers to the sun. A rain barrel sat at one corner of the house to catch runoff from the roof. No fences separated the farm buildings from fields of browning corn to the north, but both aging worm wood fencing and newer barbed wire enclosed a pasture south of the barn.

Two scrubby dogs ran to meet the wagon, barking and wagging

their tails as the horses whinnied in answer, shaking their harnesses. The wagon pulled into the farmyard past old oaks standing tall in front of the house on the west, near the road. Tall cottonwoods spread their branches a short distance from the house in the back, and were scattered haphazardly a quarter of a mile to a creek and water hole where cattle drank.

A large unkempt plot of garden ran in line with the house to the north. It seemed to blend into the corn field with its clutter of weeds overrunning pea and bean vines, rhubarb, radish greens, turnip, onion and carrot tops, its countless hills of potatoes.

Goldenrod and tough, wild milkweed crept up to the west steps at the front door, which obviously were little used. The house had neither porch nor flowers to soften it. The farmyard was scarred with bare earthen paths fanning out from the house to the outhouse and various buildings. Walnut, maple and fruit trees had been planted by the owner in a grove behind the barn. Cherry, pear, Winesap and Snow Apple limbs drooped with ripening fruit, the sight of which made Anna's mouth water.

Petr explained that the owner had built the house more than twenty years before, but had moved with his family to the bigger place as he accumulated more land. The barn he had left the Valendas now was leaning; its roof sagged. Straw and hay lay in piles nearby. A smoke hut stood off by itself. Near the house a cast iron pump, a handy tin cup wired to it, was anchored with bolts on a wood platform that was hinged on one side to open so that pails of water could be directly drawn from the well below. There was no windmill.

Dozens of chickens scurried away from the approaching horses' hooves, squawking madly. Three grown cats stared with curiosity at the homecoming activity from the barn door as a litter of kittens among them pounced at bugs and each other.

When the horses came to a halt, Anna climbed down the spokes of the wagon wheels, following the Valendas. The biggest dog, a mixture of collie and the unknown, immediately jumped on the girl, tail wagging. Its paws hit her shoulders, nearly pushing her over. Clarence, smiling for the first time, pushed him down, saying "His name's Old Boy. He won't hurt you. He just takes on raccoons and fox." He grabbed his cousin's trunk and the troupe headed for the back of the house, the usual entrance. Fifteen-year-old John led the team and wagon to the barn.

Behind the house a wash shed had been added sometime to the original building. It served to funnel people from outside through it to the original back door leading to the kitchen. About twenty feet behind the shed a root cellar had been dug and reinforced with stones, wood and cement. Two splintered wood doors leading down to it were closed tightly. Anna wondered what doors flat to the ground could lead to.

Once inside the shed the girl could see daylight through chinks in its board walls. There were no windows, but a tattered screen door allowed eastern light and breezes inside. Nails pounded without pattern here and there held a washboard, dirty farm jackets, shirts and frayed gloves, a threadbare apron. Spider webs stretched at every corner. Work boots caked with manure, their toes curled up with age, were piled haphazardly in one corner on the rough pine floor next to a wooden ironing board. Shelves at the end near the kitchen held crocks, a butter churn, cream separator and cast iron pots resting in disarray. Two wash tubs stood on a low table on one side, dirty clothes within them waiting to be scrubbed. Opposite, tucked in a corner, stood a battered metal cot.

Clarence dropped Anna's trunk on it saying, "Here's where you sleep." Its rusty springs squeaked. The girl's first thought was that it would be the only time in her life she would be sleeping in a bed and space all by herself. This would be "her room." She spied a worn-down broom in a corner, eager to give the place a good sweeping.

The first floor of the farmhouse consisted of a kitchen and small dining room on one side, a parlor the length of the other. All were strangely dark due to the drawn green shades. Even so, heat radiated inside. A kitchen worktable was piled with dirty dishes, flies and roaches swarming over them. On the top of the stove rested a covered pan; Anna's keen nose recognized that there should be chicken inside. She also smelled potatoes under the lid of a pot nearby. Pangs of hunger made her stomach ache. Green/red apples were scattered at one end of the table. At the other end a loaf of bread was covered with a cloth held down by Mason jars, to keep bugs from it.

A filthy wood box was partially filled with split pine kindling and a few corncobs. Next to it a large old Acorn cast iron stove claimed significant space with its firebox, water reservoir and warming oven. It was caked with grease on almost every inch. Anna knew that the Scavenisks' cook would be horrified to see it.

Shelves on one side of the kitchen, near a stairway door which lead upstairs, held a few clean but chipped dishes, tins of sugar, flour and coffee, cooking utensils, and baskets of potatoes and vegetables from the garden.

Just inside the door from the shed a table along the back kitchen wall held an enamel wash pan. A pail of water from the pump sat beside it, floating a tin dipper. On a shelf above the wash area a small square mirror was propped next to a shaving mug and brush. Towels hung from nails nearby, as did a worn razor strap. Lye soap smeared the table, and a gooey lump of it lay in a puddle of water. To Anna it all seemed like unattended clutter compared to the crowded but organized rooms of *Teta* Anna in New York City, or even *Maminka's* one room in Velký Lunec.

The girl noticed in the dining room that the rectangular handmade table had around it only five assorted chairs and one small barrel to sit on, one short to seat the seven now in the household. A door from the dining area led to the parlor, which was furnished sparsely with a table holding a kerosene lamp, a horsehair-covered settee and a battered Singer pedal sewing machine.

On the table lay *The Old Farmer's Almanac* and a *Montgomery Ward's* catalog. The furniture was clustered near a Ben Franklin wood stove waiting for Iowa winter and long frigid nights. The stovepipe shot up to an outside chimney through the ceiling and the rooms upstairs. An oval, braided rag rug, the only floor covering in the house, lay over pine boards that at one time had been painted a dull brown; only faint color remained. All walls were papered, their designs of flowers and leaves stained and faded. By one window a few family portraits and a 1903 calendar had been nailed to catch the light.

Petr explained that his father would sleep upstairs with the three boys in one of the areas under the roof. Anna followed as they all climbed the stairs from the kitchen to show the place to the old man.

To get to the boys' room they had to go through the tiny space where Joe's son and his wife slept. A rod with faded gingham sewn over it separated the sleeping areas between parents and boys and, now, their grandfather. Joe would sleep with John; Clarence and Charlie shared a small single bed. All bed legs rested in cans of kerosene to ward off bed bugs. Clothes were hung on hooks and nails, or piled under beds on the floor. A pail in one corner helped avoid outhouse visits at midnight.

Bare pine rafters, stained from leaks of rain and snow, sloped down over the beds each side of the room. Windows at both ends of the upper story provided circulation when and if there was a breeze. There were no screens to ward off bugs, and Clarence shooed a wasp back outside through one opening. The quarters upstairs were stifling as the gathering stood in the small space at the end of a sizzling day.

"You're the only one who gets a room of your own, *Aničko*," Petr then said to his niece. "Now you and Georgina get that chicken out. Supper's due." The boys clamored that they were starved. Old Joe grunted eagerly. Anna's stomach growled.

The young Czech learned a lot about the expectations of her that first evening meal at the Valendas. She pitched in with her fast steps and efficient worker's hands as she had been taught as an eldest child to do. After fetching a damp rag to wipe up spills from previous meals on the dining table, she quickly set seven places with an assortment of cracked dishes and bent forks. There were only three table knives; diners would share. There were tin cups for everyone.

A fire had to be started to again boil the coffee left over from breakfast and lunch, which made the heat even more unbearable in the kitchen. Anna and her aunt were dripping with sweat as they sliced bread and put cold boiled potatoes in a dish for passing. Only one chicken was in the pot; Georgina cut it into multiple sections.

The aunt didn't talk much; when Anna asked questions, her answers were brief and preoccupied. She moved slowly, filling the space with her bulk and seeming overwhelmed with just getting the meal organized from the clutter.

The woman finally told the girl to fetch milk and butter from pails lowered in the coolness of the well. The fourteen-year-old went to carefully open the trap door by the pump. She peered down into the darkness with squinting eyes to watch the pails rise slowly as she pulled them up by ropes fastened to both their handles and hooks underneath the wooden platform.

Once that task was finished, Georgina sent the immigrant to notify the men and boys that food was on the table. They had gone toward the barn to tend to livestock, first fetching water from the well to fill the animals' trough. *Petr's* three milk cows had been separated from five sheep in the pasture, in order to enter their stalls in the barn. Four horses and eight pigs needed feeding. The woman showed her husband's niece where the dinner bell was kept in the wash shed, and told the fourteen-year-old to clang it loudly outside so that her husband could hear it wherever he was.

Anna had never rung a bell. She did her best with this one, which was heavy and almost as big as her head. She held its handle with both hands and rang it as hardily as she could, just as she had seen Sister *Marie Helena* do at school. She liked the sound of it and the power of making noise, grinning as she clanged it with gusto over and over. Finally Georgina stepped to the door yelling, "That's enough, girl! You're hurting my ears. Anyway, they're coming," she added as men and boys came around a barn corner, hurrying toward food.

Once the seven gathered at the dining table, Clarence perched on the barrel and chairs scraped the bare floors loudly as all but Anna claimed a seat. She was left standing. *Petr* told his five-year-old son to shift to one side of his chair and share it with "little Anna." The uncle added, "She don't take up much room, Charlie," as everyone snickered at the girl's size once again.

As for supper that night, it was portents of things to come during Anna's years at the Valenda farm. The boys, their father, bulky Georgina and Joe took from the lone chicken both drumsticks, thighs and breasts. Old Joe also was given sparse pickings from the back and one wing. Anna was left with the remains: one wing and the neck. The fourteen-year-old managed to spear the last half potato from its bowl with her fork.

After watching Georgina slather three pieces of bread with butter and devouring them noisily, the girl decided to reach for a second piece of bread herself. The large, fat hand of her aunt quickly grabbed her small wrist as the woman cautioned that the rest of the loaf was to be for breakfast the next morning. Anna pulled back, embarrassed. She left the table hungry, devouring a small green apple that later gave her a severe stomachache and sent her to the outhouse twice in the dark of night.

After dinner Georgina watched the quick work the new girl in the house made of organizing to wash the dishes, heating water and whittling flakes of soap. With that observation the woman shuffled outside to sit in the shade on a felled tree trunk under the cottonwood trees with *Petr* and his father. The sun was low in the west. The boys busied themselves with chores around the barn.

Anna was left alone in the kitchen to scrub the dishes and pots and pans from supper, as well as those from earlier in the day. She did so with her usual fast steps, and after all dishes were clean and dried, she decided to scrub the stove with an old brush already blackened with grease. She raised the shades in the waning light so she could see better to also sweep the floor and tidy the kitchen. Surely that would please *Petr's* wife, she thought. Her stepaunt would see how helpful she could be, just as *Teta* Anna and Mrs. Kinkel had.

Dust flew; the sweating girl had a sneezing fit. The stove responded somewhat to her scrubbing, although most of the grease was baked beyond removal. Anna's hands were reddened and black by the time she gave up scraping and picking at it. When she glanced at the mirror over the washstand she saw that her cheeks were streaked with black as well. With a dirty towel she scrubbed her face until it hurt.

Light of day almost had disappeared as she wiped clean and rearranged the shelves in the kitchen and shed. She sorted like utensils together as Mrs. Scavinisk's cook had, to make food preparation easier.

As twilight of her first night in Iowa cloaked the isolated farm, Anna greeted the boys, who noisily trouped into the kitchen after throwing their filthy boots in the corner of the shed. They lit a kerosene lamp for their cousin, then tromped upstairs to bed, pushing and teasing each other boisterously.

By lamplight the girl continued to clean, next sweeping the shed floor and shaking out the worn and not-too-clean bedding stacked on her cot. From a disorganized pile of newsprint in one corner she made a place for the mound of stinking boots and lined them up neatly. Then, soaked with perspiration, she sank down exhausted on the cot next to her small trunk. It did not seem possible that at dawn that day she had still been east of Chicago.

Beneath a thin and grimy mattress the rusty springs of the cot squawked with Anna's every move. The fourteen-year-old bounced up and down to make rhythm of the noise, wearily smiling. Even with the squeaking it was much better than the straw mattress over a lattice of rope she shared with her sisters at *Maminka's*. And she had her own room with a wooden floor, even though the worn pine boards were tracked with dirt, mud and manure carried in from the barnyard.

At that point *Petr,* Georgina and Old Joe walked into the wash shed, bringing a swarm of mosquitoes with them. When the girl's uncle lit his own lamp in the kitchen, he was very surprised at the unaccustomed tidiness he saw around him. He swung the kerosene lamp around the room, taking note of the girl's helpful changes.

"Good, little Anna!" he commented, smiling at her. The girl glanced at Georgina, seeking her approval also, but the woman was looking at her husband strangely; she said nothing, immediately turning away to climb the stairs to her bed.

At long last at the end of her difficult trip from Velký Lunec, the fourteen-year-old was left alone in another strange bed, another strange place. The whispers of Iowa farmland surrounded her—a welcome breeze rustling cottonwood leaves, the occasional grousing of chickens and livestock settling for the night. It was all so different from the noises of the Kronprinz, Ellis Island, the overcrowded streets in the Lower East Side, the clickity-clack of the train wheels that had brought her here. But smells were familiar, much like those in Velký Lunec at the close of summer days. Anna breathed in the dust, manure, the odors of fecund farmland and its ripening bounty.

The girl opened her trunk and moved her few rumpled clothes to hang them on nearby nails, then she carefully unfolded *Babička Marie's bábuška.* There lay the tiny American flag, her rosary, the 1889 Indian Head penny and the few coins she had remaining from her work for Mrs. Kinkel.

After removing her skirt, blouse and boots, and spreading the cot with the old quilt and blanket provided, Anna prepared for bed. She regularly swatted pesky mosquitoes, and decided to sleep in her patchwork petticoat for protection. Before turning down the kerosene lamp, the young Czech found a chink on the wall over her bed to poke the little flag into, and a tip of a nearby nail to hold her pale pink rosary.

Once in bed she lay staring at them and listening to the prairie night, thinking about her incredible journey and this rugged land in which she had finally alighted among strangers. The flag reminded her of *Teta* Anna and the feel of her warm hug when they met at Ellis Island. The rosary reminded her of *Maminka* and her sisters and brother in Velký Lunec, all sleeping near one another as Saint Barbara's Cathedral protectively peered down upon them.

Taking the beads in her hands she prayed yet again that her family would not forget her, and that *Teta* Anna's baby would be healthy. Tears were streaming down the girl's cheeks as she finished her petitions and turned out the flame of the lamp. Her stomach growled with hunger as she burrowed under the ragged quilt to escape the whines and bites of determined mosquitoes. Into the chatter of Iowa katydids, frogs and night owls flowed the muffled sobs of a frightened and homesick fourteen-year-old separated by thousands of miles from her home and family and all things familiar.

August quickly turned to September as young Anna rose each morning to meet the challenges of her new life. She watched carefully the interacting roles within the Valenda family, trying to find her place. Georgina shortly told her to serve the meals to the family and to eat afterwards. *Petr* said nothing, not wanting to cross his wife. The arrangement meant even less food for the girl, as there seldom was much left for her but scraps.

The woman clearly considered her husband's stepneice to be a servant. She addressed the fourteen-year-old as "Girl," not "Anna," and she often was sarcastic with her. At the Kopeckýs' and the Scavenisks' the young Czech had been treated with firmness, but not hostility. The girl lay awake on her rusty cot many nights distraught and crying, wondering why *Petr's* wife disliked her so.

More worrisome still was how long she would have to stay with the Valendas, and how she ever would manage to get away from the household to find paying work in this Iowa. There was no *Maminka* or *Teta* Anna to help her sort through it all, nor sisters and caring neighbors. Surrounding farms were out of sight; she couldn't go anywhere without the Valendas taking her.

Soon Anna heard her aunt and uncle arguing upstairs after bedtime, or rather, Georgina railing at her husband over something or other, *Petr* answering in tired grunts and monosyllables. Sometimes "the Girl" or "Anna" could be heard sprinkled among her complaining words, even where the young immigrant lay downstairs in the shed.

The woman also singled out Clarence, her middle son, to vent her anger. To her the boy was too slow with his milking or picking beans for supper, he didn't cut wood the right length for the cook stove, or he muttered complaints back at her under his breath. She boxed his ears regularly.

Within a week Georgina had assigned most of the household duties to her husband's fourteen-year-old stepniece, and the girl worked with her quick steps from dawn to dusk caring for a household of seven. She swept up dirt that sifted throughout the drafty house, mopped footprints of mud and manure tracked in by the men and boys.

After beds were changed the bedding had to be washed on a washboard, along with frayed clothing. Water had to be pumped from the well and carried to tubs heated on the stove. Clothes were dipped in and out of steaming tubs with a broom handle, to try to get them clean. Anna's hands quickly became red and rough, chapped and bleeding. She smeared them with lard to sooth them. And after all the work to clean the clothes and pin skirts and shirts and pants to rope clotheslines stretched from the shed to a tilting T-shaped pole, quick storms sometimes rinsed them again.

The slightly built fourteen-year-old fell into her squawking bed exhausted and hungry at the end of every day. Gradually, as her work routine settled to a rhythm, she began to face the reality of her situation. Tears receded; anger toward Georgina and a grim and stoic determination emerged to replace them.

Lying in bed in the dead of night she thought at length of her long trip, and how she had made the difficult journey to guide Old Joe safely to Iowa. She had survived the sickness on the Kronprinz, the confusion and anxious waiting at Ellis Island. She had earned money with Mrs. Kinkel, who was pleased with her work. Her first American job had been a good experience, especially when the twins taught her English words. It was disappointing that only Czech was spoken within the Valenda household. The girl wondered how she would ever learn the language that she needed to become an American.

She often walked again in her mind through the trip she had made to meet the cigar-making Matějíček family, realizing that even at the Valendas she was better off than the destitute Czechs in their grimy tenement in the Lower East Side of New York City. Some day, some way, she would find paying work again. In the meantime, Anna realized that she had to shift from trying to please the mistress of the house to concentrating on how to cope with her hunger and isolation under Georgina's control.

At least little Charlie liked her. *Petr* was pleasant enough, but he was away from the house most of the time. He didn't interfere with his wife's management of "woman's" work. Godfather Joe kept to himself, trying not to be in anyone's way. Anna had to accept that she alone must figure out how to deal with her aunt and the woman's unending demands. Without realizing it, the fourteen-year-old began to shape her own survival.

As she cleaned up after meals, and when able to do so unnoticed, she spread thin slices of bread with butter or lard and hid them in the bodice of her petticoat. Later she'd sneak to the outhouse to eat them. When everyone was busy elsewhere, she'd slip behind the barn and pick up fallen fruit from the trees and snatch berries from vines, eating them hurriedly and licking each drop of sweet juice from her lips and fingers before she went back to the house and Georgina's eyes.

Most days the aunt took it upon herself to gather eggs from the hen house, one chore she seemed to enjoy. She swore and fumed when the hens weren't laying well because she sold the eggs Saturday evenings at Urbana or Center Point general stores for six or seven cents a dozen. Because of this she allowed only adults and John to eat them at breakfast;

Anna and the younger boys were not included in that privilege. Extra eggs were carefully stored in the root cellar until market time.

Five-year-old Charlie was supposed to weed the large north garden, which at Anna's arrival remained stubbornly filled with stinkweed and creeping jenny. Even tall prairie Bluestem grass encroached the plot from the nearby cornfield, its foot long roots defying removal. Anna discovered soon that the garden neglect was due to the child being afraid of the snakes and spiders among the rhubarb choked with nettle and the cucumbers snarled with burs.

One morning she heard a commotion outside as she was scrubbing pans, and she looked out an opened window to see what was happening. Georgina had Charlie by the ear, slapping him soundly because she had found him standing stationary in fright at the rim of the garden. The woman was screaming at her small son, "Mother of Jesus, you just kill the snakes with the hoe!" The boy then stepped into the thicket crying and miserable as his mother stormed toward the orchard to pick apples.

Anna remembered her own terror of snakes when she was six and carrying buckets of water to farmhands near Velký Lunec. She eventually had beaten one to death with a dead tree limb as she gasped for breath, her heart racing.

The next day Anna offered to help Charlie with the weeds. She lured him to stick to the job along side her by promising to give him crust trimmings from the apple pie she had been told to bake later. She said she would specially sprinkle the dough with sugar and cinnamon, just for him. At that the boy perked up a bit and cautiously followed the older Czech into the bramble of garden. Before the two quit that day, the fourteen-year-old had killed both a bull and a garter snake with the hoe, trying her best to hide her own fear from the frightened little boy.

"See, it's not so bad," she reassured him as parts of the snake wiggled gradually to stillness, and then, while Georgina was out of sight, she stuffed fresh peas in her pocket to eat later.

Anna left the garden to do the baking with her work skirt littered with burrs and nettles, her hands patterned with scratches. At bedtime, as she sat on her bed picking away at the stubborn stickers, little Charlie came to the shed to give his cousin a hug, careful to do so when his mother was not around. Anna hugged him back with tears in her eyes, missing her sisters and brother. She was thankful finally to find someone in the Valenda family who seemed to like her. It was her first hug since *Teta* Anna had bid her farewell in the Lower East Side of Manhattan.

The fourteen-year-old continued to help the boy as she had time away from all her other duties, and she ate extra picked vegetables as she could do so out of everyone's sight. Georgina didn't seem to care who weeded the overrun garden as long as she didn't have to do it, and as long as Anna completed her other tasks. The aunt barely watched the weeding and made no comment.

The two cousins managed to get the garden somewhat under control by the time bright orange pumpkins and squash were ripening and nights were growing chilly. A large bin of potatoes, turnips and rutabagas were by then stored in the root cellar for winter. Cucumbers and beets were ready for pickling, cabbage for sauerkraut.

The day after his arrival, Old Joe had joined his son and two older grandsons to work daily with neighboring threshing crews. After dawn breakfasts, John hitched the horses to the wagon and the four trotted off toward one farm or another.

Anna was thankful to learn that she, Georgina and Charlie were expected to join them two or three days weekly to help wives, sisters and daughters, mothers and grandmothers, prepare dinners and suppers for the threshers. The days briefly rescued the immigrant from the isolation of the Valenda farm. The baskets aunt and stepneice carried along held their contributions to the hearty meals: pickled beets, Anna's *koláče*, dumplings and noodles, fresh pies.

Huge meals were served at the farmhouse of whichever fields were being worked. Tables groaned with piles of food as women brought their special dishes in quiet competition. Anna was able to enjoy the food shared by the cooks after the men were fed and back in the fields.

The girl liked sitting squeezed in among the women after noon dinner as they joked and laughed and gossiped; she felt a part of a larger group effort of great accomplishment. From time to time all eyes scanned the dust rising from fields around them as acre by acre was cleared of its harvest. Good crops involved incredibly hard manual labor and months of preparation. Skies were examined regularly for signs of threatening weather.

At the table German, English, Czech and Swedish all were spoken at times. The girl gleaned as much as she could from conversations before women and girls moved on to wash dishes and prepare for supper. She managed to understand the clucking about a young girl north of town, pregnant and without a husband. Georgina occasionally passed on to her snippets of other news.

An elderly grandfather was ill with painful shingles. A farmer further west fell fixing the roof of his barn, and he fractured his right arm and left wrist; the vet set them. Now relatives farming nearby were having to help the wife and children with the crops. The pork they were eating came from an unfortunate sow that somehow had broken its leg; it had had to be slaughtered before the regular fall schedule.

There was an upcoming dance at Yost Hall in Center Point. Anna's interest peaked, but she was disappointed to discover soon that only the older John at the Valendas' rode a horse to attend the dances, if he had finished his chores. The fourteen-year-old missed the twirling camaraderie of polkas and schottisches on the Kronprinz and at Ellis Island.

Several cooks at harvesting spoke of articles in the *Center Point Journal*, their only touch with the broader world. A story had been printed about a bigamist with wives in Marshalltown and Clemons. Women guffawed at the ability of one man to deal with two women. They also shook their heads grimly over news that a wife south of Lafayette had been returned to the asylum in Independence, quite mad.

And the two-ring Busby Circus was coming to Center Point early September. Two young women captured everyone's imagination as they told of a circus they once had attended. They described elaborately how tiny women flew back and forth between trapezes. They told of fire-eaters, contortionists and hilarious tumbling clowns. Anna had seen jugglers at Kutná Hora fairs. She wished she could see the American circus.

The girl usually was able to eat her fill at the threshing meals, a relief after her slim portions left to her from Georgina's table. And neighboring farm women spoke kindly to the slight young Czech, encouraging her to eat hardily. Many understood too well the plight of new immigrants making their way alone, isolated by their inability to communicate easily in English or to understand a new culture. Most were immigrants or children of immigrants themselves.

At the third threshers' gathering the fourteen-year-old attended, she was pleased to meet Libbie Kusak, a twelve-year-old her sister Mary's age. Libbie spoke a Slovak dialect of Czech and also English. She helped to interpret things for the new immigrant. The younger girl was taller than the older Anna, who was becoming more self-conscious of her short stature daily due to the comments and teasing of the Valenda family.

Together the girls minded a gaggle of small wild and unruly children as older women controlled affairs in the kitchen. Free of their lonely farm lives, boys and girls screamed and hollered and raced every which direction, playing tag or taunting each other. Anna and Libbie had to be careful that none strayed into a nearby cornfield to become lost in its tall and uncut rows.

The two also helped place tables under oak trees for the men who would swarm in from the fields at the clanging of a bell. Very quickly the girls were sharing their stories and giggling in annoyance at the spitting of grasshoppers in the dry grass beneath their skirts. They were vexed by overhead birds leaving their marks on clean tablecloths so carefully laid out for the meals.

Anna told Libbie about steerage on the Kronprinz and her trip across the unending ocean, about sleeping near the Netherlanders and people from all over Europe. She chattered about her exciting times in New York City, clams and the Fourth of July. She vividly described her night at "The Great Train Robbery."

The eyes of the twelve-year-old grew wide as the older girl recounted each detail of the cinema, adding sweeping exaggeration and gestures. The fourteen-year-old pretended to be tied up like the telegraph operator, she twirled in dance like the crowd asked to form a posse, and she pulled an imaginary gun on her new friend as she described the last bloody scene.

Libbie flinched with fright and gasped, "Did robbers stop your train to Iowa, too?"

Anna paused, enjoying the suspense before she said, "I saw men on horses chasing my train. They could've been outlaws!"

The younger girl was overwhelmed, hesitating to tell this Anna of the world about her mundane life, but she wanted to share her story. She had been born just a few miles away at her parents' eighty-acre farm on the Cedar River. Her two older brothers helped her father to work the neighbors' fields. They also cleared trees along the river and hauled the wood to markets. The younger of the brothers, Henry, had lost his left hand at the wrist when he was twelve in an accident while felling an old oak.

The brother now wore a shaped wooden hand Libbie's father had carved for him from a limb of that very tree. The blacksmith in town had helped fashion a leather attachment to secure the artificial hand to the boy's stump. Anna's pale eyes widened at that. She had seen people with missing hands and arms in Kutná Hora, but she had never seen any of them wearing a hand made of wood.

The Kusaks had moved to Illinois from Slovakia shortly after they were married, but had later joined a group to move on west of the Mississippi. They had heard of the Czech settlements around Cedar Rapids, built in the midst of rich Iowa farmland.

Libbie had learned English in the nearby one-room school, which she missed terribly during the summer months; she loved her teacher and reading. Listening to the girl talk about her studies, Anna wished again that she could read English words, that she had been able to do more than look at the pictures in the Ellis Island books.

The Kusak girl also said that she attended the Methodist Church just a few miles away, and asked whether Anna might like to go to church with her family some time. The fourteen-year-old replied that she was Catholic, and said that she didn't think her aunt and uncle attended church much. They all worked seven days a week. Her rosary was the only one she had seen in the Valenda household, and there were no etchings of the Blessed Mother in a special corner anywhere in the house. No one ever spoke of going to church.

"My father would pick you up. He leads *Bible* study and brings new people all the time." Libbie added, "I'll ask him," she said before they both moved on to fetch pails of water from the pump so that dusty threshers could wash before eating.

One evening shortly afterward, the Kusaks showed up at *Petr's* little-used front door to ask whether Anna could attend church with them the following Sunday. Barking frantically, Old Boy had announced their arrival. Georgina and Anna, alone in the house, watched through a window as the whole family alighted from a handsome buggy. The aunt shuffled to the front door sniffing in her usual ill humor about people stopping by uninvited.

Mr. Kusak, speaking in his native Slovak tongue, introduced his family as they all stood in the front yard. Libbie waved shyly and smiled at Anna, who was doing her best to peek around the bulk of Georgina. The Czech girl's eyes quickly moved to the wooden hand of Libbie's older brother, curved like a cup, peeking from a shirtsleeve. She did her best not to stare at it.

The father explained that his daughter had talked to Anna about visiting their nearby church. Georgina was silent; she did not invite the guests into her parlor. The man went on to say that the Valendas and their boys would be welcome, too, of course. "You'll find us a friendly church," he added, smiling.

The woman of the house just stood at the door as the group waited awkwardly outside, the three children behind their parents. The Kusaks obviously had anticipated a social chat between neighbors. Anna smiled, pleased that Libbie's father had made a trip especially to invite them to his church. But she was embarrassed for Georgina, mindful that *Maminka* and *Babička Marie* always welcomed friendly visitors to come inside when they came to their doors. And Mrs. Scavenisk usually offered her guests tea and *koláče.*

Petr's wife seemed annoyed, however. She mumbled through the tattered and closed screen door, "We're busy in the fields now. The girl is needed here."

Mr. Kusak was quick to feel the dismissal, but he smiled as he nodded and stepped backward, saying "Maybe later in the winter, then, when work slows down. Have a good evening, both of you." He and his wife both glanced sympathetically at their daughter's thin young friend as they turned to leave.

Georgina said nothing as her niece sadly waved good-bye to the Kusak girl. The family headed back to their wagon to depart as the aunt went grumpily back to the kitchen. Her lonely stepneice sadly went outside to watch the Kusaks move on down the dusty road. She and Libbie continued to wave at one another until the shiny buggy was nearly out of sight.

Most Saturday evenings the Valendas loaded their wagon for a weekly trip to town. Anna only occasionally was told she could go along. The girl grew to long for the outings, eager for a break from her lonely drudgery at the farmstead.

It was her chore to heat water and fill the washtub in the shed or kitchen for a weekend bath for everyone before the trip. Baths were taken in the shed in warm weather, but moved to the kitchen by the fire as cold weather arrived. Sometimes, after rainstorms, Anna was able to dip water from the rain barrel rather than having to pump or lift it laboriously from the well. Her size still made it difficult to carry much weight. The lack of protein in her diet sapped her energy. Filled buckets were more difficult for her to maneuver as time passed.

In the pecking order established, *Petr* and Old Joe were the first to bathe, then Georgina, then the boys. Charlie and Anna were in last place. Even though the water was by that time murky, the girl carefully unwrapped her precious Pear's soap from New York City's butcher paper. She lathered herself with sweet-smelling suds, thoroughly enjoying getting to a clean body after seven hot and sweaty Iowa days and nights. Times when she was allowed to join the Valendas' trip to town, she had to rush to finish and dress in order not to keep the wagon waiting. As she ran from the house Georgina usually was yelling, "Mother of Jesus, Girl, come on!"

Once on the rutted dirt roads leading to Center Point, Anna eagerly watched for wagons coming from different lanes and roads, all heading the same direction in plumes of dust. She felt excited as they pulled into town and she quickly became immersed in the activity she saw—farmers gathering supplies for the next week, families sauntering the wooden walks and socializing, young people her own age huddled in groups.

Center Point couldn't have been more different from Kutná Hora or New York City, but in 1903 it was an extremely bustling spot in

Lynn County nevertheless. Settled first in 1839, the city had been incorporated in 1875, the same year most of Main Street's wooden buildings had burned to the ground. A two-story brick business block had replaced them to serve not only the nearly eight hundred citizens who lived in the city, but also families who regularly came to market from surrounding farms.

While the town certainly had no centuries-old stone European buildings, by the time of Anna's arrival it did have more than one hotel, the *Center Point Journal* newspaper office, the City Meat Market, druggists, Dunlap Millinery, and the Bonton, Neighbor, and McCoy Restaurants. There were beer saloons and furniture stores plus a Center Point Laundry. The railroad connection to the much larger city of Cedar Rapids had brought forth shoemakers, portrait photographers, wagon makers, lawyers and doctors. Kubias' Harness Shop and blacksmith businesses were gathering points for rugged farm men keeping buggies and wagons in working order.

Often, almost before *Petr's* horses were hitched to their posts, twelve-year-old Libbie Kusak emerged from a tangle of young people, searching out Anna Mrkvička. She wanted her new Czech friend to wander the crowds with her. The Valendas went every which direction. The boys found their friends, *Petr* headed for the barbershop and Georgina shuffled toward grocers with her baskets of eggs.

Anna again was amazed with the plenty of things to buy in America. Behind the windows of the prairie stores were goods of all sorts, much like those in the shops of New York City. Packed along crowded aisles were barrels of crackers, sugar and flour, shelves of baskets, blankets and cooking utensils.

Cuticura Soap was promoted for hair growth and as a "great skin cure." Bromo Seltzer cost ten cents; nickel-plated sad irons, three to a set with stand and handle, all could be bought for 95 cents. Cascarets, a candy cathartic, lay in tins beneath a sign saying it was a cure for constipation, appendicitis, sour stomach and bad breath.

The markets the girl wandered through smelled of pine floors, foodstuffs and sweaty shoppers, Saturday night baths notwithstanding. Sweet aromas greeted children crowded around jars of striped hard candy and licorice strips, pleading with their eyes to their parents for a treat.

Women pondered the latest fancy hats in milliners' and tailor shops, or bantered with clerks at general stores over bolts of colorful gingham for curtains, dresses and men's shirts. Men tried on suits advertised on sale for $7.85, regularly $10, $15 or $20. Almost everywhere Anna looked she saw something she wished she could buy, but the few coins she had left from New York wouldn't allow it; neither her aunt nor uncle ever mentioned giving her money to spend or wages for her work.

But the first time Libbie was at her side to help her as translator, the fourteen-year-old decided to spend some of her pennies to buy a post card and a stamp at the post office counter. She wanted to let *Maminka* and her family know that she and her godfather had arrived safely. The new friend helped Anna choose a card with a pale picture of an Indian wearing a headdress on it, IOWA printed above his head.

"Have you seen these Indians?" Anna asked.

"They don't look like that," Libbie answered. "They camp sometimes along our river to fish, but they don't wear feathers like that." They both shrugged. They liked the card anyway.

Anna borrowed a pencil from the mail clerk and then wrote carefully in Czech to her family:

> I am safe. Grandfather made it too. I could have
> been robbed on the train by outlaws but I wasn't.
> Antonia, write to me. I miss you. *Anička.*

The fourteen-year-old then carefully copied the Iowa farm address as written out for her by *Petr* on a scrap of paper. Then she proudly dropped her message into the box marked "United States Mail." She hoped that this time her message would bring an answer from home. Each day she thought of her family and their lives in the shadow of Saint Barbara's Cathedral, and each night she prayed to the Virgin Mary that they were well and would not forget her.

The two girls moved on to wander the streets. At the barbershop men were lined up waiting for a shave and a haircut, although many of their heads obviously had been sheared from time to time at home by their wives. They saw *Petr* taking his turn in the barber's chair, a huge cape over his shirt.

Men waiting for service smoked Royal Blue five-cent cigars, told ribald stories, discussed crops and complained about the weather. They mulled market prices printed weekly in the newspaper: cattle selling for $3.00 to $5.15 a hundredweight, butter eighteen to twenty cents a pound, potatoes sixty to eighty cents a bushel.

Along the walk Libbie introduced her new friend to other boys and girls from her school. A couple of them knew some words of Czech. Many were barefooted. Boys wore overalls; girls mostly wore hand-made dresses passed down from older sisters or aunts. Anna always wore her Kinkel blouse with the blue flowers to town, and she tied her fine brown hair neatly into her only ribbon.

The girl was pleased when she looked at her reflection in wavy store windows. It was comforting to be strolling beside Libbie, a new American friend. It was like walking again in Kutná Hora with her school class and seeing herself in old casement windows, one within a group to which she belonged.

Anna always dreaded leaving those evenings in Center Point to return to the grim loneliness of the Valenda household.

When farmers completed harvesting that first fall of 1903, as well as corn picking and husking, *Petr* and John began to prepare their rented house for winter. Old Joe helped them pack bindings of straw around the stone foundation to try to keep icy drafts from the wooden floor. Anna and Georgina together canned and prepared food they hoped would last through a long Iowa winter–a frigid, howling one of a kind the girl never had experienced in the hamlet of Velký Lunec.

The flat doors to the root cellar, those that the girl thought to be so odd her first day at the farm, were entries to an amazing underground storage space. It also served as shelter during frightening summer storms.

Before Anna's first August in Iowa had ended, black roiling skies warned of tornadoes. They brought men and boys dashing pell-mell from the fields, branches, dirt and loose boards blowing around them.

Everyone packed into the crowded cellar among put-aside potatoes and turnips, churned butter, and eggs waiting for market.

Listening to the terrible winds, Anna sat gripping her knees, her stomach tight with fear, her young Czech eyes large. She had heard many times about *Otec's* own father dying in a storm before he was born. She watched with fright the cellar doors above her head bend and creak as roaring storms battered them. She covered her ears as hammers of hail pounded the worn and splintery boards that separated her from ferocious elements above.

Anna was relieved when tornado weather subsided and the leaves on nearby trees turned to burnt orange, Sumac scarlet and burr oak yellow. White oak became subdued purple and brown against skies floating a harvest moon and billowing autumn clouds. Cooler weather and the beauty of Iowa Indian summer calmed both the rugged plains and the heart of the lonely girl.

The young immigrant smiled as she watched squirrels scoot here and there to hide hazel- and walnuts. Back in Velký Lunec she and her sisters had wondered each fall how the "bushy-tails" could find their hidden treasures throughout the winter.

The girl also watched with amazement as large Canadian geese began to honk their way south over the farmstead. She and little Charlie both ran outside when they heard them overhead, peering upward with awe at their V-shaped formations. Sometimes the flocks swooped down to land and pick at dropped kernels of corn in nearby fields. Then they noisily rose in dark swirls, on their way again.

Anna awoke in the shed one midnight in late October chilled to the bone by a frigid north wind sweeping through the plains. Ice-like drafts whistled through the chinks near her creaking cot. She wrapped her quilt around her and shuffled to the horsehair couch near the parlor stove, where she would be destined to sleep until the warmth of April. It was a lumpy and prickly bed.

As the snow and ice of November and December arrived with fury, it became the girl's job to keep the fire in the parlor stove alive through the night, and to get flames going in the kitchen work stove for coffee before the family came downstairs. By turns everyone splashed their faces in the enamel kitchen basin and slurped coffee before heading for chores or school. The water stored in the pail beneath the wash bench often was flecked with crystals of ice, even in its spot near the morning warmth from the cast iron range.

Everyone in the household, everyone but Anna that is, had accumulated meager collections of warm but ragged winter coats and stockings and boots to shield them from the cold. One frigid morning *Petr* gave his stepneice an old scarf of his; Clarence passed on to his cousin a pair of stockings with darns on darns. Georgina never offered any of her old clothes to the girl. They were too big for petite Anna anyway.

The girl had little in her small Bohemian trunk that would help protect her from Iowa winter. She could tie *Babička Marie's* old *bábuška* on her head, but otherwise she was driven to wear odd layers of the clothes she had, piling her brown suit coat over blouses and two petticoats, using the gifted darned stockings for mittens.

Early in November, the last time she was taken to town before snow no longer melted in the noon sun, the girl had to make a difficult decision about protecting herself from frostbite through the winter. She decided that she had to spend most of the few coins she had left from New York at a used clothing store in Center Point.

Once there Anna pawed through cluttered bins to find a serviceable pair of brown wool stockings, mittens and a black wool boy's coat frayed at the cuffs. She was pleased also to find not-too-stained long underwear that was about her size, a few of its buttons missing. *Teta* Anna's negotiation lessons in New York again came in handy as the girl tried to communicate about purchases with a woman clerk who spoke only English.

The two finally solved the language problem by showing each other in their palms the coins they were discussing as the cost for things. The woman would hold out a nickel and a dime and point to an item Anna had in her hands, but the fourteen-year-old usually nudged the clerk down to a dime or nickel only, pointing to wear or tears, and pleading with anxious young eyes. Finally the woman acquiesced, noticing with sympathy the strange collection of layered clothing on the small, young immigrant obviously having to struggle to get by day to day.

In late September Clarence had reluctantly started back to school, soon to trudge by foot through progressively icy winds and winter storms. He had warmed up a little to Anna by that time, especially when she flattered him by asking him to read and translate for her what was in the *Center Point Journal.*

The newspaper was printed each Thursday and delivered on rural mail routes, weather permitting. The evening the paper arrived, Anna, and most times *Petr* and John, sat around the dining room table to listen to the boy tell of the latest news from the outside world. Anna's isolation made her eager to know what was happening beyond her lonely existence.

Through Clarence's awkward translations she learned that "Kit Carson," the first Wild West movie, premiered in New York City the fall of 1903. It gave her opportunity to brag once more to her uncle and cousins about the "Great Train Robbery," and to tell of her fear of train robbers on her way to Iowa.

In December, headlines announced that Wilbur and Orville Wright flew their 25 mph engine-driven air machine over the beaches of Kitty Hawk. Black drawings showed an image of the strange winged machine. Shaking heads in disbelief, everyone wondered how anyone could trust it to fly. Clarence tried to make a winged paper plane from a limp page of the Ward's catalog. When he thrust it into the air it quickly crashed.

Once the front page even gave space to the woman who discovered the mysteries of radioactivity, Madame Curie. She was the first woman to receive the Nobel Prize in physics, beginning a long line of "first" women who were moving out of their historically accepted social status in early twentieth century society.

Women in America had begun organizing and marching for rights in the 1800s, to eliminate slavery. By the time of Anna's immigration, suffragettes had turned their attention to a woman's right to vote in order to gain political and economic equality.

Educated at the State College of Iowa, Carrie Chapman Catt became an early leader in the women's rights movement. Even when Anna grew to voting age in Iowa, she could not vote. Had she become a widow without a husband's will, she would have inherited only one third of the man's property, his children two thirds. Men had the legal right to their wives' earnings, but wives had to assume their husbands' debts, even though those wives had no voice in financial decisions. The majority of American women acquiesced to their roles in society, not even aware of feminist strivings to bring them equality.

Of course no one in the Valenda household understood all that was printed in the newspaper. They couldn't comprehend what radioactivity was all about, or the Nobel Prize, for that matter. That a woman was involved in such a thing was all the more strange to them.

The *Center Point Journal* usually focused on articles that fit the concept of women's roles of the era. Wives and daughters were supposed to be delicate and protected, even if most women's lives didn't fit that myth. The paper's "Health of Women" column (actually a pitch for Lydia E. Pinkham's vegetable compound) contained prescriptions for women that most could not attain:

> Health and beauty are the glories of perfect womanhood. Women who suffer constantly with weakness peculiar to their sex cannot control their beauty. Preservation of pretty features and rounded frame is a duty women owe to themselves.

On the run-down Valenda farm in Linn County, young Anna had little energy left to devote to the "glories of perfect womanhood." Grooming and keeping clean was a backbreaking and time-consuming chore for her. She had little time to follow the advice in one article in the newspaper, how-to drawing included:

> Women, dry your long hair. Cut a box to sit on your head and draw your hair up through it outside the box. Sit in front of a window for an hour, then run a warm flatiron over your head to make it drier.

Saturdays, at bath time, Anna scrubbed her body and head with her rapidly-diminishing Pear's soap; its sliver finally disappeared. Then with lye soap she did the best she could to clean her long, fine hair of the week's sweat and dust and flour. Its limp strands then hung below her shoulders to dry, often tied back with twine.

Fourteen-year-old Anna Mrkvička began her first long and trying Iowa winter working through an endless routine of food preparation and cleaning. *Petr* Valenda marked an "X" through each day on the parlor calendar after his morning coffee. The young immigrant watched the X's slowly march through her long and tedious days.

She was always cold and hungry, wearily struggling with feelings of helpless isolation and loneliness. But as the girl cooked and scrubbed clothes and her fingers bled and cracked, daydreams of "wonderful" New York City with a caring *Teta* Anna, along with a few sweet memories of life with her sisters near Saint Barbara's, helped see her through.

When the newspaper announced that the subways she had seen being dug in New York were completed, she imagined herself traveling through the sprawling city underground, and she wondered if *Teta* Anna and Adolf were taking the new trains to see "Kit Carson." She wondered whether her aunt had saved enough money to move to Brooklyn with her new baby. The immigrant was disappointed that no word from the Ziemans came to the Valenda farm about the birth. It was as though no one anywhere gave a thought to the occupants of the scruffy clapboard house on the Iowa prairie.

As winter snow drifted around the farm and wind roared incessantly one long frigid spell, Georgina became even more unpleasant and unpredictable. Christmastime had come and gone with little notice in the household, a day of the week like any other. *Petr's* wife was angry about almost everything. Her husband worked as long as he could outside to stay away from her, but Anna heard the couple quarrel late in their bed often, Georgina's angry voice piercing the silence of the cold house.

And Clarence was slapped more often by his mother. He even was forced by her to kneel on a broomstick in the kitchen for punishment because he had cut wood too long for the kitchen stove. Anna's heart ached for the boy as his torment increased. She tried to separate herself from his agony by retreating to the outhouse or the icy wash shed. She covered her ears to shut out sounds of his pain, much as she had in *Maminka's* one room when *Otec* Karel had been brutal to everyone after evenings of too much beer.

It was during that long first winter that Georgina's temper lashed out full force at her husband's stepniece the first time. One evening at suppertime Anna was especially hungry. She speared a small boiled potato with her fork from the bowl she was preparing to take from the kitchen to serve the rest of the family in the dining room. The aunt appeared in the cooking area unexpectedly, just as the fourteen-year-old stuffed the potato in her mouth.

The girl felt the woman's hand hit the side of her head before she even saw the movement. Her vision blurred and her ears rang as she stumbled backward clutching her jaw. The fork and half-eaten potato smashed to the floor.

"Don't you ever eat before my family's had their fill," Georgina snarled.

From the dining table *Petr* glanced through the kitchen doorway to see what had happened, but he only shook his head, saying nothing.

"Now, get this food on the table for us," the aunt warned.

That night, after everyone else had gone upstairs to bed, Anna was still scrubbing pots and pans by lamplight. Over the wind howling outside the girl heard the creaking of the stairs. The heavy steps could only be those of Georgina. In the flickering lamplight, Anna went rigid with fear when she saw the fierce look of her stepaunt's face appear in the stair doorway.

The woman moved directly to the broom leaning in a corner and threw it on the floor; the fourteen-year-old backed away, terrified of what she realized was coming.

Georgina stepped to the girl quickly, grabbed her arm and twisted her frail body downward. "Kneel!" she snarled through clenched teeth. The woman was twice the size of the young immigrant, who lacked the strength to wrest herself free.

Anna felt the broomstick dig into the skin and bones below her kneecaps as her aunt pressed her down. She gasped as piercing pain shot up and down her legs. A questioning murmur began in the bedrooms upstairs. Hearing it, the girl hoped desperately that *Petr* or her godfather would come down to her rescue, but she waited in vain. There was no more creaking on the wooden stairs.

Threatening the fourteen-year-old with the back of her hand, the woman ordered the girl to stay put, then moved her bulk to pour herself what was left of coffee on the stove. She noisily dragged a chair to sit down near her victim. Georgina's twisted face was but inches from Anna's own, her eyes glittering ominously in the lamplight.

"Don't you ever, ever do that again, d'ya hear? We get fed first. D'ya hear?" she said over and over again, her huge shadow quivering across the kitchen wall behind her. Anna nodded, the pain by then cutting her legs like a knife.

Finally, only after she drained her coffee cup, Georgina slowly rose, turned and heaved her weight back up the stairs. Anna was left alone to tumble sideways onto the cold floor, moaning and rubbing her numb legs. After a time she lifted herself up and slowly began to limp around the kitchen table like a caged, hurt animal.

"It's not fair," she cried to herself. The Virgin Mary would know that it was not fair. *Maminka* and Antonia would have tried to help her had they been nearby. But they weren't there. They were far across half of America and the vast ocean. She felt the full weight of aching anguish that she was all alone and isolated on the Iowa prairie.

Gradually, rage at Georgina's treatment of her swirled up through Anna's pain. She raised her fist toward the upstairs bedroom and cursed her tormentor silently with every blasphemous word she could remember. "God will punish you," she muttered over and over as she patted her tear-stained face and burning knees with cold water from the enamel basin. The exhausted fourteen-year-old finally stumbled by lamplight on her aching legs to the horsehair settee in the parlor.

As she laid her head down on it this night, the couch's prickliness on her body reminded her of the crown of carved wooden thorns on the weeping head of Jesus in the school chapel of Kutná Hora. The image filled her mind as she hugged her shivering body, her trembling hands tightly clutching the pale pink rosary from her childhood.

Even after she extinguished the kerosene light she couldn't sleep. She lay there in the dark listening for Georgina's every movement above her or on the stairs. Finally she painfully crept through night shadows into the kitchen. There she grasped the broom and carried it back to the parlor, hiding it under the settee.

The next morning the exhausted girl rose before dawn and replaced the broomstick in its kitchen corner. It was a routine she would follow each night through the rest of the long winter. She stiffly walked through her usual chores before breakfast that morning, grim and braced for she knew not what.

But when Georgina came downstairs she acted as though nothing had happened between them. *Petr,* John, Clarence and Old Joe kept their eyes from meeting those of the hapless girl as they passed through the kitchen to the dining room. Only five-year-old Charlie, following the rest, looked sympathetically at the Anna who had rescued him from snakes in the garden.

After breakfast, when all but the small boy had left the house for chores, little Charlie helped clear the dining room table, carrying dishes almost too heavy for him to his cousin in the kitchen. He made a point to hand Anna his own plate. On it he had saved most of his single piece of slab bacon for her, as well as a thick slice of rye bread slathered with butter. He'd taken only one small bite out of one corner.

The grateful girl quickly embraced the five-year-old, and the two hugged each other tightly for long minutes, without words.

Never again did the young immigrant try to eat before Georgina and her family had had their fill. The girl became bone thin. Bread and butter stolen in her bodice to the outhouse became brief respite from hunger, along with small raw potatoes she ate hurriedly when she went to fetch food from the root cellar for the Valenda's meals. When his mother was not in the house, Charlie sometimes sneaked to Anna his apple from lunchtime, or good portions of the remains of his meals.

The rest of the winter the fourteen-year-old struggled with nightmares as she lay restless on the settee, her ears attuned to every creaking movement in the house. Georgina, however, did not repeat the terrible incident that winter. Instead, she increased her ill will toward her middle son, Clarence. *Petr* and his wife hardly spoke to one another. Anna did as her aunt told her quickly and efficiently, her different eyes newly watchful.

It was springtime of 1904, on her fifteenth birthday, when Anna managed due revenge for Georgina's torment of her. She watched *Petr* after his breakfast mark "X" on the calendar through April 6. The girl's birthday was not acknowledged, nor was that of anyone else in her stepaunt's household.

That day would turn out to be the day of Anna Mrkvička's declaration of independence in America, one she had planned through tedious winter days and nights. She had prepared bacon and eggs and *koláče* for the Valendas; as usual, her only breakfast had been their leftover scraps.

She watched the entire family, including Old Joe, drive away in the wagon to a funeral for *Petr's* cousin, and when they were out of sight, she hurriedly marched directly to the henhouse. Chickens scattered from her path, their waddles and combs jiggling back and forth with their jerky steps. Once inside the smelly coop, Anna collected four large eggs from the nests of Georgina's best Longhorns, and she then carried them carefully in her apron to the kitchen.

The old iron skillet was still warm from the Valenda's breakfast, so the girl stoked the cooking range fire and carefully broke the four eggs into lard sizzling within it. Once the egg whites were browned and sputtering around their edges, Anna slipped them with anticipatory delight onto a cracked white plate. The yellow yokes looked up at her like four bright suns lighting up the day.

Then the fifteen-year-old went to the dining room and pulled out Georgina's chair to place it at the head of the table. With ceremony she sat down by herself to feast with great satisfaction on each bite of the forbidden food. But when all four eggs had vanished, the girl was still hungry.

She immediately got up, put another log on the fire, and marched right back out to the henhouse to gather four more perfect eggs. Those she scrambled and placed on a thin slice of rye bread and butter, consuming them again in Georgina's chair at the head of the table. Still she was hungry.

Another trip provided four more eggs to poach, after which water was heated for an additional four boiled eggs. Those were consumed after the girl cracked and peeled each carefully. That brought the total eggs Anna had eaten to sixteen, one more than the years of her neglected birthday. Nothing remained on the old cracked plate in front of her but yellow smears in the center of a ring of broken shells that circled the rim of the old plate like a crown.

Even though her stomach felt uncomfortable, unaccustomed as it was to so much food, the girl smiled ear to ear. Her step was light as she carefully cleaned the kitchen of her deed before she walked to the henhouse to scatter the sixteen crushed eggshells among the chickens. She knew that they'd be pecked to pieces before the family returned from the funeral. Georgina need never know.

On her way back to her chores in the dismal Valenda house, Anna noticed the sweet smell of early clover sprouting near the turned loam of the garden. She gazed upward at billowing April clouds overhead, thinking that they looked amazingly like pools of egg whites spreading through the bluest sky she had seen for months. The sun caressed her face. For the first time since her arrival in Iowa the girl was very full.

Deliberately, Anna moved back into her "own" room in the washhouse that evening, to close the door on her difficult winter. She was energized by the new life bursting into bloom around her, and she didn't want the prickly horsehair under her back another night. If Georgina's fury approached her in the washhouse, she could escape through the door outside and run as fast as *Babička Marie* had warned her to do.

The gritty dust from spring planting soon was blowing through the opened windows and cracks of the clapboard farmhouse. Getting to town to market became easier unless rain and mud made the roads impassable. Occasionally the girl was permitted to ride with the family in the wagon to town Saturday evenings. Anna looked forward to escaping Georgina's house and her grinding work.

On the other hand, she was ashamed to have others see her in her shabby clothes. She carefully studied her face in the piece of mirror in the kitchen. Her eyes had dark circles under them, her cheeks were hollow, her hair dull. Even with her lack of proper food her breasts were budding beneath blouses now gaping and tight. She scrubbed and ironed the clothes she had as best she could before her first spring visit to market, and tied her hair with the fraying blue ribbon.

Then the immigrant sat through the bumpy ride to town with anticipation mixed with anxiety. She hadn't seen her friend, Libbie, for months. She'd wished each Sabbath that she had been allowed to attend church with the Kusaks throughout the winter; Georgina had never permitted it.

Notwithstanding Anna's worn appearance, the Kusak girl was delighted to see her Bohemian friend again. Almost the minute the Valenda wagon was hitched to a post on Main Street, Libbie appeared on the wooden walkway rushing to embrace little Anna. Her warmth and touch were much-needed balm to the discouraged fifteen-year-old.

While the Valendas went their ways, the two girls wandered arm in arm as if no time had passed since their last time together. Libbie chattered about school and a crush she had on a farmer's son. She blushed telling that he had paid a quarter for her pie at the oyster supper box social. He and his parents had joined her family at a bobsled party the last winter snow.

Anna listened to tales of a happier young life, but had little to say about her days of washboards and hot stoves, her nights of tension with Georgina. She couldn't bring herself to speak of her stepaunt's meanness and her ordeal with the broom.

The girls wandered into the general stores to see and feel new things being offered for sale. Anna stopped at a bin of Pear's soap, the pretty maiden with curly hair pictured above it just as the poster had been in New York City. She picked up a bar to breathe in its sweet blossom smell, and she could feel again the lushness of her very first bath with *Teta* Anna's precious bar. She reluctantly put it down, as she had no money to buy another. The lye soap she was forced to use had made her skin rough, her hair lackluster.

Anna was stopped by one yellowed newspaper ad in a store window. It showed a drawing of a nun like Sister *Marie Helena* in Kutná Hora. When she asked Libbie what the ad was about, the girl read, "Sisters of Charity use Pe-ru-na for coughs, colds, grip and catarrh."

"What's catarrh?" Anna asked. Libbie didn't know, but there was another ad pasted to the window for Ayers Sarsaparilla, good for weak nerves, and Libbie did know something about that. Her aunt drank sarsaparilla sometimes for headaches. The girls shrugged their shoulders and moved on.

On one such excursion to town Mrs. Kusak strolled briefly with the girls. When she parted from the two young friends, she mentioned that her daughter had some dresses she had outgrown that would fit and look nice on Anna. Even though Libbie was two years younger than the immigrant, she stood taller than her friend already, and was more robust.

After that the Kusak mother and daughter carried a package for Anna to market each time they went, until one day Anna was able again to join them in Center Point. Then Libbie passed on to her friend two fresh gingham dresses, which brought tears to Anna's eyes. Her rough hands smoothed the blue and yellow checkered garments carefully before she held the items to her body to be sure they fit, grinning when they did. The gifts were carried to the Valenda's carefully and tenderly placed in her trunk. The immigrant thought them too good to wear for every day. They would be saved for town outings and harvest dinners, which would be sweeping very soon across Iowa fields.

The summer months passed quickly. Anna worked dawn to dusk with food preparation and washing and ironing and cleaning and helping Charlie with weeds in the garden. Together the two often killed snakes slithering around peas and cucumbers. They gathered wild gooseberries and elderberries. Honeybees buzzed around them and were traced to combs that provided sweet honey for biscuits.

The men of the household, now including Clarence, were in the fields by sunup, rain or shine. Old Joe struggled each day to keep up with the younger men, trying to shoulder his share in return for his keep. Georgina lumbered through the chores she chose, grousing at everyone about everything, although warm months seemed to make her less depressed.

One very important event occurred for Anna that summer. The postman finally brought a letter addressed to her from Velký Lunec. It was the first communication from the Mrkvička family since the girl had left for her long trip over the Atlantic more than a year before. The Czech script of her sister, Antonia, scrawled across the envelope. When Charlie came running from the post box gripping the envelope with strange writing on it, Anna grabbed it from his hands and tore it open.

The letter began with news that thirty-five-year-old *Marie Barbora* had delivered another son, named *Anton* (Antone), and that now both Antonia and Mary had quit school and were working out to help *Maminka* buy food and clothes for the growing family. The postcards Anna had sent from America were propped up on the windowsill near the hearth so that they all could see them every day. Little Frank especially liked the card with the Indian head ringed by sprouting feathers.

Antonia asked whether her sister lived among Indians like that. The last line of the letter wrenched Anna's heart. "*Aničko*, I miss you so much. Your America sounds grand. I wish so much to be with you and the Indians in Iowa." Tears came to Anna's eyes. She desperately wanted her family near her. A wave of homesickness for Antonia and her mother caused her to sob well into that night, the letter clasped to her heart.

The girl read the message from her sister dozens of times daily, carrying it in her bodice to read each time she went to the outhouse. She was both sad and happy about having another brother. She realized that her mother must have been pregnant when she sent her away to America. Now there was yet another mouth to feed and clothe in the tiny Mrkvička room.

Anna remembered how worn and tired *Maminka* had looked when she left her to board the train. The peasant mother was constantly suffering with toothaches and rotting teeth. Her shoulders sagged from nursing and carrying babies in her arms and on her back in the fields, and she was burdened with both her own and those of the stream of foster children. The girl wished she could find some way to bring her weary mother and all her family to be with her, but she knew not how to do it.

For the first time Anna realized fully that she did not want to return to the difficult Mrkvička life in Velký Lunec. While she had longed to be home with her family her first months in Iowa, she was beginning to sense the hope of life in America, to dream of a better future.

She'd watched in March as farm renters moved down muddy roads in overflowing wagons to try to improve their lot, find better land and better arrangements. Their furniture and belongings were piled every which way around them, pots and pans banging, mirrors sending slivers of light over the landscape with each rut conquered, each stone hit by dusty wheels. Even the limited interaction she had with neighbors had shown her that Iowa people had hope of rewards for their hard work at farming.

As unhappy as her time was with Georgina, she had a wooden

floor to walk on and to clean, and she had a space and bed of her own in the wash shed. She would find a way to get paying work somehow; she would find a way to get away from *Petr's* wife and her bitterness. She was becoming more determined day by day to find a way.

So as Anna pondered her future and hid bread and butter in her bodice to survive under Georgina's spiteful eyes, days passed and news of the broader world filtered to her through Clarence and the *Center Point Journal.* The Saint Louis Expedition opened. Caruso recorded "Rigoletto." "Recording" was foreign to everyone in the household. Singing coming from a round black cylinder was beyond their comprehension.

It was threshing time in 1904 when the fifteen-year-old met for the first time the woman she would describe the rest of her long life as her American "champion." As they had the year before, Anna and Georgina in September prepared baskets full of food for the threshing crews, and they traveled regularly from farm to farm to help other women feed the workers. The girl looked forward to the tables always heavy with food. She never went hungry at threshing time.

Additionally, not only was Libbie at a few of the farm gatherings that year, but also a young woman fair of hair and pleasant in manner. She quickly befriended the struggling immigrant. Her husband farmed the large Gilbert spread a half-hour wagon ride from the Valenda place. Claire Gilbert had a year-old son. Anna was taken right away with the woman's cheerful manner and her ready laugh. The farm wife knew a few Czech words, and she took the time to ask the girl about her home and family. Haltingly the two were able to get through conversations, Claire laughing and giggling as they both fractured the other's language.

All the women at the gatherings recognized young Anna's difficult situation. Georgina did not go out of her way to be sociable with anyone, including neighbors at the threshing meals. The girl from Bohemia was terribly thin and small for her age, and she was obviously exhausted. She had no blood family to look out for her.

Mrs. Gilbert seemed particularly concerned about the immigrant's life with the Valendas. She would have been horrified had she known of Anna's abuse with the broomstick and her lack of food, but the girl told no one about her trials. She was ashamed to have been treated so.

Anna was sorry to see threshing season end, even though it was a time of a tremendous workload for her. Canning time added additional chores. When the weather turned cooler and the trees started draping a kaleidoscope of fall colors across the horizon, the socialization that accompanied warm weather diminished quickly. She seldom was taken to town after harvest time, making it impossible to visit with Libby. Claire Gilbert and the kind threshing women were lost to her for another year. She dreaded facing another long winter with her stepaunt.

In November Teddy Roosevelt was elected President for another four years. His plans for the Panama Canal were well under way and he was taking on big business greed and national racial issues. *Petr* and John often talked politics at the supper table, ranting and railing about the "Big Wigs in Washington" who didn't understand how tough it was to make a living in the Midwest, with low farm prices and rising costs.

It was again during the height of winter, January 1905, with winds howling incessantly through cracks of the sagging Valenda house, that *Petr's* wife once again slipped into her winter depression and became increasingly angry with Clarence and Anna. In their own way, the two victims of her unhappiness found ways to briefly ease their torment.

Clarence by this time was nearly twelve, and he had shot up considerably in the months Anna had been on the farm. He was now taller than his mother, but thin like his father. One night when Georgina tried to box his ears for sassing her at the supper table, the boy stood his ground and batted his mother's hands away. When she tried again to hit him he held her wrists so that she could not. The woman became furious with frustration, screeching at the boy.

Petr and John got up and left the table to avoid the rift, heading for the barn. Old Joe finished the pork on his plate in haste before he followed them. Charlie cringed down into his chair, his large frightened eyes peering over the edge of the table. Anna listened tensely from her station in the kitchen.

Infuriated with her son and her life in general, Georgina finally left the table herself and stormed upstairs to her bedroom, vitriolic words continuing to take aim at Clarence. The boy finished his supper with a steely calm, then rose to head for the barn himself, his jaw taut, his head held high. He and Anna exchanged knowing glances.

Anna at least had more leftover food that evening. *Petr* and John had not eaten all their servings. Charlie brought her his plate still half full. But even as she ate her fill for a change, she did so with apprehension, wondering what the rage of her aunt would bring. Her stomach was in knots as she scrubbed pots and pans into the dark.

Once again, after all were in bed but Anna, the creaking stairs announced Georgina descending. Anna froze at the sound, but she quickly recovered and moved to the corner to take charge of the broom. She had it in her hands, pretending to sweep the already-cleaned floor, by the time her aunt came through the doorway to the kitchen.

With glaring eyes Georgina began. "I noticed you goin' to the barn this afternoon just when my husband was out there working on the harnesses. Why'd you do that? What were you doing with him out there in the barn?"

Anna had made a trip to the barn with a secret piece of bread and butter, but when she had seen *Petr* busy there, she had moved on to the outhouse to be alone. She didn't dare share with Georgina that she had been looking for a place to eat bread stolen from the larder. She said nothing as the woman stepped toward her, big and formidable, her menacing shadow in the flickering lamplight smearing the walls.

The woman stared down at the girl with hostility in her eyes as she reached to grab the broom from Anna, but the girl gripped it tightly and quickly stepped away to put the center worktable between her and her aunt. *Petr's* wife again was frustrated. First her son, now this bit of a girl dared test her.

"I don't want you sneakin' off around my husband, d'you hear? I don't forget you're no blood kin to him, or any of us," she raged, lumbering to get her girth around the table to catch the girl. Anna's quick steps easily kept the barrier between them.

"I don't look at Uncle *Petr* that way," the girl answered, her courage rising. "You should know that."

"You don't sass me, girl. I give you room and board. You eat my food," her aunt screamed, awkwardly lunging again. Anna could hear mumblings upstairs, just as before. Everyone obviously was awake. Anna knew Charlie would be under the covers, frightened. Clarence, who had gotten the better of his mother earlier, would be listening carefully. The woman stepped toward Anna again, only to be out-maneuvered by a thin young girl very nimble on her feet and spurred on by fear and a growing anger of her own. Czech words flew between the two.

"I need more than eats and bed. I was paid in Velký Lunec for my work. I need some money to buy what I need. My toes are poking through the tops of my boots, they're so small. I need better boots in the snow, some pay for my work." The words from *Petr's* usually compliant niece shocked and stopped the woman.

"Pay? Pay? You get a bed to sleep in, your meals. That's enough for an immigrant girl off the boat."

"It's not enough. I need money for boots, a bar of sweet soap all my own."

At this Georgina threw her head back and began to laugh. "First Clarence smart and sassin' me. Now you." She stepped back from the girl, chuckling wickedly. "You know where the door is, you stupid little Bohunk. Who do you think will take you in, anyway, and pay you on top of it? There's the door," she said contemptuously as she turned to lift her bulk back up the stairs.

Anna took the broom to bed with her that night, and she listened to every move of Georgina overhead. What was she to do? How could she find another job? She understood little of the language of America. How would she ever get out of this unhappy house? The girl was gripping both the broomstick and her pink rosary to her heart when she finally fell asleep.

Just as after the previous broom incident, Georgina acted the next day as though nothing had happened. That night after supper, however, as *Petr* passed through the kitchen to go upstairs to bed, he quietly slipped his niece a quarter and a nickel before he climbed the stairs, saying nothing. Anna was surprised and thankful.

A few more coins slipped to her privately every week or so by her uncle enabled her to finally buy a pair of second-hand boots that fit her. On a rare visit to town she carefully picked a pair with good laces and an inch in length beyond her toes to spare, just for good measure.

The next month, February, a letter arrived for *Petr* from his sister, Anna Zieman. He read it to everyone after supper. Anna had delivered a little daughter some months before, and Adolf had named her Opal after his mother. *Petr's* sister also wanted her brother to note that her new address was in Brooklyn. The Ziemans had moved to a small row house with a fenced-in front yard that even had a tree in it. Adolf had transferred to the rail line in Brooklyn; his wife had found a job near her neighborhood sewing for a seamstress. She took Opal with her as she worked.

Anna Mrkvička smiled at the news. Her godfather's New York daughter had managed to move her family from the tenement in the Lower East Side, just as she'd dreamed of doing. The girl knew that her aunt's trips to the bank had helped her do it.

Teta Anna sometimes had taken the girl with her paydays when she marched to the bank. Before a stern-looking teller behind a bank cage, the woman counted out carefully-saved crumpled bills and worn coins. Each time, after the teller marked the Ziemans' special little book with a new balance, Adolf's wife looked hard at the final figure. When she was sure it was correct, she said to her niece, "Save your money, *Anička*, so you can buy your own home in America."

The girl was happy that now Walter and his new sister could go to good schools in Brooklyn. They would not have to spend hot summer nights on a noisy roof with knives by their sides. They never would end up like the destitute, cigar-making Matějíčeks.

Petr read on with a message from his sister to his niece, "Tell little Annie hello, and give her a hug and a kiss from me. Does she have her eye on a nice 'Bohemie' boy yet?"

The man looked at the girl smiling, but thought better of acting out the hugging request under his wife's watchful eye. It also was painfully evident, even to him, that his niece had no opportunities to meet young men of any kind. Georgina sniffed and left the table.

It was enough for Anna that her kind and helpful aunt in New York had remembered her. She missed *Teta* Anna's caring guidance and her ready laughter. Giggling with her as they sat side-by-side gossiping on the roof of the tenement seemed like a lifetime ago.

During 1905 more immigrants deluged the United States as Anna coped with her delicate relationships within the Valenda household. The

Russian-Sino War and bloody conflicts with Czar Nicholas II pushed peasants to escape Europe for more freedom in America.

One late winter Saturday evening, after John had ridden a horse to a dance in Urbana, he told his family of seeing a "Rooskie" lay down a nickel for a Coca Cola at a drug store soda fountain. The man was wearing a strange, tall fur hat and had a long, curled mustache. Everyone stared at the foreigner and giggled. The Russian laughed loudly along with them good-naturedly, even though he didn't understand that he was the butt of their amusement.

The *Center Point Journal* also related in detail facts about the First Transcontinental auto race. As Clarence read aloud to her about it, Anna realized that the Oldsmobile Curved Dashes involved in the race were like the first car she had ever seen in New York City the day she rode the elevated trains with *Teta* Anna.

In forty-five days, beginning May 8, Dwight Huss and Milford Wigle drove their Oldsmobile, dubbed "Old Scout," from New York to Portland to the Good Roads Convention. June 20 they were handed the first place $1000 prize. The men then reported their first-hand trials with the terrible condition of rural roads across America, which was not news to Iowa farmers. They struggled with poor roads daily.

When threshing season finally arrived that year, Anna was thankful to be with Libbie, neighboring farmwomen, and especially Mrs. Gilbert once again. As before, the woman went out of her way to visit with Anna and laugh with her. She asked even more questions about the Valendas than she had the year before, and what the girl's duties were there. When the threshers moved to her husband's farm, the woman had a pile of skirts and blouses she no longer used waiting to give to little Anna Mrkvička.

The immigrant loved to be with Claire Gilbert in her rambling white farm home. Fresh curtains hung at windows; zinnias and marigolds framed a pleasant front porch; there were books in the parlor. The large kitchen and pantry were well stocked with a cream separator, scales, crocks and the necessary tools of cooking, just as the kitchen of Mrs. Scavenisk had been.

Off the spacious dining room another space held Claire's quilting loom. Anna carefully ran her fingers over a colorful, half-finished pattern spread across the loom, wondering where all the little squares came from— an apron? a dress? a blouse? a worn shirt of Mr. Gilbert's?

Even the barn and outbuildings were painted and cared for. There was an order and crispness about the place that pulled at the girl. Her eyes feasted on the sights in every nook and cranny. Again she hated to see threshing season end.

That autumn of 1905 President Roosevelt declared Thanksgiving Day a national holiday to be celebrated the last Thursday of November. Churches in town and country planned dinners of turkey and goose and duck, inviting everyone to join in a potluck of prayer and fellowship. Hand-written signs of invitation were placed in store windows of small town America. Georgina didn't want to go to any of the churches, but at *Petr's* urging she instructed Anna to cook a special meal for Thanksgiving.

John chopped the head from a fat duck and carried it to his cousin to pluck and clean; Charlie walked through fresh snow to the storm cellar to collect potatoes and turnips, beets and sauerkraut. Anna churned fresh butter for the bread she would serve hot from the oven. The stove's heat and moisture from cooking steamed the kitchen window, which quickly coated to ice.

The girl grew excited at the challenge of a special meal. It broke the monotony of her days and reminded her of more pleasant times at Mrs. Scavenisk's during holy days, although the differences in the kitchens, houses and available foods couldn't have been greater. Anna did her best to make a banquet with the food at hand. It spurred her on that the men of the household were looking forward to it so, nodding and breathing deeply the pungent smells of the kitchen when they came and went during the special preparations.

Anna made apple *koláče* to match her artful creations at the Kinkels in New York, and she even found sufficient makings to mix up *bábovka*, the sweet poppy seed cake of her homeland. By nightfall Thanksgiving Day, sweet potatoes, pickles and rich gravy were spread across the table along with other heaping dishes. A rare abundance of food swirled around the roasted duck, now browned to perfection.

Everyone ate until their bellies ached. Anna served them. *Petr,* her godfather and the boys voiced their delight with noisy belches. The sixteen-year-old felt great satisfaction with the pleasure her efforts had brought to the day. Appreciation of her cooking was something to grasp in the midst of the mainly unappreciative Valenda household. Her tasty meals were one way she could be considered special.

Georgina was miffed at any hint of praise of Anna's work, of course, but she ate two and three helpings of everything on the table, all doused with thick gravy. Even the immigrant cook had enough to eat that first Thanksgiving, there was so much food left over.

Anna worked well into the night cleaning up the kitchen afterwards, storing leftovers in the frigid washhouse and storm cellar for later meals. No one offered to help her. They barely managed to groan with satisfaction as they lifted their added weight up the creaking stairs to their beds.

Weeks passed, and the only thing that happened at the Valenda house over the Christmas Holiday was that everyone, including Anna, came down with a flu that had spread through Iowa. The illness started with Clarence and went through the entire family. Hacking coughs were followed by dizziness and painful vomiting.

Because the sixteen-year-old also was down, a pail near her by the horsehair settee, everyone else was forced to fend for him- or herself. When the siege was over, however, it fell upon the girl to clean up the mess and air the house. All the bed linen had to be washed and dried, the floors scrubbed. She threw the windows and doors open the first day she felt well enough to tackle it; cold winds were better to deal with than the remaining stench of sickness in every room.

It was March of 1906, near the end of that long hard winter, and but a month from Anna's seventeenth birthday, when Georgina and her stepneice had another battle of wills. Snow driven by a vicious north wind had drifted around the Valenda farm, sifted through chinks in the washhouse walls, encased outbuildings and fences. The pump froze each night.

One evening after supper, *Petr* and his wife argued about spending what little money they had left from fall harvest. They had only enough either to buy a fresh horse for spring planting, or to replenish the flock of hens supporting Georgina's egg money. There were not enough dollars kept beneath their mattress for both. As tempers rose, the boys and Old Joe fled the dining room table and left the house for night chores in the barn.

Harsh words led to more harsh words, until Georgina angrily confronted her husband about how much money he was wasting on "the girl." Anna's different boots had not gone unnoticed by her. In the kitchen Anna froze, listening as she scrubbed dishes and pans with her calloused hands.

In anger *Petr* shouted at his wife, "She pulls her load and then some here. She needed something decent on her feet to do her work." For once the husband held his ground. "John Rubek, south down the road, has a fair mare for sale. I aim to buy it." That was that. The incensed husband rose from the table and stormed through the kitchen, slamming the door as he left to join his boys in the barn.

Anna's stomach clenched in fear. She heard the screech of Georgina's chair push back across the bare wood floor. The woman stepped quickly into the kitchen to face the young immigrant, fury lining her puffy face. The girl looked anxiously toward the corner broom, but it was too late for her to reach it. Her aunt already had moved to grab it.

Holding onto the broom like a baseball bat, Georgina swung it in a wide arc at Anna as the terrified girl tried desperately to stay away from the blows and shield herself. Even putting the center table between her and her tormenter didn't keep the woman out of reach. Bristles hit Anna's face and arms, lodged in her hair, whacked her small body.

"Stay away from *Petr,* you *česká* bitch," the woman screamed. "You're not taking my hens and egg money from me."

It was only when Georgina heard voices approaching from the barn that she hurled the broom across the table at the girl as hard as she could and marched upstairs. When Clarence and Charlie came through the wash shed to enter the kitchen, the men close behind them, welts were forming on Anna's face and arms, one dangerously near an eye. The bruised girl picked broom bristles from her hair and turned back to dirty dishes and pans, biting her lip and stifling sobs.

With her back turned to them, she could not see the sympathetic glances of the men and boys as they crossed the kitchen to climb the stairs to bed. *Petr* shook his head grimly. Only Charlie lagged behind to give Anna a longer-than-usual goodnight hug.

Anna lay awake long into the night, the broom stowed beneath the horsehair couch, a new sense of urgency boiling within her. She gripped her pale pink rosary in her hands, reciting every prayer Sister *Marie Helena* had taught her as best she could remember. She pleaded with Saint Barbara, patron saint of the poor miners who had worked beneath Kutná Hora so long ago, to help her. She knew that she must find a way to escape her stepaunt's wrath. And as soon as possible.

Georgina ignored the girl from that time on, only speaking to her to give her orders. *Petr* continued privately to slip her coins from time to time, without comment. Charlie hugged her more often, helped to clear the table of dirty dishes. He fetched more things from the storm cellar for her.

Spring finally ushered in Anna's move to the washhouse, which coincided with market day news of a train wreck in Colorado that killed fifty people. Anna again gave thanks for her own safe train trip to Iowa. She shuddered remembering the creaking wooden spans over the rivers she had crossed.

But soon balmy breezes joined with new green shoots springing up from warming black soil. Anna and Charlie spied the first robins. Canadian geese once again flew over Iowa heading north.

April 6, 1906, the girl's seventeenth birthday came and went, but an "X" on the parlor calendar was all that celebrated it. Anna Mrkvička had been separated from her family and with the Valendas on the isolated farm nearly three long years.

The next time *Petr's* stepneice was allowed to go to Center Point turned out to begin a pivotal change in her young life. First that day there was the excitement of a rare glimpse of a horseless carriage in the town. People everywhere were buzzing about it. One of the local doctors had purchased a Ford Model A; a crowd milled around it all the while the doctor was in the barbershop getting his regular haircut and a shave.

As soon as *Petr* hitched his horse to a post on Main Street, Anna joined the cluster around the unusual machine parked among rows of horses, wagons and buggies. Unlike the Curved Dash Oldsmobile she had seen in New York City, the Model A had not one but two leather seats. Its back seat was curved and tufted. The car looked somewhat like an open carriage. Men in the crowd murmured about the reported 30mph speed of its two-cylinder engine.

Scores of men, women and children stood waiting for "The Doc" when he emerged from the barber shop donning a dusty loose muslin coat over his suit, and carrying his black physician's bag. He was shorn of hair and clean-shaven. Everyone stared in awe as he cranked and started the car and chugged off down the street; horses whinnied and stomped their feet, ears twitching, their eyes frightened at the racket.

One driver in a wagon coming toward the Model A nearly lost control of his two mares. The terrified animals quickly tried to swerve away from the strange and loud contraption. Shoppers along the wooden walkway scattered to get out of the way lest they be trampled.

As the doctor disappeared, the crowd slowly dispersed. They had enough excitement and chatter about the Ford to last all day, on the long trip home, and through many conversations at their supper tables.

While Anna was disappointed that her friend, Libbie, didn't emerge from the crowd that day, she soon came upon Claire Gilbert struggling along the crowded walkway with her little boy, John, by then a rambunctious two-year-old. He was acting out and pouting. Nonetheless, the harassed mother greeted Anna warmly; smiling as she noticed that the girl was wearing one of the blouses and skirts she had given to her the year before.

Instinctively the seventeen-year-old took the boy's hands and tweaked his nose to make him giggle. She distracted him with her playful "Tst, Tst, Tst," just as she had her siblings and the Kinkel twins, and then she offered to go with Mrs. Gilbert to keep the boy occupied so that the woman could do her marketing. Georgina would be busy with shopping for awhile; her uncle was at the blacksmith's. A relieved

Claire was able to proceed with her helper and son to the general store and the dressmaker.

Soon she and the girl picked up where they left off the previous threshing season, laughing and communicating the best they could in Czech-American and with gestures. Again Mrs. Gilbert pointedly asked about Anna's duties at the Valendas, this time asking what pay she received for her work.

Anna explained awkwardly, "I get no regular money, Missus. Just a bed and some food." The woman was taken aback.

"Really? No pay?" she said, shaking her head. She looked hard at the thin, worn immigrant before her with a concern in her eyes that nearly brought the girl to tears. "Well," she finally went on, "I'll be looking forward to visiting with you at threshing time. Very much looking forward to it!" She hugged the girl as they parted, thanking her for helping with John. "I wouldn't have gotten much done without you," she said, taking off to meet her husband with her little boy squirming, but in tow.

That Iowa summer passed slowly for the seventeen-year-old. Days and nights were sweltering and buggy. Mosquitoes tortured her nightly in the wash shed. The holes in the screen near her bed never were repaired. Months of non-stop cooking and housework for Anna seemed never to end, nor did the backbreaking field work for the men of the household.

Evenings, after the supper dishes were cleaned and neatly put away, Anna sometimes stole time to drift into the back yard and sit alone on the felled tree to watch fireballs of sun sink beneath the horizon. Often their red/gold glow was dulled by air heavy with moisture. Fog drifted up from the farm pond, along with the rhythmic chorus of frogs and katydids. A musty smell of rich black soil filled the air. Bats whirred around the cottonwood trees. Warm dampness filtered from the ground beneath Anna into her every pore. She watched darkness descend, believing with all her being that she could hear the corn grow around her.

The immigrant thought of the sunsets of her life. In Velký Lunec, woods of tall old trees blocked sunsets from the view around the Mrkvička communal building. Only Saint Barbara's Cathedral, high on its ledge above, peeked around the trees. On the Kronprinz Wilhelm she had gasped at the scarlet sunsets huge on the ocean's never-ending horizon, even as she battled seasickness and painful loneliness. She remembered how in New York the last rays of sun and starry skies emerged over the tenement rooftops at *Teta* Anna's. She felt again the stifling heat as she'd lain there staring upward among crowds of exhausted neighbors trying to sleep.

Anna decided that the sunsets over the Iowa fields around her, with green growing crops reaching toward the sky, were as beautiful as any she had seen. But she also decided that she soon must find a way to watch them away from Georgina.

Clarence continued to read from the *Center Point Journal*. An earthquake measuring 7.7 on the Richter scale destroyed San Francisco, causing a devastating fire that killed over three thousand and left many more thousands homeless. Stories of tent cities and rationed food filled the front page. No one in the Valenda household could contemplate quake destruction. They felt thankful that Midwest tornadoes at least usually gave them time to head for the storm cellar.

Petr and his father were surpised by the odd news that in Europe Finnish women were granted the right to vote, just as men were.

"Are you going to join the uppity women to get the right to vote, *Aničko*," *Petr* kidded, "push fliers in my face like those angry females at the county fair?"

Anna couldn't imagine what a right to vote actually meant; no one she knew voted in the Habsburgs' Bohemia. Finding a way to survive away from the Valenda household, not women's suffrage, was foremost on her mind when threshing season once again finally arrived.

Even Georgina looked forward to a change in her daily schedule, anticipating money from harvest that would allow an increase in her flock of laying hens and egg money. Little did she know how pending plans for her stepneice soon would be changing the availability to her of Anna's helpful hands, and how her daily responsibilities beyond the hens on the farm would be increasing.

Claire Gilbert showed up at the second farm where neighbor women gathered to feed the threshers, and she was quick to find time to pull Anna aside to talk. The woman looked kindly into the girl's questioning eyes as she began haltingly, trying to be sure that the immigrant understood her. She knew only a few Czech phrases.

"Mr. Gilbert and I have decided that I need help with this son of ours. Bessie Buresh, wife of one of our farm hands, does most of the cooking for us, but I need help with the housework and the washings and, mainly, little John. If you'd like to come to our farm to work we can pay you bed and board and $5 a week. You would sleep in John's old nursery. He has his own room now, and so would you . . . . Do you understand what I've said, Anna?"

The girl's mouth dropped with astonishment. She had understood enough to know that she was being offered a job, and she especially understood the five dollars weekly pay for her work. A smile quickly spread across her small, round face. "Ah, Missus!" she said gratefully. Then Czech/English words tumbled forth. "I make good *koláče* and liver dumplings and I clean and iron good. I keep your house spotless for you and the mister. I take good care of little John."

The woman laughed and patted the girl's arm, stopping her stream of mostly Czech words. She hadn't understood all of what the seventeen-year-old had said, but the girl's enthusiasm obviously meant she wanted to come to the Gilbert farm. "Well, I'll also help you with your English and you can help me with my Czech. Would you like that?" The girl nodded eagerly. "I know you're a hard worker, Anna. I've watched you at threshing meals. And you're good with children. Mr. Gilbert and I would be pleased to have you in our home.

"But we must talk about when you can come. Early November would be a good time. Little John won't be able to run outside as much by then. Canning will be over."

Anna hesitated and frowned. She understood "November," weeks away. "Georgina, Georgina," was all she could murmur, worry clouding her different eyes.

"Will the Valendas be angry?" Claire asked, sensing the problem.

The girl nodded her head, rubbing her arms. She thought of her beating with the broom. She knew *Petr's* wife would be furious about her leaving.

Claire Gilbert finally asked softly. "Do they hurt you, Anna?"

The troubled girl turned away before she finally could admit to the kind woman, "Georgina takes after me sometimes. She can be terrible ornery with me."

"Well, I'll talk to Mr. Gilbert, and we'll go to your uncle's farm to tell him that we want to hire you. You needn't say anything until we do that. We'll see that nothing bad happens over this, Anna. I promise. Do you understand? Don't say anything to Georgina. We'll come to talk to her and her husband." Anna nodded.

The two then rejoined the women serving tables surrounded by hungry men. The young immigrant felt a lump in her throat from excitement, gratitude and anxiety combined. She couldn't believe that she would soon be working at the Gilbert's large house. She was going to watch sunsets on another farm after all, and with a woman who was kind, like *Teta* Anna. She was going to escape Georgina and her dangerous moods. She was going to be paid for her work.

The seventeen-year-old cradled her secret within her at her stepaunt's home. She smiled to herself each time it surfaced as she scrubbed pots and pans, drew water for Saturday baths, washed and ironed clothes, swept and mopped the floors. She sneaked bread and butter to the outhouse convinced that she would not have to do so in Claire Gilbert's house.

Only once, when she and Libbie had the opportunity to walk together on a day at market, did she share her news. She swore her friend to secrecy before she told her that she was going to work at the Gilbert farm. The Kusak girl was elated. She knew that the Gilberts were Presbyterians; church affiliation labeled everyone in small communities. "They're nice folks, Anna," she said as the girls hugged happily.

One Sunday evening in mid-October, shortly after suppertime, Mr. and Mrs. Gilbert's wagon came up the Valenda farm lane; barking dogs announced them. Charlie, now eight, ran in from the yard to tell his mother that visitors had arrived. Georgina grumbled in her usual way as the couple walked to the front door through autumn weeds. Anna followed her aunt into the parlor as she talked to the couple through the screen door.

Frank Gilbert spoke first. "Evening, Georgina. Is *Petr* around? May we come in to visit with you and your husband a few minutes?" As

Claire peeked around the bulk of the mistress of the house at the nervous young woman behind her, she said kindly, "Hello, Anna."

The aunt opened the door for these neighbors. She didn't turn them away as she had the Kusaks. She had been to the Gilbert's big house with the threshers, and she knew of their position in the farming community. She couldn't imagine what they had to talk about with her husband. "Go get your dad from the barn," she barked in Czech to Charlie, and motioned for the couple to sit on the horsehair sofa.

The weather was discussed thoroughly as the group waited for *Petr* Valenda to join them. When he did, and a handshake passed between the men, Claire's husband got straight to the point. The conversation proceeded in English. Anna struggled to determine what was being said, what was being decided about her life.

"My wife and I have asked Anna to come to work for us early November, to help with the housework and the boy. We told her that we wanted to talk to you about it first, though."

Silence filled the stale air of the parlor. A sluggish October fly buzzed near the door. Cool breezes ruffled leaves in the front yard. Georgina's eyes grew narrow as she looked at the girl who had kept her household running smoothly for three years. The smoldering anger in her eyes did not go unnoticed by the Gilberts. Claire spoke.

"We know Anna is a good worker, Georgina, and will be missed here, but she is seventeen. She needs to make her own decisions." Mrs. Gilbert deliberately turned to the girl. "Are you sure coming to our farm to work is what you really want to do, Anna?" She reinforced her English words with gestures from the girl to her husband and herself.

The immigrant understood and shook her head quickly. "Yes, I want to work with you. At your house," she managed to communicate with some firmness.

Petr finally stepped in. "The girl's a good worker, Claire. She'll be a help to you and the boy. Charlie's most fond of her," he said, glancing down at his son beside him, now forlorn to hear that Anna was leaving. "And she's a damn good cook, too." Georgina glared at her husband, but at that the visitors rose to leave.

"It's settled, then," Frank said, reaching for *Petr's* hand again. "I'll send someone over to pick up Anna and her things sometime November 1st. Let's hope snow doesn't make us bring the sleigh." Both men smiled grimly and nodded.

Claire pointedly walked to the girl and hugged her tightly. Anna gratefully hugged back. The woman left with a pleasant smile to *Petr's* wife, who did not smile back.

Of course angry words commenced before the Gilberts had driven the horses from the farmyard. Czech curses flew from Georgina as she snarled that Anna was ungrateful, that she had gone behind her back to find another place. She said the girl would have a hard time keeping the highfalutin Gilberts happy in their fancy house.

After a few minutes of her tirade *Petr* interrupted with disgust, "Be quiet, woman. We were lucky to have her here this long. You best leave her alone and not make a fool of yourself over this with the Gilberts. They're good people." And he walked back out to his chores.

Anna took the broom to bed with her that night, but Georgina climbed the steps after supper and snarled angry words in bed with her silent husband. Finally snoring came from upstairs. The girl was relieved that the episode was over, but she would be watchful until the Gilberts came to get her November 1st. She would begin to count the days marked off on the parlor calendar, and to get her clothes washed and ironed for her new job.

The seventeen-year-old packed and repacked her trunk as days marched by. Tucked among her clothes were the little flag from New York City and her first Fourth of July in America, her 1889 Indianhead penny and the well-read postcard from Antonia. Some nights she was so excited she couldn't sleep, even after exhausting hours of any hard work Georgina haughtily ordered her to do. The girl had to complete most of the canning herself.

When she did have the chance to watch the sunset behind the house, by now with a coat pulled around her in the cool night air, Anna imagined how it would look from the pleasant Gilbert farm. Would she be able to see it from her room, her very own room? she wondered. Could she satisfy the Gilberts with her work? She remembered how she had learned to make Mrs. Kinkel happy on her first job in America. She determined to do that at the Gilberts'.

How she longed to share her news with *Maminka* and her sisters. They would be so proud. Each night she said her rosary and thanked the Holy Mother Mary for Mrs. Gilbert. Sister *Marie Helena* would be proud of her too, she was sure. She felt as though Saint Barbara's Cathedral was looking down upon her from its hillside with its comforting shadows once again. Immigrant Anna Barbara Mrkvička was going to be safe in Iowa after all. She was becoming an American.

Chapter Ten

A Better Life

NOVEMBER 1ST THE seventeen-year-old rose early from the scratchy parlor sofa. She closed her packed trunk. It was cold and windy under gray skies, but it was not snowing. The Gilberts would not have to bring the sleigh.

The girl worked quickly through her duties in the kitchen—starting the fire, heating water, preparing the table for breakfast. She listened to feet hit the floor from beds upstairs, happy that it was the last morning she would be awaiting Valenda footsteps. As she completed her morning work, her ears listened for a wagon coming up the farm lane; her eyes glanced anxiously out windows.

Clarence and Charlie bid Anna good-bye as they left for school, the eight-year-old pausing to give his cousin one last, sad hug in the warm kitchen. Joe Valenda shook his goddaughter's hand awkwardly and said only "*Sbohem* (good-bye)" before he departed for the barn to rip nails from old fencing. He seemed sad.

Then the immigrant waited. And waited. Hours passed slowly as she busied herself with sweeping and cleaning and picking up soiled clothes from the bedrooms upstairs. She thought of her long ordeal before *Téta* Anna came to claim her at Ellis Island. What if the Gilberts had changed their minds about her coming to work for them? She argued with herself that Claire wouldn't do that, but still she glanced nervously through windows every few minutes.

It was after lunch when a young man finally pulled into the Valenda lane. It was Claire's brother, sixteen-year-old Ralph, whom Anna had seen at threshing, but had not met. He jumped easily from the wagon and walked along the worn path to the back wash shed. The girl rushed to open the door before he had time to knock.

Ralph stood there with questioning eyes. "Mornin'. Anna?" he asked. The girl nodded, prepared to try to understand his English words. "Claire said for me to fetch you today. I'm Ralph, her brother." He removed his wool cap and held out his hand awkwardly. Anna shook it, noticing his strong farmer's grip. Her head reached only to his broad shoulders.

Anna quickly tied *Babička's bábuška* on her head and donned her shabby old boy's coat, wishing she had a better one to wear to her new job. She refused to put her worn-out mittens or darned socks on her hands for protection from the cold. Ralph didn't seem to notice. When the girl moved toward her trunk he motioned to stop her and picked it up to tote it to the wagon.

None of the Valendas was in sight outside, but then Georgina emerged from the hen house. The girl called to her stepaunt that she was leaving. The woman only grunted and walked on to the barn, as sullen at the girl's leaving as she had been at her coming. The two travelers climbed into the wagon and were off.

Anna hugged her coat around her to escape a bitter wind, her bare hands stuffed into her pockets. Ralph fetched an old blanket from beneath the wagon seat and helped tuck it around his charge. The girl couldn't help but compare his caring gesture to her awkward introduction to the Valendas three years before, and the lonely ride she had taken from the train station to the unhappy household.

She hugged herself under the blanket, and suddenly she felt safe and hopeful of her future. Ralph spoke little on the trip, but he turned a toothy grin to her often. He didn't know exactly how to bridge the

English/Czech gap to communicate with his passenger. As for Anna, she smiled back each time he looked at her, taking special note of his kind blue eyes and his expert control of the horses.

When Ralph guided the team into the Gilberts' lane, the immigrant's eyes locked on the big house. It was hard for her to grasp that she was to live in such a place. Its inviting porch and the well-kept buildings and grounds surrounding it were immediately comforting to her.

Smoke from a healthy fire came from its chimney, and straw bales were placed to keep the basement foundation safe from winter winds. Both promised welcome warmth after the cold journey. A flurry of dogs greeted the wagon. Soon she and Ralph were walking through the back door of what would be the immigrant's home for three years filled with many changes in her life and well being.

Claire greeted her at the kitchen door with John hanging onto her skirt and ogling the newcomer. The woman nonetheless managed to give Anna a hug, and then she asked jokingly whether Ralph had talked her head off on their trip. His quiet nature was well known, the butt of many family jokes.

Bessie Buresh smiled in the background as she kneaded bread dough on a large kitchen table capable of feeding multiple farm workers. Her hands and arms were covered with flour. The kitchen was warm and humid. Windows were icy.

The cook immediately greeted the girl pleasantly in Czech, "*Ahoj. Jak se máš, Aničko?* (Hello. How are you?)" Bessie could speak the language of Bohemia well because she was married to a farm hand whose parents had come to America from Prague before he was born. It was through Bessie that Claire had learned a smattering of Czech words and phrases.

A relieved grin spread across Anna's face as she answered quickly, "*Dnes je zima.* (It is cold.)" It was comforting to know that someone in this English-speaking house could help her understand its workings. Bessie was in her fifties, older than *Maminka,* her children raised and gone. She and her husband lived in a small farmhouse down the road, a remnant on a plot of land Frank Gilbert had purchased.

The brother and sister continued to banter back and forth, and the immigrant was confused at the sounds of the foreign words and the giggles that swiftly flew around her. She could only try to gather from facial expressions and gestures what was happening. She smiled and laughed along with them anyway.

Together the group climbed up stairs to the bedroom area where the girl's loving gaze swept "her" room the minute she walked through its door. Ralph deposited the trunk and went quickly on to outside chores.

A hand-made white family crib John had outgrown stood in one corner of a large room that was positioned down the hall from the other bedrooms. Another spacious room nearby served as a combination guest room and Claire's sewing and linen room. She spent hours there stitching clothing for the family, sewing rag rugs into ovals and rounds, and mending a constant mound of shirts and pants and socks.

On top of a bright quilt on the crib in Anna's bedroom was propped a teddy bear much like the one Sophie Kinkel clung to in New York City. The bright red ribbon tied around its fuzzy neck made Anna smile.

The girl's side of the space had been carefully arranged for the new arrival. It held a simple iron bed and a chest holding a kerosene lamp, a mirror hanging above it. Fresh linens on the bed were covered with another hand-sewn quilt, many yellow squares cut from a dress of Claire's patterned across it. The girl imagined it sewn by capable hands on the downstairs quilting frame.

A small wooden washstand near the door held a porcelain basin and pitcher for water. Clean towels hung on hooks nearby. A well-used wooden rocker stood on a large oval braided rug that would shield Anna's feet in the morning from cold pine floors. The girl noticed a ceramic chamber pot tucked discreetly under her bed.

"*Hezký, hezký*," she murmured. Then she searched for the English word Libbie had taught her. "Pret-ty."

Claire smiled at Anna's obvious delight with the room, and left explaining as best she could that the girl should unpack her trunk and come downstairs when she was finished, to help her and Mrs. Buresh prepare supper. The mother took little John with her so that the girl could arrange her things in peace.

The seventeen-year-old was overwhelmed. She first sat carefully on the bed and smoothed the little squares of pretty quilt patterns with her rough hands. She stared at the pale yellow flowers on tidy blue wallpaper adorning the walls. Over the washstand hung a framed and cross-stitched "Home Sweet Home." She couldn't read the words, but whatever it said, she thought it looked beautiful with its scrolled floral border.

The room was quite a step from the horsehair sofa and the freezing wash shed at the Valendas, the crowded, dirt-floored Mrkvička room and the sweltering Zieman tenement in New York City. Anna studied the crocheted doily that lay over the chest, a Mason jar filled with dried zinnias and cattails perched upon it. She jumped up and in the mirror she looked carefully at her happy face. Then she quickly removed the *bábuška* and unpacked her comb.

The seventeen-year-old was testing the creaking rocker and smiling broadly as she rocked back and forth when she remembered with a start that she was to help with the evening meal. Swiftly she unloaded her trunk. Some of her worn clothing she placed carefully in the drawers of the chest next to the now-tattered letter from her sister, Antonia. It was the first time in her life that she had drawers to hold her belongings. Skirts and her coat were hung on hooks on the wall near her bed.

Anna draped her pale pink rosary over the mirror and arranged her comb and the tiny American flag on the crocheted runner of the chest before she practically flew down the stairs and into the kitchen to get to work in this wonderful house.

That night, after the kitchen was spotless to Bessie's satisfaction, the immigrant bid the Gilberts goodnight and went to her own bedroom, where she carefully slipped into a comfortable bed between clean linens. She pulled the bright quilt up to her eyes with a sigh. A November moon eerily glowed through cold windowpanes.

A familiar feeling of strangeness engulfed her. She had yet another new place, new people to adjust to. Getting to sleep had been difficult many times of her life—in the bed crowded with her sisters at home, on the swaying trains that carried her with each clickity-clack further away from Velký Lunec, in the rolling bunks of steerage on the Kronprinz and the too-few beds at Ellis Island. She thought of her sleeplessness on the sweltering roofs of New York City, with its crowded rows of sweating bodies. And she would be forever haunted by the many nights she lay shivering in the dark with loneliness and fear within the Valenda's cold, grim clapboard house.

But this night she felt a goodness in the rambling rooms around her. She felt that her life was going to be better within the carefully papered walls. She fell asleep that night relieved and grateful for the very good turn of events in her life.

So began the immigrant's years with Frank and Claire Gilbert. Anna looked forward to each day, even though they still were filled with hard work and long hours. Most importantly, everyone treated her with respect. Claire patiently made directions clear as to what was expected of her with little John and the house.

The family home was pleasant in itself, more pleasant even than the Scavenisks' in Velký Lunec. Claire Gilbert had covered cold wood floors with warm-hued rugs, brightened each room with dried flowers and family portraits. The tub room off the kitchen was open for a bath to anyone who pumped water to it from a nearby cistern. Anna especially appreciated being able to bathe easily, and when she wished. She determined at once to buy fresh Pear's soap with her earnings.

At the end of the first week of work, Mrs. Gilbert called Anna into the parlor so that her husband could count out the promised pay–five Liberty head silver dollars. The girl felt more proud than she ever had in her life. "*Děkuji, děkuji,*" she repeated over and over before she remembered the English words, "Thank you."

That night she sat on her bed in the light of the kerosene lamp counting and recounting and examining the coins, front and back. She could not read "*E Pluribus Unum*" curved over the beautifully coifed Liberty head, nor "In God We Trust" over the eagle on the reverse, but she rubbed her thumbs tenderly in appreciation over the amazing carved images.

Finally Anna tucked one silver dollar into her little purse from New York City and snapped it closed with determination. The coin was dedicated to a bar of Pear's soap and new boots, not second-hand ones this time. Next visit to market she would find a wonderful new pair of shoes to put on her abused feet.

The rest of the girl's pay was tied in *Babička's bábuška* and placed in her little trunk. The *bábuška* already had been replaced by a warm red wool hat knit by Mrs. Gilbert. The immigrant knew that she must not spend all her earnings. She was determined to find a way to help her family join her. She took *Teta* Anna's words to heart: "Save your money, *Aničko!*" If her aunt could accumulate enough money to move her family to Brooklyn, perhaps, just perhaps, she could somehow find a way to bring her family to America. But she realized that the difference in the two tasks was immense.

By her second week in the big white house, the seventeen-year-old was her fast-stepping self, drawing on all she had learned from mistresses Kopecký and Scavinisk. Wanting desperately to impress Mrs. Gilbert, she energetically dusted and scrubbed, and she spent long hours keeping the family's clothing clean. Claire remained patient when the newly hired girl did not do something to her standards; that proved to be seldom, however.

There were mountains of piles of clothing in the bedrooms to haul down stairs to clean and care for. Even on the most bitter winter days Anna hung clothes outside to dry, if possible. Otherwise washings had to be placed on rope lines in the dark, damp basement, or in the wash shed attached to the separate summer kitchen building. It was chilly and unpleasant both places.

Clothes were ironed in the large kitchen pantry, close to the black cast iron stove where the girl heated one after another sad iron. She carefully tested the irons with spit on her finger to see if they were hot enough, analyzing the sizzles she heard with growing skill. Sometimes Bessie helped with the ironing, depending on how many field hands she had to feed at the time.

Two-year-old John immediately was drawn to "Annie," which she was quickly called, enjoying her no-nonsense good humor, her tweaking of his nose and her "Tst, tst, tst," which meant that he was to settle down. She occupied the little boy both in- and outside, chasing him, tickling him and showing him winter games she had played with her sisters in the snow of Velký Lunec. Laughter returned to her life.

Each day the trials she had endured at the Valendas faded a bit more, but sometimes at night she would awake from a bad dream trembling, sure she had heard Georgina's heavy footsteps coming down the stairs toward her again. It always took a minute for the girl to realize where she was and that what she had heard was the pounding of her own heart.

Claire soon knit red mittens for the immigrant to match her hat, and she passed on more of her own clothing, outgrown after her pregnancy. Her still-smart brown coat replaced the shabby one Anna had worn when she arrived. Nevertheless the girl saved the old black boy's coat for washdays and forays to the pump, barn and storm cellar. She was too frugal to discard it.

When she had no other duties, the young Czech helped Bessie Buresh prepare food for her hardy meals. The cook laughed good-naturedly at the girl's barrage of questions. She was flattered to teach the young woman new ways to serve food and organize cooking. Conversations of the two switched from Czech to English and back again.

The cook liked Anna Mrkvička, taking note of her hard work and earnest desire to do a good job at whatever she was asked to do. She reminded her in many ways of her own daughters. Soon she was sharing gossip with the girl about the neighbors, and other rural rumors circulating the area.

A neighbor had lost her second baby to scarlet fever. A nice young girl down the lane was marrying her beau—in good time, Bessie muttered, raising her eyebrows. A woman at the Missus' quilting session had inherited a farm in Missouri at the death of her grandfather. Anna began to feel a connection to the society surrounding her. And the cook and Claire both kept the immigrant apprized of news in the *Center Point Journal.*

Unlike the Valendas, the Gilberts insisted that Anna sit down to eat with the family after she helped Bessie set meals on the table. There she could assist Mrs. Gilbert with little John, cutting his meat and avoiding spilled milk. The two-year-old often kept both women busy. The cook and her husband, Henry, ate supper in the kitchen with whatever farm hands were working on the farm at the time.

At long last the hungry girl from Velký Lunec was able to eat her fill. Both Bessie and Claire saw to it that she would gain much-needed weight, encouraging her to take second helpings, to finish leftovers.

The immigrant no longer had to hide bread and butter to eat in the outhouse, or long for the taste of eggs. In fact, she made a point to fix an egg for herself each morning, savoring the decision to have it poached, fried, boiled or scrambled!

Gradually Claire and Anna didn't need to converse much about John's care. As the eldest child in her family, the seventeen-year-old had had much more experience with small children than her mistress, so the older woman soon left it to the hired girl to keep John on his schedule and occupied so as not to get into trouble. As for the young Czech, she couldn't remember a time in her life when she was not looking out for younger siblings or caring for others' children; interacting with little ones was natural to her.

While baking with Bessie, Anna allowed John to play with tiny balls of the dough she was preparing for *koláče*, and she made the boy small cinnamon crisps as a treat. When she and Bessie were rushed with cooking, she sometimes placed the two-year-old in the large kitchen wood box, giving him jar lids and a rolling pin to play with. Occasionally, to keep him quiet, she gave him sugar tits to suck on, made from old flannel tied around a spoonful of sugar. Her tasks were usually done by the time the sweet was gone.

The immigrant was thankful to be in a well-stocked, well-run home. The pantry and storm cellar were stacked with food from harvest, row upon row of Mason jars filled with meat and pickles and jams, baskets loaded with apples and potatoes and turnips.

The roomy house kitchen was furnished well with the large black cast iron stove, cleaned spotless after each use. A pie safe to one side of a window kept bugs away from freshly baked pastries. Anna especially liked the safe, remembering her irritation with pesky ants and flies in the past when she had to set her summer pies to cool on windowsills. The safe's four wooden feet were set in cans of kerosene to protect from pesky roaches.

The summer kitchen behind the house was used seldom during winter months, except for when an extra stove was needed for holiday cooking, or when heat was needed to dry clothes in its attached wash shed. June through August the separate summer kitchen kept cooking heat out of the big white house.

While the Gilbert home was furnished differently from that of Mrs. Scavenisk, Anna loved its rooms and its American feel. Bessie Buresh shared with the girl that the Gilberts purchased many of their furnishings in Cedar Rapids, or had them made by local carpenters. Frank himself was handy with carpentry.

The seventeen-year-old thought the dining room especially grand. Its heavy table took up much of the room; Frank and one of his many brothers had made it from oak wood hewn from old trees on the farmstead. Ten to twelve chairs could squeeze around it. A nearby breakfront was filled with delicate porcelain bowls, platters and dishes, their floral patterns fading.

Claire explained to Anna that the items must be handled with care. Many had come from Europe, belonging to grandmothers and great-aunts; after their deaths the dishes had been passed on to her and her husband. She showed Annie the undersides of pieces stamped faintly with "Germany" and "Denmark."

The parlor was furnished with a piano that had jiggled on a train from Cedar Rapids to Center Point, then down rural roads on the Gilberts' wagon; its dissonant chords clanged over every rut along the way. It had been Frank's first anniversary gift to his wife. Claire played hymns on it almost daily.

Sometimes evenings in the parlor, husband and wife sang along together. Anna listened to them from the kitchen, but the Presbyterian songs sounded strange to her Catholic ears. There was no holy corner as in Bohemian Catholic homes, but a large leather-bound family *Bible* lay prominently in the parlor on a small table near a lamp. Births and deaths were logged carefully inside its cover.

Family portraits hung on parlor walls in ornate, hand-made frames. A maroon horsehair settee sat against one wall, quite grand compared to that of the Valendas. Near it on another table lay a stereopticon viewer. When Mrs. Gilbert urged Annie to look through it one evening, Anna was astonished to see two pictures come together in depth. She kept taking the viewer away and looking at the two pictures, then going back into the viewer to see only one. Claire laughed with her.

A bookcase with a glass door housed a modest collection of books.

It was Anna's job to clean them regularly. While dusting the case one day soon after her arrival, Anna carefully opened the door and picked one up to search its pages for drawings or pictures, as she had looked through the Public Library books on Ellis Island.

The English words were frustratingly incomprehensible to her. She had taken pride, under the stern gaze of Sister *Marie Helena* in Kutná Hora, to be able to read and write Czech well. She formed her letters carefully with chalk on a slate board shared and passed from student to student. When Claire found the immigrant turning the pages of *The Farmer's Almanac*, a frown on her face, she determined that the girl's English lessons should begin in earnest.

Each time she and Bessie were involved with Anna on any task, they tried to explain the English words and phrases that described items or activities. For her part, Claire would ask the girl what the proper words were in Czech, and the two would stumble through their communication together learning new phrases. The seventeen-year-old worked hard to understand. What the Kinkel twins had taught her on their trips to the park helped a little.

She went to sleep and awakened to odd-sounding words buzzing in her ears. Self-instructions in her head were unrelenting throughout the day: It is "barn," not the Czech *stodola* that shelters horses in America. "Pigs," not *vepři*, stay in sheds. The creaking windmill pumps "water," not *voda*, to animal troughs. She had to discover how to properly refer to a "corn crib" and the "outhouse" tucked away nearby but downwind of the house. Sometimes the struggle gave her a headache; she knew what she wanted to say but the words were hopelessly scrambled somewhere deep behind her different eyes.

Lively conversations between field hands at noon dinners in the kitchen enlightened her about guns and hunting, and she learned the English words for the game they shot or trapped and brought to Bessie to be cleaned and prepared. She soon could identify the "prairie chickens" that she had seen scurrying around fields and meadows, as well as "white-tailed jackrabbits," "pheasants," "deer" and "wild turkeys." The hired men told and retold their shooting stories, bragging shamelessly about their prowess.

One day a young hired man reached out and pinched Anna's bottom as she walked by his chair in the kitchen, saying he sure did like the way her *koláče* livened up the meal after the squirrel they had devoured for lunch.

Like a flash Bessie moved to slap his arm soundly, scolding him in her most vitriolic Czech. Her husband, Henry, hooted, and told the man he'd better be careful around his wife, as she'd knock him down if the mood struck her. Said she'd put him sprawling on the floor a couple of times. Bessie laughed and tapped her husband's balding head good-naturedly with a wooden spoon.

When the men finished eating and left the house, Bessie cautioned little Annie not to go alone to the barn where the hired hands slept. "Some of them are drifters, *Aničko*. We don't know them well. They could cause you trouble."

Anna was thankful for the woman's protection, but even at twelve and thirteen at home in Velký Lunec she had learned to stand up to such advances from farm men. *Maminka,* as well as *Babička Marie,* had instructed her early on how to swat errant hands, advised her to slip away quickly. And it gave her yet another reason to strive to learn the language of America, to understand what such men were saying to her.

Before uttering English words and sentences out loud, Anna would have to think what she wanted to say in the language of her childhood, and then try to remember the proper English translation. Reactions from listeners verified her correctness or their confusion. There were many moments of laughter at her convoluted phrases, and at times she muttered a few Czech swear words under her breath at the vexing difficulty of the *anglicky* language in America.

But "*Jak se máš*" slowly became "How are you?" and "*Mám se dobře, děkuji*" was replaced with "I am very well, thank you." She understood completely that jumping somersaults from the words of her Bohemian upbringing to those of her new country was necessary if she was to become American. When she became overwhelmed by it all, she sought refuge in her room, her very own space.

It was in her bedroom in the first light of several mornings that Anna heard Mrs. Gilbert retching down the hall. Having been through so many pregnancies with *Maminka,* the girl guessed that her mistress was with child again. Sure enough, by the end of November Claire announced that the following June another baby would be filling the crib in the nursery. Anna would have another little one to care for. Her room would need to be part nursery again.

The space was ample enough. Even little John spent time in Anna's room before he was tucked into bed. The sunset was visible from Annie's windows. As the Czech held the little one in her arms, she and the boy would mutter "Ooh" and "Ah" at the beautiful colors on the snow. Anna showed John how his warm breath could fog the frigid glass, and how to press his handprint on it.

The two together gazed out at subdued white against the shadowy whites of hills and lowlands. Bare trees etched their gray against cold skies that washed from pale to darker blue. As red balls of vanishing suns disappeared, clouds whipped by overhead on frigid prairie wind. The shadows of fences, made of wood and barbed wire, scratched their way through dollops of snow bordering fields frozen until spring. In the comfort of the Gilberts' warm home and family, Anna finally could appreciate the beauty of Iowa farmland in winter.

The young woman felt a contentment in Claire's rooms that she had never felt before. It was so different from the stress of her crowded home in Velký Lunec, the long journey to Iowa and her frightening time with the Valendas. And part of her contentment came from the fact that the immigrant's three-year social isolation was over.

Many travelers with horses and wagons or buggies turned into the Gilberts' lane and were made welcome. In-laws and cousins, brothers, sisters, aunts, uncles and church friends wandered farm to farm to socialize when chores permitted. Claire always was glad to have company, particularly as her pregnancy proceeded. And she especially looked forward to the quilters who stopped by to help her stitch a current quilt. When John was napping, Anna was asked to join the women around the quilting frame. She enjoyed listening to neighbors' stories about their daily lives.

It was Anna's first attempt at fine stitchery. She did her best to pierce her needle through the material and cotton batting in a sewed line as perfect as those of the experienced quilters around her, but it took her twice as long to match their tiny ten stitches to an inch. As the girl's fingers pushed her needle and thread through the pattern, her quick mind tried at the same time to thread whatever new words whizzed around her into her growing English vocabulary.

The seventeen-year-old helped serve refreshments to guests, often in the parlor, its stove lit and warming. She passed around her best *koláče* with pride—prune, apple or cherry. She sometimes shared her poppy seed *bábovka,* which always brought compliments.

The girl was so pleasantly engrossed in her new life, that one night as she prepared for bed a sharp jab of guilt pierced her heart. After particularly busy days, Anna realized with a start that she had forgotten to pray for her family in Velký Lunec for several nights. She had not thought of them at all. She rummaged in a dresser drawer for the worn-out letter from home, and pressed it to her heart as she sank down in the rocking chair.

When she looked around her pleasant room, cozily glowing from the light of the kerosene lamp, she thought of Antonia and Mary and Frank, of new baby Antone being suckled by her weary mother. In the white crib nearby a teddy bear awaited a new life. The new Gilbert baby would not be stacked with others like cords of wood in one bed, as she knew her siblings were.

Comparing the stark difference between the crowded, dirt-floored Mrkvička room and the quilted beds in her room, the crocheted doily and the "Home Sweet Home" on the wall above her, brought Anna to tears. Her different eyes now screened all she saw in the life around her through both her Czech and Iowa memories.

She desperately wanted her family safely in America, as happy and warm as she was. She wanted their cold feet to feel rag rugs beneath bare toes, their stomachs to fill with an abundance of food they had never known, their lives to be more than the drudgery of field work and hopelessness in the beet fields of Velký Lunec.

The seventeen-year-old quickly grabbed her rosary from the mirror and knelt to plead with the Virgin Mary to help her find a way to bring her family to Iowa. She at length petitioned the Holy Mother for the salvation of each member of her family that night, carefully naming them one by one. She finally went to sleep with Antonia's letter beneath her pillow.

Ralph and John, Claire's brothers, helped brother-in-law Frank from time to time on his large farm. The two lived on their parents' section of land thirty minutes west by horse from the Gilbert spread. Claire insisted that her younger brothers dine at her table when they worked on her husband's farm. The three siblings kidded and taunted each other, laughed a lot. Anna enjoyed watching them together.

Bessie one day explained to the girl that Claire had wanted to be a teacher, but as an only daughter she had stayed to help her parents on the farm while her brothers worked the family fields. She had not married young. Frank Gilbert had been an older, settled bachelor working on his brothers' farms when Claire finally caught his attention.

He, his brothers, as well as their father, had bought up sections of land surrounding their properties as they came up for sale. Most of Frank's brothers had married and moved to farmsteads nearby. Frank had purchased land when he married Claire that included the large farmhouse with its pleasant front porch.

Anna hung on every word about the family whose lives were rapidly intertwining with her own. She was trying hard to understand how people in America could buy land and own such beautiful houses, how they made money for themselves to buy nice things. She thought the Gilberts to be very smart indeed.

One evening in late November, when the brothers had joined their sister for supper, John mentioned that they were going to a dance in Urbana the following Saturday night. Claire immediately blurted out, "Well, take Annie with you!"

Sixteen-year-old Ralph turned to the young hired girl. He had been trying to visit with her more as her English improved, and he had learned a few Czech words from working side by side with Bessie's husband. "Would you like to go with us, Annie?" he asked.

Anna completely understood the invitation and she replied quickly in English, "Oh, yes. I polka. You polka?"

Both John and Ralph said at once, grinning. "We polka. We schottische." Ralph went on, "We'll give you a spin you won't forget!"

"I'll wear my new boots," Anna murmured without thinking. Everyone laughed. She had spent a full hour at the cobbler's in Center Point the previous Saturday trying on pair after pair of high-topped boots, and had finally settled on fine brown leather ones that laced smartly over her ankles. It took more than the one silver Liberty dollar she had set aside to purchase them, but she decided that owning a shiny new pair of shoes that fit was well worth it.

"Good. It's settled," said Claire, "but you'll have to watch that these brothers of mine don't step all over your wonderful new boots with all their spinning."

The seventeen-year-old could hardly bear her excitement the following days. Mrs. Gilbert searched her closet for something nice for the girl to wear, and found a black taffeta skirt and fresh white blouse for Anna. The night of the dance the anxious girl bathed with her fresh bar of Pear's soap and, at Bessie's suggestion, washed her long hair with a touch of vinegar. Claire heated the curling iron on the stove to shape soft curls around the girl's face. Then she brushed Annie's long hair until it glistened, tying it behind her head with a large rose-colored bow she had worn herself when Frank was courting her.

The girl fidgeted and asked dozens of questions of Claire about the dance and the people who would be there. She revealed that she'd only danced outside the town hall in Kutná Hora with her sisters and other children, and briefly on the Kronprinz and at Ellis Island; it all seemed like a century ago. Her mind was whirling, wondering whether she would be able to remember enough dance steps and English to get through the night. Both Bessie and her mistress assured her daily that John and Ralph would show her a grand time.

When the brothers arrived that Saturday evening, they were taken aback by little Annie from Bohemia. She came down the stairs looking very pretty, stepping cautiously in her new boots. Her cheeks glowed like the ribbon in her hair. Her tiny waist was cinched in even more with their sister's sash. John offered his arm pointedly as the girl smiled nervously and stepped out for the first adult social event of her life. Claire and Bessie beamed.

The night of dancing did not let the seventeen-year-old down. The elder John–nine years older than his younger brother–was the talkative one. He kept the buggy ride to the dance jovial. Ralph was his quiet self, but he laughed and bantered some with the older John, smiling at his guest often. Of the two brothers, Anna was drawn to quiet Ralph, nearer her age. She noticed that his blue eyes seemed incredibly dark in the moonlight.

Excitement rose as the group entered the town. Everything seemed aglow with lanterns lit along Main Street. Sounds of voices and laughter came from shadows everywhere. Anna had not visited Urbana before. The brothers' buggy joined wagons heading from all directions for the dance hall. Ralph finally found a place to hitch the horses.

Men were crowded along the wooden sidewalk smoking cigars, chewing tobacco and telling rowdy stories. Anna's ears heard German and Swedish words coming from the din. She turned her head when she recognized Czech phrases spoken somewhere, but could not pinpoint their source. Ralph and John steered the immigrant through the ruckus, their hands on her elbows as they walked protectively each side of her. Sprightly fiddles and stomping feet could be heard inside. The girl's heart was pounding when she walked between the two handsome young men into the crowded, dimly-lit dance hall.

Once inside, the brothers greeted many in the noisy crowd; Annie was introduced at every turn. She practiced her English, saying carefully, "How are you?" and responding to inquiries with "I am fine, thank you."

She felt a twinge of jealousy when a tall and pretty young blond woman approached Ralph and John and spoke rapidly to them, laughing at their responses. They talked so fast Anna didn't understand much of what they said.

Fiddlers were playing with gusto at one side of the large room. Couples twirled around the Hall like the pale images she had seen in "The Great Train Robbery." Newspapers still ran stories about railroad bandits, and the girl hoped that no posse like the one in the New York motion picture would interrupt to break up this magnificent evening.

Very soon polka strains filled the hall and feet began to tap and stomp in anticipation. Men yelped and hooted, grabbing their partners and taking off around a dance floor worn smooth. John stepped up and took Annie's hand. They were off.

It was amazing to the young Czech how the steps came back to her. Her whole body fell into the rhythmic beat of the fiddles as her feet flew around the floor. Only John's arm around her waist kept her from flying away. By the time the dance was over, both partners' faces were flushed and perspiring, and more than a few male eyes had begun to watch the petite seventeen-year-old dancing with Frank Gilbert's brother-in-law.

Ralph was waiting alone for the two with glasses of warm cider for them from the bar. Despite his awkwardness, there was a twinkle in his eyes for Anna. When the schottische began, John took her glass and shooed the two onto the dance floor.

As Ralph grabbed Annie tightly around her waist and vigorously began a lively step, the seventeen-year-old felt a strange rush of heat ripple through her. Even the touch of his hand tingled, but soon she had to concentrate on her dance steps as the two whirled and twirled among the crowd. They giggled. They hooted.

Sometimes they crashed into other dancers, their arms, their backs, their buttocks. Everyone just roared with laughter and continued on their way, yelping in tune with the music. When Anna laughingly glanced up at Ralph, she thought that this moment well made up for her terrible years with the Valendas. She knew that nothing else would ever equal her first night of dancing in America.

That evening was only the beginning of the young Czech's happy times with Claire's brothers. She accompanied them to dances almost every Saturday, in whatever nearby town they were held, weather and farm schedules permitting. John particularly introduced her to many neighbors of the area.

Young Czech men soon sought out quick-stepping Annie as a partner, men with names like Stodola and Novák. They rushed to offer her beer or punch between dances. A Jacob Kubesch sometimes asked her to dance, but while she was spinning with him through the crowds, her eyes were searching other couples to see who was held within Claire's brothers' arms.

She felt pangs when the partner of either of them was the talkative young blond woman who had been introduced to her as "Charity." Odd name, she thought. No one in Bohemia was named Charity. She especially was vexed to notice that the black boots the blond wore were much fancier than her own.

Anna was surprised when eighteen-year-old John Valenda appeared at one dance, and made a point to seek her out. He asked about her new job. In Czech the girl rattled off all the things she had experienced at the Gilberts'–the spacious bedroom where she slept, how she sat down at the family table to fine meals served in a grand dining room. When he finally walked away she felt delight in her soul that he would tell Georgina all about Anna Mrkvička's wonderful new life.

She had seen the Valendas occasionally at market, and while *Petr* was always pleasant, his wife usually turned and went the other direction when she saw her stepneice approaching.

At that same dance, this time in Center Point, Libbie's brother, Henry, suddenly appeared and asked his sister's friend to dance. Anna was disappointed to hear that Libbie was at home with her sick mother, but she awkwardly took Henry's wooden hand in her own as he put his good hand at her waist. Away they went.

Henry explained that his father had to replace the artificial hand often; they kept getting splintered as he worked cutting trees. Anna glanced at the finely carved piece and felt the graininess of it against her fingers, then smiled at Henry and said that she thought the latest one Mr. Kusak had made to be the best one yet. Henry agreed, grinning as they twirled on.

Soon the 1906 holidays began to influence the dances and everything in the Gilbert household. In this home Christmas was truly celebrated. One day Annie trudged with the entire family through the snow to cut a Christmas tree from nearby woods, and that evening little John tried his best to help decorate it with cranberries and popcorn strung on string. Claire added to the branches dried flowers that she had hung from the rafters of the washhouse at the end of summer. Frank lifted his son up to place a hand-made angel dressed in white at its top.

Anna approached the family activities with excitement and joy in her heart. When she realized that everyone was preparing gifts for others, and after Bessie's explanation of family customs, she purchased little items in Center Point for each member of the family: ribbons for the women, a small toy for John, a book mark with a Bible verse on it for Mr. Gilbert. She mulled over each purchase, giving up her precious coins with difficulty. Gift giving was a new experience for her; no one in her family in Velký Lunec could afford to exchange gifts in this manner. As people wrapped packages in brown paper and tied them with string or ribbons saved from previous holidays, great secrets were hidden in every corner of the house. The seventeen-year-old came upon gifts slipped behind dishes in the kitchen cupboard, kettles in the pantry and pickle crocks in the storm cellar. Little John grew more restless daily, sensing the growing anticipation in the air.

Mrs. Gilbert asked Anna whether she would like to go to church with the family Christmas Eve. When the girl hesitated, repeating that she was Catholic, Claire offered to drop her off and pick her up at the Catholic Church. It happened, however, that John developed a cold and couldn't be taken into the weather, so Anna stayed alone with him in the spacious house as everyone else climbed into the sleigh to skim over snow to candlelight services.

Christmas morning John was up at dawn, anxiously pulling on his parents' covers to wake them. When everyone tumbled downstairs to see what was under the tree, packages miraculously had appeared. There was a flurry of openings as Mr. Gilbert handed out gifts.

Everyone thanked Annie for her presents, and she received special things in return: an embroidered apron that Claire had spent hours finishing in her sewing room, a shiny silver dollar from Mr. Gilbert, a red knit wool scarf from Bessie. It was the same yarn as the hat and mittens Mrs. Gilbert had made for her shortly after her arrival. With his mother's help, little John had wrapped for everyone some pretty pine cones he and Claire had collected from nearby woods.

The immigrant was overwhelmed with the family thoughtfulness around her, but images of *Maminka* and Antonia and her family kept crowding into everything she saw and felt. Twinges of guilt, comparing this American life of hers with theirs in Habsburg poverty, wove among the giggles and gift giving in the warm parlor. She especially remembered the look of her worn mother as she bid her good-bye. *Maminka* would have stroked Claire's gifted apron and its stitchery with wonder.

But the seventeen-year-old felt better as she helped Bessie work hours on the Christmas Day feast. Her special touch with food was another gift she could give the family that had saved her from the Valendas. She stirred egg yolks, flour and salt to make a firm dough, then rolled, dried and cut slivered Bohemian noodles for soup to start the courses of the meal. Bessie used the unused egg whites for angel food cake, little John's favorite.

At Mr. Gilbert's request, Anna made her specially seasoned pork-filled dumplings. Even the older Bessie did not know the secret of the recipe, which the girl had gleaned from the cook at the Scavenisks'. The immigrant sidestepped passing it on to her.

Family and friends started arriving in their sleighs and smaller cutters through the snow before noon Christmas day. They gathered around the tree in the parlor as Claire played Christmas songs and hymns. Once when Anna peeked into the room she saw with delight that sixteen-year-old Ralph was playing a harmonica. He managed to wink at her.

Guests finally sat down at the Gilberts' large dining room table about three o'clock in the afternoon. Chairs had to be brought in from the kitchen. Anna was disappointed that she and Bessie had to tend to seven of the smaller children at the kitchen table, so that adults could enjoy their holiday banquet.

Bessie at last shooed the girl in to have dessert with the rest, and Anna was able to squeeze herself onto the piano bench with Frank's tiny aunt, shrunken with age. Everyone raved about Annie's *bábovka*, and Mr. Gilbert said her dumplings were her usual tasty delight. When the girl looked at Ralph for his response to her cooking, he raised his eyebrows to her and nodded vigorously. The two grinned ear to ear.

Anna Mrkvička went to bed that night feeling very fulfilled. Her stomach and her heart were brimming over with a new sense of well-being.

After the first Christmas with the Gilberts, on an occasional Sabbath morning, the young Czech did make an effort to attend Catholic mass, but she usually was busy with Bessie fixing Sunday dinner for Claire and her after-church guests. Often John was sick with croup or a cold, and had to stay in bed for the day. Scarlet fever was circulating among farm communities, and the Gilberts didn't want the boy exposed. Then Anna was both nurse and cook, but she didn't mind. She was grateful for her new life.

Winter months continued to be highlighted for Anna by weekend dances, sometimes interrupted by heavy snows. The girl dreaded that winter storms would make the excursions to town impossible; sometimes they did. The times she could spend with Claire's brothers became precious to her.

When Ralph stayed for winter suppers she stole glances at him often, sometimes finding him gazing at her already. Claire and Frank began to smile in amusement. John developed a fixed smirk on his face around his younger brother and the Czech girl with the fast-stepping feet and the different eyes.

The seventeen-year-old spent many frigid winter nights before going to bed looking out her window at the moon, carefully noting its waxing and waning. It seemed extraordinarily beautiful to her, reminding her of the nights she returned from dances huddled in the cold, Ralph in the wagon by her side. She could feel the touch of his arm next to hers, see his dark eyes in the moonlight.

When dance trips were possible, Anna dressed carefully for them in her room, glancing at her mirror, fussing to pile her long brown hair high on her head or to tie it back prettily with a ribbon. She borrowed Mrs. Gilbert's curling iron. Part of her weekly pay began to be spent on a sash of her own, new stockings, a new blouse, colorful ribbons. Bessie showed her how to order things from *Montgomery Ward's Catalog*, which she mulled over at length; she did more contemplating than buying.

Most of the silver dollars she received continued to be added to the growing pile of coins tied in *Babička's bábuška*. Each payday she counted her savings with satisfaction. She was determined to find a way to bring her family to Iowa. She couldn't imagine how much money it would take to do that, but she began to nurse a small hope that anything was possible in this America.

The girl waited anxiously for mail from her sister, Antonia. Before the Holidays she had written to explain her new address and job with the Gilberts. She hoped for a response throughout the winter to no avail. In the meantime she began to etch indelibly her own place on the Midwest prairie.

One late February evening when Ralph and John were around the supper table with Anna and the family, Frank announced that they would all pick up after the meal and go tobogganing in the moonlight. A light fluffy snow had fallen during the afternoon, but had stopped at dusk. They could walk to the hill by the pond and light a fire. Everyone thought it a grand idea. Claire told Bessie in the kitchen to put little John to bed, as Anna was to accompany them.

Everyone scrambled to put on layers of clothes against the cold: stockings under mittens, wool hats, scarves, thick wool socks, old boots. Anna was excited to be invited. She donned her matching red hat, scarf and mittens, preening in her bedroom mirror, but decided to wear her old boy's coat. She couldn't risk damaging the brown one from Claire. She didn't know what to expect of this "tobogganing."

Once outside, the small band was surrounded by a sparkling fairyland. Their lanterns and the moon twinkled on snow-draped tree branches and dried grasses. Their feet scattered diamond dustings each step. Frank carried a long wooden toboggan he'd retrieved from the barn.

Soon Claire's brothers were at Anna's side, John joking and kicking snow with gusto. He picked up a handful of the white fluff and sprinkled it over Annie's head. Ralph followed suit. The girl gathered handfuls herself and threw it at them right back. Soon the whole party was throwing snow at each other, howling and giggling. Then Mrs. Gilbert began to sing "Oh, My Darlin', Oh, My Darlin', Oh My Darlin' Clementine." Frank joined in, their voices clear in the pristine night.

Once at the hill the men made a fire and soon everyone was taking a turn at hurling downward into the strangely sparkling darkness. Anna was put on the toboggan for her first ride, John in front of her, Ralph behind. The seventeen-year-old snuggled into Ralph's arms and hung onto John for dear life. They zoomed downhill. She was terrified, at one point muttering a prayer to the Holy Mother.

Halfway down, all three spilled into the feathery snow, screaming and laughing, the toboggan finishing the run without them. Ralph and Anna had tumbled side by side, his arms still around her to keep her safe. John took off running to fetch their wayward ride. Ralph pulled Annie to her feet and gently dusted snow from her red hat and cold cheeks. He bent to kiss her cheek; his lips cold against her skin. Anna suddenly found it hard to breathe.

When everyone tired of playing, they put out the fire and much more quietly trudged back to the warm kitchen where Bessie would have hot cider waiting for them. Frank and Claire walked arm in arm, John beside them pulling the now-empty toboggan. Ralph and Anna followed behind, young Ralph's arm still around the Czech hired girl with the very different eyes, helping her through the fluffy snow.

When the seventeen-year-old at last fell into bed she was exhausted, but too exhilarated to sleep. For a very long time she watched the way pale moonbeams lined through the bedroom windows and across the floor to touch her bed.

As soon as March sun and wind softened the warming fields, intense work on the farm began. The men started to plow the soil, sow seeds. Mr. Gilbert invested in a new Robinson manure spreader. Lambing season commenced. Pittsburgh wire fencing welded together by electricity was installed during wet days when workers couldn't deal with the mud in the fields. The fencing would enable cattle and sheep to be sent into expanded pastures.

The master of the house fired a new hired man because he caught him beating a recalcitrant horse. No one on Frank Gilbert's farm was allowed to abuse livestock. It made Anna feel good when she heard of it. She felt certain that she could judge a good man by the way he handled his livestock. As a child carrying water to the workers in the beet fields, she had cringed when she saw burros or horses beaten and bloodied.

Inside the house the women took on spring cleaning, wiping winter grime and smoke from walls and woodwork, taking beds apart, hanging mattresses and covers outside in crisp fresh air. The garden plot near the house was prepared for planting.

Mrs. Gilbert was over her early-pregnancy nausea, and helped with these chores, but her back hurt and she was tired most of the time. Frank was delighted with the prospect of another child. He was enlarging his acreage to accommodate as many children as God gave him and his wife. As a special gift to Claire he came home from market one day with a new Royal treadle sewing machine. It had six drawers, carved intricately. The plain older machine handed down in the family was given to Bessie.

The women all sat down to test the Royal stitch and found it fast and straight. Mrs. Gilbert set to work sewing fresh baby clothes, as John's were worn and faded already. She also kept herself busy making clothing for the Presbyterian ladies' group and their drive to help needy children. She constructed shirts and nightwear for everyone in the household. Most evenings she darned socks, knitted and embroidered as Frank caught up with his reading.

On Anna's eighteenth birthday, April 6 of 1907, Bessie baked her a special apple cake. The women celebrated with little John around the kitchen table midafternoon; the men were busy in the fields. Claire gave Annie her very own curling iron. That evening at supper brothers Ralph and John promised to celebrate her special day at the Saturday dance in Center Point. The girl thought it a perfect day, completely unlike the birthdays of her past.

Iowa farms soon were in rhythm with sun and rain. Pastures bloomed with pink four o'clocks, yellow lady slippers, purple and fuchsia spiderwort. Spring commodity markets were discussed around the supper table along with other news from the weekly *Center Point Journal.* There was a crash on Wall Street. J. P. Morgan locked bankers in his private library in New York City and didn't let them leave until they pledged $25 million to prop up the stock market. The young immigrant couldn't imagine so much money.

Norwegian women received the right to vote. Claire was ecstatic about it, her husband silent. "Uncle Tom's Cabin" toured Iowa, its performances in tents, as lynchings of black Americans continued their horrors in the southern United States. Oklahoma was made the forty-sixth state of the Union.

In Washington D.C., Congressmen raised their pay to $7500 annually at the same time they determined to give Spanish war veterans $12 a month at age 62. Frank Gilbert was appalled at the disparity of incomes. An aging uncle had fought in the war and placed his life on the line for his country. At the supper table actions by the federal government often brought angry words from Frank Gilbert.

Late in May the Ringling Brothers Circus came to town. Claire decided that her son must see the animals, so she convinced her husband to schedule his farm work around taking the whole household to watch the circus train unload and to see the big tent being hiked to the sky.

Mid morning, watching her very first circus performance, Anna's eyes grew wide at seeing an African tiger, and she watched gasping as a Gypsy-looking woman acrobat in scanty costume spun through the air above her. No safety net was spread below.

Early in June, during what had been an ordinary day, the farm erupted into panic. Anna was watching toddler John play midafternoon as she hung washing to dry, when Mr. Gilbert came running pell-mell from the barn shouting. Bessie's husband, Henry, had fallen from the haymow. Two other farm hands were rushing behind their boss carrying the writhing man. John sensed trouble and began to cry as he ran to Anna and gripped his arms around her legs.

Claire, now large with child, held the kitchen door open so the men could take Henry into the house and up the stairs to the extra bed in the sewing room. A distraught Bessie followed her moaning husband, his arm falling askew from his body. Anna knew that the arm was fractured the minute she saw it. She had seen many such accidents on the farms of Velký Lunec.

Mr. Gilbert immediately ordered one of the farm hands to take a horse and fetch the doctor from Center Point. Everyone else clustered around the bed where Henry lay muttering with pain and disgust about his carelessness. A broken arm was a terrible setback for a farmer. Summer fieldwork was heavy; he knew all hands would be needed.

Anna was sent with John to watch on the porch for the doctor. It seemed to take forever for the man to appear, but finally, after well over an hour, the girl heard the sound of a Model A chugging up the road to the Gilbert lane. Once by the house the car backfired with a loud bang and stopped with a jolt. The farm hand who had fetched the doctor came galloping up behind the car, his horse in a lather.

In the upstairs hall Anna and the boy joined Bessie and Claire, who were pacing nervously as the doctor rolled up his sleeves and examined Henry's arm. He determined that it was broken in two places below the shoulder socket. The man had fallen awkwardly on the edge of a corn picker, and while he was scraped and bruised, the doctor was relieved that the broken bones tore no skin.

Anna was instructed to take little John outside as Frank fetched a bottle of his whiskey from the dining room and Henry Buresh took a good long swig of it. Then his boss gave him a piece of wood to bite and held him down as the Doc pulled and straightened the arm. The Doc secured wood splints around the break with an old sheet torn in strips. The injured man groaned in pain as Bessie covered her ears and cringed. Claire held the frightened woman in her arms. Anna, outside, could hear the commotion, and tried to busy little John with the Czech "Prune Song," singing every verse she could remember as loudly as she could.

Then it was over. There was silence. Bessie went to her husband to comfort him, stroking his balding head. Frank Gilbert brought out two silver dollars to pay the doctor for his work, but the physician immediately said that his wife would appreciate more two dozen good large fresh eggs and a couple of chickens for her pot. Frank nodded and set out with him to gather the food.

Soon the doctor cranked his Model A as Anna and John watched with fascination, but when the machine backfired, the little boy began to cry and hold tight to Anna's skirt. The chugging of the car turning back out the lane and down the road mingled with his sobs.

Accidents were not unusual on the Gilbert farm, or any farm. Hired hands like Henry Buresh were at the mercy of their employer during illness or injury. Even though Bessie's husband was worried because he would be disabled for a time, he and his wife were fortunate to be working for the Gilberts.

Frank quickly assured both of them that as he was able Henry could do what he could with one arm. He could still feed livestock and round up the cattle using his good arm and the dogs. The Bureshes would not lose pay over this. As Bessie and Annie prepared supper that evening, the cook repeatedly wiped tears of relief from her eyes with her apron.

The incident reminded Anna vividly about the farm workers in Velký Lunec who lost limbs from farming accidents, or who were crippled or became critically ill. Landowners seldom took care of them or their families. Injured workers' only recourse was to move in with relatives as poor as they were, becoming a burden to everyone. In her parents' communal building two such families were stuffed in one small room. A brother had taken in his sister's family when her husband lost a foot from a scythe accident that developed into gangrene.

Henry recovered quickly, wearing his arm in a sling and wincing with each movement for a time. Nevertheless, he soon fed the livestock and learned to do much with his one good arm. After each meal Bessie rubbed his cramping shoulders before he left the kitchen to face more chores.

Shortly after the accident, two o'clock in the morning of June 28, Claire felt her first labor pains. The baby was overdue. Frank's younger half-sister, Glynnis, had come to stay at the house to help with what seemed to be a delayed birth. Claire hardly could walk up and down the stairs; sometimes she slept on the settee in the parlor.

Anna awakened when she heard concerned voices in the Gilberts' bedroom. By the time she lit her lamp and dressed, Glynnis was by Claire's side and a visibly worried Frank was leaving to fetch the doctor with the buggy.

"Of course it's raining," he muttered. "Babies only come when it rains or snows." The weather would make it difficult to see the mud of the roads and the way, and he didn't trust a hired hand to make haste as needed. Anna was instructed to set water to boil. Old towels and worn sheets were already stacked near the mother's bed in preparation.

It took two and a half hours for Frank to return with the doctor, whose Model A was not usable because it could not handle the slippery mud. Even using two horses and a buggy it was slow getting the two men back to the Gilbert farm.

As they waited, Anna and Glynnis changed bedding, soaked when Claire's water broke. They held the laboring woman's clutching hands and mopped her brow as she lay moaning and grinding her teeth. Pains came closer and closer together. Glynnis nervously decided that she and Anna might have to deliver the baby themselves, and she sent the uneasy eighteen-year-old to boil scissors and find thread to tie the umbilical cord.

The infant's head had begun to emerge when the doctor finally entered the house and hurried up the stairs into the birthing room, Frank close behind him. The rest of the delivery came with a rush as the physician ordered the husband to the parlor and told Glynnis and Anna how to assist him. Very soon a healthy, squalling baby girl, to be named Rose, was delivered into the world.

Anna never actually had been involved with a delivery before, although midwife *Maminka* had told her daughters tales about many. The girl's stomach was in a knot until the baby was safely swaddled and in her mother's arms. Everyone heaved a sigh of relief. Frank and Claire smiled broadly.

Mrs. Gilbert didn't bounce back as she had after the birth of little John. At Rose's christening she appeared exhausted. Anna went with the family to their Presbyterian Church for the baptism, John in tow. She had laundered and ironed the christening dress herself. Both Frank and little John had worn it. Baby Rose slept through the entire event.

The new mother paid as much attention as she could to John as he adjusted to someone new demanding her attention. Anna sometimes rocked the infant to sleep, the brother watching, but because Claire was breast-feeding, most of Rose's care fell to the mother. Anna had her hands full with the three-year-old, the laundry, cleaning, and helping Bessie in the kitchen as she could.

She and the cook soon were busy picking elderberry and gooseberries for pie. They watched apples ripen and began to pull fresh vegetables from the kitchen garden. Anna savored the taste of fresh food, and the fact that her belly was empty no more.

1907 rushed by for the hired girl. One afternoon the family managed to get to the city to watch the Center Point Bloomer girls play ball. Anna cheered and hooted with the rest of the crowd; little John was quickly bored.

Field work and the care of crops and livestock from dawn to dusk kept everyone too busy to go to many dances through the summer. Anna was thankful that Claire's brothers were able to sit often at the Gilberts' supper table. She looked forward to Ralph's grin, his blue eyes twinkling back at hers, their shared giggles.

One day in August the girl finally received another letter from her sister, Antonia. When Bessie brought it to her she ripped open a wrinkled and soiled envelope, eager to read her sister's careful Czech script. *Maminka* was again pregnant. Foster child *Anton* Procházka was living with the family once more. He had been removed at two years of age, as was the custom with foster children, but he had cried until he became ill, refusing to eat. When *Maminka* heard of it she asked the authorities to return him to her for a time, at least until he started eating again.

Antonia once more closed with, "*Aničko*, I miss you. Your big farmhouse sounds grand. What is a porch? You have your own room for sleep? I want to be in Iowa, too."

Anna read and re-read the letter each night the following week. She sat sadly in the rocking chair by her bed, thinking of her family in their crowded little room in the compound in Velký Lunec. She knew her mother was exhausted already, and she certainly was not well enough to have another baby to nurse and carry on her back into the fields.

The girl took *Babička's bábuška* from her dresser drawer and spread its content on her bed. She had saved $151 silver dollars and two quarters working for the Gilberts, but it would not cover the cost to bring the sizeable Mrkvička family by train and ship to Iowa. As the family grew, so did the money needed.

The eighteen-year-old confided in Bessie about the money she was saving in her bedroom. The cook immediately urged her to put her savings in the bank where it would be safe, but the immigrant was not ready to have the coins she could count and feel in her fingers replaced by a small book like the one that held *Teta* Anna's deposits in New York City. She was proud of each dollar she had earned, and she looked forward to counting her savings every payday.

Busy threshing season soon arrived. The three women of the Gilbert household baked and filled their wagon with sweet potato pies, freshly churned butter, applesauce, and ham from the smoke house. Bessie steered the wagon from farm to farm. Anna sometimes was able to see and visit with Libbie Kusak, now sixteen and convinced that she was in love with yet another boy at her church.

When Georgina Valenda appeared at the gatherings, Anna pointedly ignored her and felt satisfaction in it. Claire's friends always welcomed the Gilberts' hired girl, and many told her how fine she was looking with her dark brown hair tied back in her favorite blue ribbon. She had gained a little weight; curves were appearing. "You look so good," they said, beaming.

The men being served at the long tables under the trees talked of Howard Taft running to be the 27th President, along with the "Tin Lizzies"–Model T Fords–that were coming off production lines in Detroit at the rate of one every fourteen hours. A drawing of one appeared in the *Journal.* They seated two, cost $850. The farmers around the table speculated about who besides the doctors in the area would be rattling down their roads in one of the new contraptions, spooking their chickens and cattle. Certainly it would not be one of them, with hog and crop prices what they were.

A Zeppelin exploded near Stuttgart, Germany, home of the grandparents of one of the farmers at the table. Terrifying flames had plunged to the ground. The men decided that it served the Count who developed the floating thing right. They concluded that if Man was expected to fly through the air the good Lord would have given him wings.

Of course they discussed the market for their harvested grain. The nearby Alburnette Bank was paying 4% for certificates of three months or longer.

Women buzzed about the wife of an implement dealer in Center Point who had acquired an Edison Phonograph; someone had heard that the lazy woman listened to its cylinders all day while her hired girl did all the work. The machine cost nearly $35 of her husband's hard-earned money, they clucked. Then they quickly turned to bragging about the quarts of foodstuff they'd canned already that summer.

Anna enjoyed listening to all of it; her English was improving. Her conversations were interspersed with words and phrases from both her native and new language, but she was getting better at understanding and speaking "American," muttering and cursing to herself about it less.

After threshing, the process of canning wound down, although its schedule always was determined by the ripeness of fruits and vegetables, the timing of butchered hogs and cattle. Bessie and Annie shouldered most of the work with food preservation. They picked cabbage, squash and pumpkins, as well as berries and grapes for jams and jellies. They boiled Mason jars and melted paraffin to cover row upon row of bright jars filled with preserves. They made pickles, and whenever the men butchered, they filled Ball jars with every edible animal part of hogs, cattle and sheep. Bessie continued to care for the chickens and gather their eggs.

Anna and the cook carried basket after basket of canned goods to the storm cellar and basement because the pantry quickly overflowed. The eighteen-year-old never tired of looking over the stash of food, remembering the countless evenings of her life she had gone to bed with a gnawing stomach. She never tired of holding treasured scarlet and purple jars of jellies up to the sunlight to see them sparkle like jewels.

The eighteen-year-old regularly counted how many jars were completed, once in Czech and once in her new English, to see if she could do it. The women quilters often recounted their inventories of food as they sat together sewing their tiny stitches into intricate patterns. Anna always looked forward to telling them how much she and Bessie had accomplished.

Finally Indian summer arrived along with golden harvest moons, and dances began in earnest. Anna had waited not-too-patiently for time to sit regularly beside Ralph and John on their way to dances again. She and the brothers resumed their trips to Urbana and Center Point. Sometimes the beauty of the moonlight, the chill of rich land finally at rest, made even the usually talkative John speechless. They all three bumped in the buggy down the road quietly drinking in the glowing country night.

But the stillness ceased when they arrived in town at dance time. Yelping and hollering and fast steps around the halls, mixed with beer and warm cider, provided relief to workers in farming communities after months of profitable field work and preparation for another long, cold Iowa winter.

Anna noticed with some annoyance that fall that Ralph and his brother both began paying more attention to the blond with the lovely boots, Charity. No matter who from the rows of farm men spun little Annie around the floor–the Novatnys, the Kubesches, the Kubias–the eighteen-year-old kept her eye on Claire's brothers. Her heart was pierced with an unsettling jealousy new to her; she didn't like it.

Christmas was even sweeter for Anna than the year before. She anticipated it with excitement, hiding her gifts along with those of the rest of the family. She baked special Bohemian rye bread Christmas Eve Day for John and Ralph to take to their farm and table. The brothers gave her ribbons for her hair; their sister had helped choose the colors. Annie hung them over the mirror in her room beside her pale pink rosary, so that the rose one from Ralph would be the last thing she saw when she turned out the lamp before going to bed in her wonderful room.

Claire presented little Annie with a grand present: a recently completed quilt. The eighteen-year-old had stitched a small portion in its corner one day, not dreaming that it was destined to be hers.

"For your hope chest," the older woman said smiling, "the wedding ring pattern you liked." The girl was fascinated as she looked again at all the cut pieces of material and the rows of tiny stitches. She recognized patches of cloth from a discarded dress of Claire's, an apron of Bessie's. She would carefully treasure the quilt forever.

The girl tucked the handiwork carefully in the bottom drawer of her dresser, and she started paging through the *Montgomery Ward's Catalog* to see what large trunks were available, so the gift would have a proper home. She supposed that she should have a "hope chest." Libbie spoke of having one already. Anna decided that she really was truly becoming American.

February 18 a severe blizzard brought outside movement to a standstill in the Midwest. Blinding snow buried the inhabitants of the Gilbert house. Farmhouses were isolated even more than usual. Anna's days were filled with just keeping warm, corralling rambunctious little John, who couldn't go outdoors, and looking anxiously for clearing skies. There were no dances until the snow began to melt in earnest.

It seemed to the eighteen-year-old that the spring of 1908 took forever to arrive, but when it did, the countryside sprouted lush wildflowers and trees went gold to green. She and little John clapped their hands at the first robin.

It was March when everyone realized that farm work soon would fill all schedules. Dances and rides to and from such good times now became more special. With Claire's brothers Anna savored each spectacular sunset as they rode over the prairie. By this time Ralph and Anna giggled a lot, pinching and poking each other. Elder brother John rolled his eyes at their playfulness. In the shadows of the street outside the dance halls the two teenagers exchanged soft kisses, then went inside to float through dances together.

After her nineteenth birthday in April, again celebrated with a special cake from Bessie, the girl and everyone on the farm was buried in farm work. Nursing things to grow from Iowa's rich loam helped everyone quickly forget the cold of winter.

On Decoration (Memorial) Day in May, cemeteries throughout Iowa's countryside bloomed with remembrance. Anna joined old and young who paraded by gravestones to place handfuls of wildflowers near tombstones marking their departed. Summer Sundays Claire took zinnias and dahlias in rainbow hues from her garden to the churchyard graves of cousins, aunts and grandparents.

Frank's wife had gained weight with her pregnancies; gray hairs wove through her hair. But Anna thought the woman who had saved her from Georgina to be quite beautiful as she wandered and placed flowers lovingly on graves.

Sometimes the immigrant went to church with the Gilberts, even though the Presbyterian services in the simple church gave her little comfort. More than she thought she ever would, she missed the pained, hand-carved face of Jesus looking down at her in school chapel in *Kutná Hora,* and the striking spires of Saint Barbara's Cathedral.

One late June day at market, Anna finally asked Claire to help her open a bank account. Bessie at last had convinced the girl that she should not expose her savings to fire or theft in a dresser drawer. After much thought about it, the nineteen-year-old decided to bank at least one hundred of her silver dollars. The rest would stay in the *bábuška*; she couldn't bear to part with all her earnings.

With Mrs. Gilbert beside her for encouragement, the girl signed "Anna Barbara Mrkvička" in her finest Sister *Marie Helena* script on bank papers, frowning nonetheless at the shrinking pile of dollars she could touch and count. Then she walked out with her shoulders back and her very own bankbook in her little New York City purse. She was just like *Teta* Anna, she thought, even though her different Czech eyes were clouded with a vague uneasiness. She was the very first in her Mrkvička family to have enough money to put in a bank.

That experience became the highlight of her summer. Every two weeks or so she would march to the bank and push her silver dollars into a cashier's cage. She'd then walk away studying hard the new figure in her little black book, double checking its sum. She still was very good with numbers; she knew the Sisters in *Kutná Hora* would be proud.

One sweltering day in August another letter arrived from Velký Lunec. Anna ripped open the envelope to learn that *Maminka* had delivered twins, but that one had died immediately. A tiny baby girl, Louise, was managing to survive. Anna's mother had lost more teeth and she found it difficult to chew. Antonia again finished the letter with, "I miss you so much, *Aničko*. How I want to be with you in America."

Anna immediately went to count her coins once more and confirm the numbers in her little black bankbook. They were far from enough for the growing Mrkvička family. The cost for just her one trip had amounted to well over sixty dollars for ship and trains.

During the threshing season of 1908 the topic among workers around the heavily laden threshers' tables concerned newspaper reports about an auto race from New York City across the country. "Imagine! Cars driving ocean to ocean," farm men exclaimed. Automobiles going through Iowa were hopelessly bogged down in mud on the terrible roads. Experienced farmers snorted, "Even a stupid horse knows when to stay out of Iowa mud."

The month before Taft was elected president, autumn dances began in earnest. John and Ralph and Anna began their treks to dance halls once again. Claire watched them go as she nursed little Rose, envying the trio their youth and fun.

The three donned their dancing shoes and rode in the buggy through the Indian summer fields to town. John was his jovial self. Ralph kidded mercilessly with the Czech hired girl about her fractured English. When they arrived with the crowds and began to step around the floor to raging fiddles, they fell into the comfortable rhythms from previous years.

That season Charity became John's regular partner at the dances. Young farm men, and sometimes those not so young, asked the Gilberts' petite hired girl to dance constantly; she was a whiz at the polka and amazingly swift at the schottische. Her round face grinned and shouted with the festive numbers and the raging fiddles. Sometimes during Czech polkas she would shout out the Czech words, her hair growing damp with exertion from her rapid steps.

During a dance in Center Point in early October, Jacob Kubesch asked Anna to dance yet again. While she'd been his partner from time to time, she remembered little about him. This time she managed to notice that he was very light on his feet, not like some of the men that evening who had tromped on her good brown boots. And she took note that he was handsome in a rugged farmer way.

Jacob had the black curly hair of his Yugoslavian mother, which he parted in the middle in the fashion of the day. His hazel eyes and strong farm hands came from his Czech father. Work scarred fingers and calloused palms encircled Anna's small fingers as he twirled her around the floor. It was obvious that the young man had nicked his square jaw badly with a sharp straight razor as he scraped away a week's tough, black whiskers for Saturday night socializing.

Nevertheless, he looked dandy that evening in his black string tie and blue chambray shirt, which showed off his broad shoulders. He was not as tall as Ralph, but petite Anna still reached only to his nose.

As a bonus, the Kubesch man could speak to the girl in fluent Czech, even though he seemed shy and did not talk all that much. It was a relief to Anna not to have to translate every word in her head into English. After one polka Jacob bought her warm cider and the two went outside in the cool autumn moonlight to stroll the street and share snippets of their lives.

The man was so shy, talkative Anna felt frustrated having to wrestle conversation from him. She did learn that night, however, that Jacob's father, John, and his mother, Mary, also were immigrants from Bohemia. They had come to Iowa separately when they both were sixteen. Jacob had two brothers and two sisters. Czech was spoken in his home, but he had learned his English in a nearby one-room schoolhouse. His family had deliberately left the authority of Catholicism behind them in Europe; they attended no church.

"Everybody just calls me Jake," he concluded quietly.

Anna began to tell the young man of her own immigrant journey, of leaving Germany on the Kronprinz in Bremen and arriving at Ellis Island only to be stranded until her aunt came to claim her and Joe Valenda. She regaled him with her description of New York City, its Fourth of July, its elevated trains and the museum with amazingly huge dinosaur bones reaching to the ceiling.

She described "The Great Train Robbery" in every detail and added that she could have been the victim of train robbers on her long train ride to Iowa, just as in the moving picture, but she wasn't. She added that she was told there were armed guards on her trains to scare bandits away. Jacob was impressed. The farm boy had never been more than thirty miles from his parents' land near Center Point.

After the two returned to the dance floor and at last stepped through a closing polka, their faces scarlet and wet with sweat, Jake asked his little partner if he could take her home and pick her up for another dance the following Saturday. The girl replied quickly that the Gilbert brothers had brought her and that they would expect to take her home, but then she hesitated.

Ralph and John and Charity were standing nearby deep in conversation. Anna had taken note that the brothers had danced with her often the entire evening. Jealousy overcame Anna once more. She turned back to look hard into Jacob's eyes. There was a quiet gentleness there. After an awkward pause she said, "But you can come for me next Saturday, if the weather's right."

Jake replied quickly, grinning, "I'll see my horses get me there by six!"

So it was that twenty-seven-year-old Jacob Kubesch, listed with his brothers in the 1907 Farmers' Directory of Leading Farmers in Linn County, Iowa, began the courting of Bohemian immigrant Anna Barbara Mrkvička.

The following Saturday Jake pulled into the Gilbert lane a bit early. Frank, head of the household, came from the barn to shake the hand of the young man calling on his hired girl, and to inquire about the Kubesch family, their farm, their crops. The men knew each other from threshing seasons.

Bessie and Claire Gilbert watched the two from the kitchen window and called for Anna to come down from her room; her gentleman caller had arrived. The older women were more fidgety about the girl's first beau than the young Czech herself.

Maminka's eldest daughter had half-heartedly dressed for the evening. At the last minute she tied Ralph's Christmas ribbon in her hair and looked hard at her reflection in the mirror. Anna was startled to see the glum face staring back at her, and she shook her head, determined to enjoy the evening. At least this "Jake" was a good dancer. Gradually her faint, crooked smile appeared in the mirror.

When the hired girl entered the kitchen, an uncomfortable Jacob was standing at the back door, wool cap in hand. Bessie Buresh was already making pointed inquiries about this stranger, trying to determine his nature and background. Claire was a bit less obvious. The two finally seemed satisfied that the young Kubesch man was indeed a safe and worthy escort for the nineteen-year-old, and bid the two on their way.

Each following Saturday buggy or sleigh rides to and from dances provided time for Anna and Jake to learn more about each other, their families, their dreams. The girl continued to be vexed at times with the shy farmer's lack of conversation, but she slowly learned more about his background.

Jake's paternal grandparents, Jacob and Annie Kubesch, had traveled to Iowa from Bohemia with their five children by sailboat in 1872. The trip had taken 31 days, which astounded Anna. She couldn't imagine enduring more than the six days and nights of the seasickness she had survived on the Kronprinz Wilhelm.

One of the Kubesch children on that sailing ship had been Jake's father, John (*Jan*). He eventually married Mary Kupse and they worked hard to own two 160-acre farms to support their growing family of three sons and two daughters. Their land nestled among neighbors whose names represented the growing ethnic mix of Iowa: Dworsekse, Zaboketsky, Kozina, Heins, Jones and Yost. Nearly one in ten persons in America by 1910 had been born on foreign soil.

In 1907 father John and Mary had sold one of their farms and retired to Cedar Rapids, leaving their sons to work the remaining L-shaped 160 acres near Urbana in Grant Township. By the time Jake and Annie were traveling to dances together, one of Jake's two brothers,

Joe, had already married Ida Laker and had left the family farm to rent acreage nearer Center Point. More than the parents' land was needed to support the extended family.

Even though Jake's brother John was younger, he was married to Anna Rabik. Jake and the couple lived together on the Kubesch homestead, sharing the work, raising livestock and harvesting crops of wheat, oats, rye and corn. Both sisters in the family had moved away with their husbands. Shy, soft-spoken Jake remained the only of his parents' children unmarried, and he was the subject of much family prodding to find himself a suitable wife.

Anna shared with her escort her dream of bringing her family to America, how difficult life was in Velký Lunec, how slowly her savings were growing to bring her parents and siblings to be with her. Jake understood. His farming family lived frugally and had left at great risk the poverty and class system in Europe, determined to start new lives in the midlands of democratic America. A striving for family success on the Iowa prairie flowed through Jacob's Czech and Yugoslavian blood.

The often-tongue-tied bachelor was intrigued by the nineteen-year-old and her animated ability to talk as fast as she whirled through dance steps in his arms. The girl balanced his awkward shyness. Jacob admired Anna's feistiness as she spoke of her longing to bring her family to Iowa, and he was taken with the way her chin could tilt with stubborn determination as she talked about it. The two soon fell into a pattern—the girl rapidly speaking in Czech, gesturing with her able hands, her escort listening and nodding his head.

As the farmer continued to call on Anna, the girl warmed to being with a man who shared her immigrant background and loyalty to family, even though she missed playful fun with younger Ralph. As she and Bessie visited in the Gilbert kitchen, peeling potatoes or baking bread, the older woman listened to the girl's chatter and ambivalence about Jacob Kubesch. He was so shy, and it was hard to get him to talk, Annie complained. The cook generally remained silent, but occasionally she spoke her mind.

"You have to look forward, *Aničko*. Jacob seems to be a hard-working man," and she quickly added, "I've noticed he's very gentle with his horses." Anna already had taken note of that. It is a good man who shows kindness to his animals, she repeated to herself.

By November the girl stopped wearing Ralph's rose ribbon to the dances, deliberately choosing another to tie back her long brown hair. And she usually was smiling as she checked herself in the mirror before going downstairs to meet Jacob.

At one dance Jake introduced Annie to his brother John and his wife, Anna. Soon the couple asked the girl to Thanksgiving dinner at the family home; brother Joe and Ida would join them. The young Czech understood that it was now her turn to be the object of family examination.

The nineteen-year-old nervously approached Jake's home that holiday, sitting primly beside her quiet escort in his wagon. She wore her matching red gloves, scarf and hat, and held in her lap special prune *koláče* tied in a clean dish towel, her gift for the meal.

The immigrant was startled and disappointed when Jake's place came into view. The house looked at first glance very much like the Valendas', reminding her of her grim ordeal there. But unlike *Petr's* rented place, the Kubesch self-owned buildings were repaired and cared for. There was a windmill creaking in the farmyard amidst a cluster of sturdy buildings—a large barn, a machine shed, and a sizable chicken coop that appeared to accommodate twice the number of hens under Georgina Valenda's care.

Three dogs greeted Jacob with wagging tails as he and his guest stepped from the buggy. Anna noticed a boot scraper anchored near the back door. It obviously was well used by men trained by a stern mother to clean their shoes before entering her scrubbed house.

Inside, rooms were warm and pleasant. Two generations of Kubesch women had papered the walls and insisted on fresh paint on the woodwork. The one-and-a-half-story farmhouse had the usual slanting roof with two bedrooms beneath it, one for Jake, the other for his brother and wife. The sleeping rooms were separated for privacy by a partial frame wall and a worn blanket on a rod.

Family pictures hung on walls in the parlor on the first level. There was a dining room and a large kitchen with a properly cleaned stove.

Furnishings throughout were worn but neat, the space simple but adequate.

Anna found herself thinking as she strolled the rooms how different they were from those in the rambling Gilbert home. The Kubesch bedrooms were cramped, not large and pleasant like the spacious bedroom that now held her meager belongings. Then she reminded herself that Jake's home still was almost luxurious compared to the dirt-floored room in Velký Lunec where she had been born.

As the girl joined Jacob's sisters-in-law in the kitchen to help with the meal, the men withdrew to the parlor to smoke their cigars and discuss farm business. The women soon were quizzing their guest about her family, her background, any common acquaintances they might have. Anna Rabik and Ida asked many questions about the Gilberts, considered very well off by their neighbors. What was the house like inside? Was Claire still nursing her youngest? They built up to asking Anna what she was paid for her work.

The room was awkwardly silent as the girl paused. Then she replied, "A good amount," firmly tilting her jaw. She would know Jake's sisters-in-law the rest of her life, but she never would share with the two either her financial matters or her recipe for pork-filled dumplings. "Nobody's business," she often muttered beneath her breath.

When Ida asked what was in Anna's hope chest, the girl could only tell of the beautiful wedding ring quilt lying in her dresser drawer. At that moment, as Anna Rabik and Ida bragged of the holdings in their own chests before their marriages, the nineteen-year-old decided that she was going to spend her precious silver dollars for this "hope chest" of America.

It would be one as handsome as the one John's wife showed her with pride, carefully placed upstairs at the foot of her marriage bed. The trunk of Jake's sister-in-law held extra quilts and carefully embroidered and starched linens. The woman also pulled from it her white cotton wedding dress and the pressed corsage she wore at her parlor wedding.

Shortly thereafter at Saturday market, Anna walked deliberately through two general stores, stroking displayed trunks with her fingers, studying their size and shape. She stepped back from each one squinting, her different eyes trying to visualize how they would look at the foot of her bed.

At long last the girl selected a wooden humpbacked trunk covered with black metal. It had shiny, two-inch wooden braces circling its outside, and fine leather handles. The metal in the center of the hump and down the front, back and sides was hammered into a floral design highlighted with dark blue. A large black key protruded from the lock on its lid.

Anna thought it more beautiful than that of Anna Rabik, and as grand, even, as any of Mrs. Scavenisk's. She determined to have it, all the while wincing at the cost—nearly a week's salary. Nevertheless, it was a fitting chest of hope for her beautiful wedding ring quilt.

Mr. Gilbert carefully loaded the trunk on his wagon, and Bessie, Claire and Anna fussed during its bumpy journey over frozen roads and up the stairs to its place at the foot of Anna's bed. Then the whole household watched as the girl carefully placed both the wedding ring quilt and *Babička's bábuška* inside it and locked the lid shut. Everyone was beaming. Claire fetched string from her sewing room so that Annie could tie the key around her neck.

For days Anna opened and closed the lid of her trunk to view its treasures, and she looked at it the last thing before she went to sleep. She knelt with her pale rosary to thank the Virgin for her new life, and to ask that she be able to show her family some day soon how successful she was becoming in America. She especially thanked God for Claire Gilbert.

The first Saturday in December, after a dance at Center Point, Jacob was even more quiet than usual when he brought Anna home. The landscape surrounding the two was painted eerily with the glow of a blue-white winter moon. The girl, by now used to Jake's shy manner, rattled on about the dance, who danced with whom and the work to be done at the Gilberts' the coming week. Finally, sitting in the Kubesch buggy before the big white house, the farmer reached for little Annie's hand as he blurted out abruptly, "Let's get married, *Aničko.*"

He had practiced this moment all week, but he felt miserable that his words had been so awkward, especially as he saw the girl's different eyes grow large and startled in the moonlight, almost like a deer in a gun site when it spies the hunter. He had never even had the courage to kiss this nineteen-year-old who had so quickly captured his heart.

Anna was taken off guard. The man in the buggy beside her was a stranger still. It was so soon to speak of marriage. She knew that she didn't share the warmth she had felt for Ralph, but on the other hand, Claire's younger brother seemed like just a boy compared to established farmer Jacob Kubesch.

While Jake's touch did not excite her when they danced, and the feel of the sturdy farmer's hand that held hers didn't take her breath away, she realized that she felt comfortable with him, secure. But marriage!

She quickly turned to climb down from the buggy, saying that it was time for her to get to bed. There was much work tomorrow. She had to help Bessie prepare for Sunday dinner guests.

Jake walked beside her to the back door frustrated about his clumsy proposal, but he collected his thoughts enough to urge Anna to see him the following Saturday. She nodded and quickly disappeared into the house.

The following week was a time of inner conflict for the young immigrant. She well understood the responsibilities of a wife. She thought of her harsh father and his treatment of *Maminka,* her mother's many pregnancies. On the one hand she liked that the nature of Jacob Kubesch was so differently gentle from that of *Otec,* but on the other, she was confused about her feelings for the quiet man.

In addition, she was comfortable living with Claire and Frank Gilbert. The two years in their home had given her a sense of life she had never known before. She was happy there. Mrs. Gilbert was a considerate mistress of her home; Mr. Gilbert was the head of the family, clearly, but he was protective and caring with his wife and children and all else on his farm.

Bessie listened to the young Czech's concerns about Jake's proposal as they cooked and baked, again reiterating that the young Kubesch man seemed responsible and hard working. Anna certainly could do worse than having Jacob for a husband, she added. Marriage was a big step for everyone, but things usually worked out somehow if the couple had mutual goals in life.

The girl slowly began to consider the possibilities of a life with Jacob Kubesch and how it would impact her determination to bring her family to Iowa. The man lived with his brother and his wife. Where would they live were they to marry? How could she accumulate the money needed for the Mrkvičkas' trip if she gave up her wages?

And a part of Anna continued to wonder if quiet Jacob was forceful enough to head a household, a family. If she were his wife, there soon would be children. *Maminka's* physical condition and her multiple pregnancies again gave her pause.

But another part of her concentrated on how unlike her father and the other uneducated, poverty-stricken farm workers in Velký Lunec Jacob was. He could speak in Czech and read and write the English of America. His parents owned land. She would not have had the opportunity to marry a landowner's son in Velký Lunec. Perhaps with this Iowa man she could build a good life in America.

After the next Saturday dance, Jake parked the Kubesch buggy once again in the Gilbert farmyard, horses stomping in the cold. This time he pulled from his pocket a bracelet and a ring. "Let's marry, *Aničko,*" he said again, but this time he was quick to reveal plans he obviously had thought through carefully.

Married, they could live at the farm with his brother and wife until March, when John already had decided to lease land nearby to increase the acreage the two brothers would manage. Their incomes should increase. By springtime Annie would have the Kubesch house to herself, and she could take over as her own the egg money from the bulging hen house.

"We'd have a good start," he added, his eyes pleading for acceptance. Then he placed the bracelet on Anna's small wrist, but when he slipped the ring over the young woman's finger he was crestfallen. It was much too large for her small hand.

The girl again would not give Jake Kubesch the answer he wanted, but this time she leaned over to kiss him on the cheek and thank him for the bracelet before she readied to climb down from his buggy. "It's time to go to bed, *Jakube,*" she said once more, this time showing a bit of her crooked smile. Her escort grinned all the way to the back door, Anna's encouraging kiss lightening his steps. Once there, however, the girl abruptly entered the kitchen, whispering back at him, "Sleep well."

Another week passed as the nineteen-year-old thought of little else but Jacob's proposal and her future. She argued with herself in Czech and her limited English as she cleaned diapers, managed the children, washed and ironed piles of clothing. Sometimes Bessie and Claire had to address her twice to get her attention, she was so preoccupied with thoughts of marriage tumbling through her mind.

With Jacob as a husband, she could have her own house to live in, her own egg money. A smile spread her face at the realization that she could have more hens under her care than Georgina Valenda. She chortled at the irony of it.

Also, if she ever was able to get her parents, sisters and brothers to America, the Kubesch house could hold her seven-member family until they could find work and a place of their own. There would be an extra bed upstairs for her parents, with Jake's brother and wife gone; with sufficient blankets the children would be able to bed down on the dining and parlor floors.

And finally, she reminded herself that she was nineteen, soon to be twenty, older than many brides she knew. Libbie had married the previous spring at seventeen and already was pregnant with her first child. Slowly, Jake's proposal began to sound somewhat promising.

The Saturday before Christmas a determined Jacob Kubesch picked up Anna and talked more than usual on the way to a dance in Urbana. He had had to bring the sleigh that night, and the two glided over crisp snow bundled together under a lap robe. Jake even had heated rocks brought from his kitchen stove to keep the girl's feet warm as they traversed the prairie to town.

Jake asked little Annie how much money was needed to bring her family from Europe. She wasn't sure; prices might not be what they had been when she made the trip. Jacob offered to check in town as to how much it would take to bring the Mrkvičkas to Iowa. Anna shared with him the size of her savings, nearly $400 in her locked trunk and the bank. He was impressed, realizing that the girl had spent little on herself from her wages. He loved her all the more.

The farmer was especially swift at polka steps that night. He kept his arm around Anna the entire evening, even when they stopped dancing. He seemed happy but anxious. His fast-stepping partner well understood the question in his eyes, but still was unsure of her answer.

After the dance, when they pulled into the Gilbert farm yard one more time, Jacob drew from his pocket the ring he'd had made smaller for Anna's finger. He heaved a big sigh of relief when it fit, and he quickly put his arm around the nineteen-year-old to pull her tightly to him before he kissed her with a longing that surprised them both.

Little Annie sensed his earthy smell and the warmth of his lips on hers, even though his cheeks and nose were December cold. She tasted faintly the tobacco he chewed during chores. Most of all, she realized that she felt safe and comfortable within the two strong arms of farmer Jacob Kubesch.

"All right then," she said softly, adding quickly that she needed time to order a proper wedding dress from *Montgomery Ward's Catalog*. Jake threw his head back and laughed; Anna giddily joined him as the two hugged each other tightly. Their life together was to fall into place after all.

A happy Bessie and Claire were beside themselves with the news, although Mrs. Gilbert hated bidding the immigrant good-bye. The girl was not only a good, hard worker, the children loved her, and Claire had grown to depend on her greatly. Anna Mrkvička had carved a special place within the family, but the older woman well understood the girl's desire to marry and bring her parents to join her, to move on. The nineteen-year-old had endured so much to get to this place in her American life.

When Anna said that Jake did not want to seek a Catholic ceremony, and that she agreed, Mrs. Gilbert insisted that her wedding take place in the Gilbert parlor. She would play the piano; her minister could read the vows.

Anna leafed through the *Ward's Catalog* and Bessie and Claire helped measure her for a sure fit when she ordered a white cotton dress, veil and matching shoes. They all thought the outfit beautiful. The pictured dress had a high collar and sleeves to the elbow; white lace decorated the bodice and ankle-length skirt. A small crown of tiny white satin roses would anchor a fingertip veil to Anna's upswept hair. The girl ordered matching white satin shoes, a luxury.

The date and time for the wedding was set for Wednesday, January 27, 1909, at two o'clock. For the nineteen-year-old time until then either rushed by like a whirlwind or crawled like a garden slug.

That Christmas was one of excitement for Anna and the entire household. Baby Rose was almost standing by herself; four-year-old John was readying to be a wise man Christmas Eve in the church tableau of the manger scene. Claire Gilbert was busy making her son's costume. And of course the coming wedding was on everyone's mind.

The house was a flurry of baking, cooking and hiding gifts. The bride-to-be gave Jake a watch fob; the groom-to-be gave his little Annie a cameo brooch to wear their wedding day.

As soon as he was able, Jacob inquired in town about the cost of bringing the Mrkvičkas to America. Anna was aghast to learn that the price for train travel had doubled since her own journey. She and Jake determined that it would take at least $80 for each member of her family to make the trip, or $560 for the family of seven. And that wouldn't cover food on the way.

Anna was distraught until Jacob offered to add the sum needed from his savings to the girl's $400 as a wedding gift. It was all he could manage. Spring soon would require investments in seed. The Kubesch brothers needed more livestock for the two farms. Hopefully the crops would be good the coming year so that he could set more money aside after bank loans were paid.

A rush of gratitude swept over Anna. She became more excited daily, even though she regretted that her family would not be at her wedding. She was convinced, however, that she soon would be seeing them again. It had been nearly six years since she had left Velký Lunec and felt *Maminka's* arms around her. Now there were a brother and sister she had never seen.

Jake and Anna agreed to send a $560 international money order to Antonia; they soon withdrew money from the bank and entered the Post Office together to pay cash for the little piece of paper that would change the Mrkvička lives forever.

Anna could only hope that her family would find a way to cover the rest of their travel costs somehow. She knew from Antonia's letters that she, Mary and Frank all were working out and providing money for *Maminka's* household. Little brother Antone would be carrying water in the fields this coming summer, his sixth. Hopefully they could manage the rest of the cost. Others in Velký Lunec who had sent relatives to America could help the family with the details of buying tickets and making travel arrangements, just as they had for Joe Valenda and her in 1903.

The young Czech eagerly composed a letter to her sister. She could imagine Antonia reading to the rest of the family about her coming marriage to Jacob Kubesch, of Czech background, and that she would be living on farm land that his parents owned. She explained about the enclosed money order that should cover most of their travel costs to America, and that Jake's house was large enough for them to stay in until they found work in Iowa. She closed, "I've missed you all so much. Write right away with your plans. Come soon." She knew *Maminka* would weep when Antonia read her the words.

Anna carefully folded the letter around the money order with tears in her eyes, all the while trying to imagine the joy in the poverty-stricken Mrkvička household when they received her news. Her hand trembled as she handed the precious envelope to the Center Point Post Master the next market day, only to be informed that the price of a stamp for her letter from America to Europe had increased 100% in November, from one to two cents.

Then Anna Barbara prepared for her wedding, waiting not so patiently for an answer from her family. She knew that mail delivery from rural Center Point to Velký Lunec took an undetermined time. It had to be sorted and carried to New York by train, then taken by ship to Europe. There country borders had to be negotiated and crossed before her letter could be delivered to the farmers' hamlet near Saint Barbara's Cathedral.

She didn't comprehend how the money she'd handed to the Post Master in Iowa could be exchanged for Czech money in Bohemia, but she had faith. She believed that she had received all of Antonia's letters, even though the dates sent and received were sometimes months apart.

All thoughts began to turn toward the coming wedding day. Fortunately, the women in Annie Mrkvička's life stepped forward to help the young bride and groom, as women do. Everyone realized that the nineteen-year-old immigrant had no family beside her to help her face one of the most important choices of her life.

Maggie Cisler and Mary Bontty, Jake's already-married sisters, provided a blue-squared quilt for the couple. Claire's sewing group quickly stitched up another of pinks and reds. Ida and Anna Raker provided the fourth one for Anna's hope chest, fulfilling the "four quilt requirement" for newlyweds. Four quilts would keep the couple warm in their marriage bed their first winter together. Puffy goose down pillows in black and white striped ticking came from Kubesch cousins. Bessie gave little Annie sensible towels for her first kitchen, and her prized recipe for bread and butter pickles.

The new year of 1909 dawned cold and crisp. By January 5th a severe cold wave hit the Midwest. Wedding arrangements were awkward, and determined only when people were able to get together to plan. Jake and Anna wanted a portrait taken of their wedding day, to add to the line of photographs in the Kubesch parlor. The photographer agreed to travel with his gear to the Gilbert farm, weather permitting.

The catalog dress arrived, and Annie ripped open the box with anticipation. Even though it needed her expert ironing, it was as beautiful as she'd imagined. Claire tucked it in to fit the petite young woman, murmuring that she looked lovely, and that the veil made her look angelic. The shoes were a bit big; Anna stuffed cotton quilt batting in them to keep them on.

The immigrant felt that she was floating through a dream. She carefully pressed the veil and dress and hung them on the back of her bedroom door so that her different eyes could scan them each time she prepared for bed after full days of cooking, washing and ironing clothes. She also was determined to have the Gilbert house sparkling and clean by January 27th.

The immigrant who had grown up in a dirt-floored room with one window, sometimes wearing gunny sacks on her hands and feet to school in the winter, was about to be married to an American, and she would wear a pretty white bridal gown. With matching shoes. It all overwhelmed her.

One week before the wedding, January 20, to complicate the bitter cold, a vicious winter storm blew through the midlands of America.

Wind and snow roared across the Iowa prairie for two days and nights. Snow drifted midway to first story windows, which covered with ice; pumps froze. White-outs isolated everything.

Frank Gilbert stretched rope from the house to out buildings so that workers could get to meals in Bessie's kitchen and still feed the chickens and find the barn to bed down and care for the livestock. He didn't want anyone disoriented and lost. Anna watched closely Mr. Gilbert's decisions as he managed the farm, wondering how her future husband would fill such a role.

To warm everyone, Bessie made hot soups from chicken stock stored in the basement, and she kept a pot of strong coffee steaming on the cast iron stove. The wood box in the kitchen was filled to brimming with drying wood to stoke all fires. Housebound John, bundled in sweaters, raced through the big house noisily, and was admonished often. Anna prayed that drifts would not be so high that Jake and the minister could not get to the Gilbert farm January 27th.

Two days later the winds died away and a white, glaring sun emerged. Shifting snow had enveloped the land, burying outhouse and chicken coop. Farmers up and down rural lanes crept from their houses and shoveled their way to scattered farm buildings. Then they mounted their sleighs and cutters to make drifted roads passable, to slice and shove away snow crests so that horses could travel to neighbor and town. By the 27th guests with sleighs could head for the marriage of the Gilberts' Czech hired girl, Anna Mrkvička, and farmer Jacob Kubesch.

Anna awoke before light on her wedding day. She had fallen into bed the night before exhausted from finishing the family's ironing for the last time, and from thoroughly cleaning the house in preparation for the wedding.

She pulled her good coat over her nightclothes and padded on bare feet over the cold floor to peer through crystals etched on frosty windows. The sky was clear; the trees were black lines against a sky lit with stars and a setting moon.

The nineteen-year-old felt excited, apprehensive, sad, all rolled together. She glanced across the large room to Rose sleeping in her crib nearby, her eyelids flickering. The quiet child reflected how she herself felt safe and happy in Mrs. Gilbert's caring household. Her heart hurt to leave it.

And Anna missed her family this day. She wished they could share with her the beginning of her new life as a married woman in America. She longed for reassuring hugs from *Maminka*, Antonia's giggles, Mary's quiet eyes.

Surely soon they would be joining her. She anxiously awaited an answer to her letter and the money order. The anticipation of seeing them step from the train in Center Point, of sharing their lives again, helped to see her through this day and an unknown future.

The cold on her bare feet reminded Anna of her childhood scampers through the damp trails of the forest to visit *Babička Marie*. She had always felt safer clasped within the old woman's arms. *Babička* would not have been able to comprehend the path her great-granddaughter's life was taking in America.

She also thought of *Teta* Anna and the twinkle in her eye when she said, "Find yourself a nice 'Bohemie' boy to marry, *Aničko*." Jacob was that. She felt her stepaunt would approve of the hard-working farmer.

As the girl hugged her arms for warmth, her fingers felt Jacob's bracelet. When she looked down at it, shining faintly in the wash of moonlight, its glitter pulled her back to this day, this time, her ties to her husband-to-be.

She felt that she had prepared as best she could to be an Iowa farm wife. The beautiful wedding dress hung on the door. Her working girl's trousseau—fresh underwear, bloomers, stockings without holes, aprons and one good dress—was washed and ironed and packed carefully in her small trunk. She reluctantly had dug into her few remaining silver dollars to purchase new shoes. Her old ones were wrapped in used butcher's paper for coming barnyard work. Four wonderful patchwork quilts filled her lovely humpbacked trunk. She was proud that she was not going empty-handed to this marriage.

As the sounds of Bessie stoking the stove in the kitchen broke the early morning silence, the obedient hired girl sprung from her reverie. She quickly moved to clear the skim of ice in her washbasin, to splash her face and to begin this very important day.

Soon the rambling house, scrubbed and polished as only Anna

could manage, was stirring with arriving guests. Women helped to lift the best china from cupboards, to wipe each item clean for company. Watching all the bustle, the girl humbly accepted that all the commotion was for her. For the first time in her work-filled young life she was the center of much attention and many good wishes.

Anna managed a hurried bath as the smells of burning wood, coffee and Bessie's best apple and spice cake wafted around her. She scrubbed her hair, combing and brushing it dry by the washroom stove, coaxing it with her curling iron as she peered into a foggy mirror.

As the hour for the wedding crept closer, Jake's sisters and sisters-in-law arrived to buzz around the bride-to-be. At last their bachelor brother had found a wife. The immigrant tried to feel comfortable around the Kubesch clan, but she felt like an outsider among them. They all spoke English much better than she; their conversations were of relatives and happenings about which she knew little to nothing.

Two-year-old Rose sat in her crib sucking her thumb and clutching her teddy bear, sensing that Anna was leaving. Her eyes were wide with the excitement in the air. Her brother pouted that he wasn't allowed in the room to watch Annie and the commotion first hand, and he fussed when his mother informed them that he must dress up in his church clothes, even if it wasn't Sunday.

With twinkling eyes the Kubesch women hustled back and forth between the bride's room and the parlor to report when their brother had arrived. "He looks so handsome. You're a lucky bride," they said. Anna hoped so. Her stomach was clenching with apprehension.

Claire whispered about which guests were present and joined the other women to murmur "Ooh" and "Ah" as petite Anna at last pulled her dress over her shoulders and the hair she'd so carefully curled. After the white veil was fastened to the crown of her head, Anna pinned Jake's Christmas brooch at the neck of her gown and looked with surprised eyes at her reflection in the mirror. Her slow, crooked smile soon matched the broad grins of all the women crowded around her.

Mrs. Gilbert rushed with tears in her eyes to hug the girl, then left to go to the parlor to settle at the piano. The other women kept glancing back at the bride as they walked away to join husbands already seated for the ceremony. Anna was left to descend the stairs the minute the music started; at the bottom she was to join Mr. Gilbert, who would escort her to Jacob and the minister. She was alone with her last thoughts as a nineteen-year-old unmarried immigrant far from her homeland and family.

Looking again in the mirror, she felt detached from the person in the bridal gown and veil. Further, who was this man she was about to marry? At that moment Jacob Kubesch seemed an intrusive stranger she hardly knew, even though he had so readily planned a life for them together and pooled his money with hers to bring the Mrkvičkas to her. What seemed right in the buggy and the moonlight suddenly was unsettling, but the tinny sounds of the piano from below left her no more time to pause.

The girl's different and anxious Czech and American eyes guided her down the open stairway she had polished with such pride the previous day. She soon saw guests peering at her through the door to the parlor. Mr. Gilbert was waiting for her, smiling. She took a deep breath and put one foot in front of the other, aware suddenly that her too-large shoes were slipping with each step. Panicky thoughts that they would fall off and send her tumbling down the stairs consumed her as she descended, but she made it safely.

As she finally entered the parlor, Anna's future husband came into view. He stood by the minister in all his wedding day glory. The girl was amazed at how stylish he looked in his black suit, white shirt and vest. He even wore a white bow tie, and his shoes were spit-and-polish black, laced smartly up to their high tops.

Both the bride and groom looked wary, but when their eyes met, the two remembered the fragile bond they were building between them. Anna saw again the kindness in Jacob's eyes she had noticed at the dance hall the first night he had paid her special attention. As for the husband-to-be, he was visibly touched with the glow of his girl-like bride, pretty as all brides are pretty in their white bridal gowns and their hopeful, nervous smiles.

Mr. Gilbert escorted Anna toward Jacob and the minister, then took his seat. The couple took deep breaths and stepped forward to be side by side so the wedding could begin. It was the first Protestant marriage ceremony Anna had ever experienced, and it seemed strange to her. But it also seemed somehow truly American.

Among sweeping snowdrifts on an isolated farm in the heartland of Iowa, over the sounds of a creaking windmill, gusts of wind, and the muffled sobs of women in the audience, words of a traditional ceremony were heard by those collected together in the parlor.

> Dearly beloved: We have come together in the presence of God to witness and bless the joining together of this man and this woman in Holy Matrimony.

Anna didn't understand all the English words, but when it came time for the young immigrant to repeat her vows, she carefully mimicked the English sounds spoken by the minister, her Czech accent struggling through:

> In the Name of God, I Anna, take you, Jacob, to be my husband, to have and to hold from this day forward, for better for worse, for richer for poorer, in sickness and in health, to love, honor and obey, until we are parted by death. This is my solemn vow.

The deed was done. The couple who would become "Annie and Jake" to friends and family proceeded from that day on to carry out their vows and to live and sleep as husband and wife side by side for the next forty-seven years, over seventeen thousand days and nights, until they were separated by death.

Chapter Eleven

The Gathering of Family

A FTER PHOTOS BY the traveling photographer, many good wishes and tearful good-bye hugs from the entire Gilbert household, Anna Kubesch changed her clothes and joined her husband in his sleigh to skim over the snow to her new home. Her two trunks, holding all her worldly belongings, were snuggled safely behind her.

John and his wife were not at the Kubesch home when the newlyweds arrived. Jake grunted, suspicious of their absence, but said nothing. The house was cold and growing dark. The two unloaded the trunks and placed them in their side of the sleeping area under the sloping rafters of the roof. They both felt awkward about their first night together. Jake was especially quiet.

As her husband stoked the kitchen fire, the new wife lit a lamp and wandered room to room, the glow of the burning kerosene surrounding her like a bubble of moonlight. In each room she began to plan changes that she would make when she finally became mistress of this house. She would sew fresh curtains for the kitchen; all corners invited her thorough scrubbing. The new wife went on to examine the foodstuffs in the pantry as Jake sat at the kitchen table . . . waiting.

When it was fully dark a racket outside startled the two. Jake laughed and swore as his brothers and sisters and their mates banged with wooden spoons on dishpans and pails, shouting for the newlyweds to get out of bed and let them in from the cold. The family shivaree Jacob had expected was in progress. He'd been part of the same when his brothers and sisters had married. He rose to open the door, chuckling.

Once everyone joined together in the warming kitchen, whisky was passed around, ribald jokes exchanged. John elbowed his brother's ribs and said his gift to him was that he and his wife would stay with Joe and Ida this night, to give the newlyweds one night of privacy. Then the noisy bunch left, chortling raucously as their sleigh lanterns bobbed away in the night.

"Let's go up," Jake then said, slipping his arm around his bride. Anna nodded. Once in the still-icy sleeping room, the nineteen-year-old pulled the wedding ring quilt from her trunk to dress her bridal bed before she donned a fresh flannel nightgown and extinguished the lamp. Once she joined her husband under the quilt, his quiet passion surprised her. By morning she was indeed a wife.

After that night, and until John and his wife moved to another farmstead, there was little privacy for the newlyweds. Jake resumed farming duties early the morning after the wedding; Anna made breakfast for him of fried eggs, ham and pancakes, rummaging here and there to locate the makings. She assumed her job to prepare her husband for his multiple chores. She piled his plate high, not wanting to waste even a morsel of food.

John and his wife returned to the farmstead midmorning. There were pigs to feed, cows and goats to milk, horses to groom and exercise, wood to cut and split. The men had farm equipment to keep in working order and buildings to repair before spring planting would consume all their time.

The new bride was left to try to fit into Anna Rabik's ways. The house was still the first wife's domain and it was clear that things were to be done as she desired. The immigrant would bite her tongue often when she disagreed with the amount of salt in the soup or the time spent soaking the laundry.

The two women had butter to churn, eggs to gather, water to

draw, stove fires to nurse, and often additional wood to chop, split and size for the stoves. There was laundry to wash and iron, gaping holes in socks to darn, clothing to sew, rooms to dust and scrub. The farm had to provide the means now to sustain the growing Kubesch family. No one would have dared to be a slacker, let alone immigrant Anna of the fast moving feet. Sunrise and sunsets were stitched together with work. Everyone had to adjust to weather that made everyone's chores either easier or difficult.

At the supper table, conversations often dealt with news from the *Center Point Journal*, just as they had at the Gilberts'. Geronimo, the Apache Chief, died in February. Anna learned that Meskwaki Indians sometimes camped on Kubesch land near the back savanna of oaks. They quietly appeared and disappeared.

Jake and John had made a special trip to town to vote the previous November. William Howard Taft delivered his inauguration speech as the 29th President of the United States in early March. Their Iowa wives had until 1919 and the passage of the 19th Amendment to the Constitution before they would be allowed to vote in a national election. The states of Idaho and Wyoming had granted full suffrage to their women citizens by 1869; Utah followed in 1870; Colorado in 1893.

Taft faced many problems. The country was plagued with labor strikes in industry; small farmers like the Kubesches struggled with railroad shipping prices if they had any excess grain to sell after harvest.

Racism was present throughout the country. Wounds from the Civil War did not heal easily, although a few black Americans lived in eastern Iowa. Newspapers reported that a black and a white man were lynched in Cairo, Illinois. Congressmen left the House of Representatives restaurant when a "Negro" official and his guest were served there. The Panama Canal was plowing with great difficulty through Central America as its builders swatted mosquitoes and fought yellow fever.

Threats of war were rising in Europe, which especially drew Anna's attention. Unrest was building in the Balkans south of Czechoslovakia. In Serbia that regime was advised by visiting ex-President Teddy Roosevelt to give up claims on Bosnia-Herzegovina. The thunder of approaching major conflict was beginning to be heard in many European nations, and it reverberated even to rural Iowa towns.

Anna and Jake were drawn into conversations about the problems of Europe at market when they sought to buy staples like coffee, sugar, salt, yard goods and shoes. Because of Iowa's immigrant population around Center Point and Urbana, many men and women in the area had relatives still in Europe; Anna's worry about getting her family to America grew as the clouds of war gathered across the ocean near Bohemia.

Whenever possible, the four Kubesches headed for dances on weekends. The new bride twirled the floor, drank beer and cider, greeted neighbors. She joined in raucous jokes as a married woman, giving the men tit for tat with their kidding. Her hard upbringing in the beet fields near Kutná Hora brought an edge to her replies when tobacco-chewing, tipsy farmers pushed her too much.

She also joined in conversations about the temperance movement sweeping the country. Temperance workers traveled around the state supporting the Anti-Saloon League; the country was moving toward the National Prohibition Act. In Ohio most counties already had closed saloons; Tennessee had banned alcohol statewide.

Beer and liquor had been such a part of the lives of both Jake and Anna that they didn't understand what the fuss was about. They thought that working people needed to relax with their drink after long hours struggling to make a living. Anna wasn't afraid of speaking up about her beliefs on that issue or any other, for that matter. To anyone.

And that included her new husband. The young immigrant quickly developed a roughhouse humor with Jake. Often she would pat her husband on his head with a wooden spoon, pretending to bang him with it. They both laughed.

But Jacob had to learn to handle his wife's temper and opinions in little upsets in their new life together. Jake's slow deliberation sometimes frustrated fast-stepping Anna; her vibrant energy made him tired. She soon was pushing him this way and that to get something done that she considered a priority. He usually quietly listened, nodding, but sometimes he stomped out to the barn to cuss at his cattle and hogs.

Jake's brother, John, and his wife prepared to move mid-March, joining all the other renters lugging their belongings over muddy dirt roads. Some days it seemed as though armies were passing in carts and wagons, livestock shooed ahead and behind. Anna heard them coming and going, their wagons creaking, dogs barking, cattle lowing, pigs snorting. Movers from all directions traveled to better land or larger or smaller acreage, depending on their circumstances.

That same March a federal income tax was proposed in Congress for all U.S. citizens. Small hardscrabble farmers like the Kubesches had little income from their hard work to tax.

Anna helped crate a portion of the chicken flock for Anna Rabik. Jake promised to replace the numbers for her egg money. She and her sister-in-law counted out the few canned goods remaining in the cellar: pints and quarts of peas, string beans, jellies and tomatoes. Barrels of Irish and sweet potatoes and apples were nearly empty. Earthen jars of sauerkraut and cucumber pickles had been eaten long ago. The two wives split everything that was left, realizing that the work of the summer would have to replenish food for the next long Iowa winter all over again. John's wife talked her husband into a new stove for the rented house, leaving the family stove for the newlyweds.

Jake and Annie helped the brother and wife clean their new place and they listened to Anna Rabik fuss that it wasn't as nice as the Kubesch house she was used to. The four moved pieces of furniture from the family home to the rental property by horse and wagon. The new bride's rooms would be sparsely furnished for a time; but that problem seemed less important than her daily struggle with merciless backaches. She also began to awake mornings nauseated.

When Iowa breezes began to warm and late March winds heralded the beginning of prairie spring, Anna was relieved to see a house wren build its nest under the eaves. As her twentieth birthday approached, she could throw open windows to fresh breezes, hear meadowlarks singing on fences. She spied the first robin with glee. She not only recognized what seemed to be the special beauty of that particular spring, she recognized that she, too, was bringing new life into the world. She was pregnant.

Amidst all her work of the farm, Anna dashed to the privy at inconvenient times to throw up. Her weight went down; she was tired much of the time. The new wife reckoned that the baby's birth would occur in December, and Jacob smiled broadly at the news, saying it would be their special Christmas present. All the more, Anna wanted her mother and sisters to be at her side when her first child was born. She waited anxiously for the postman daily, hoping for an answer about the money she had sent across the ocean.

Jake kept his promise and brought chicks to Anna to replenish the laying hens. She nursed them in a wooden box behind the kitchen cook stove until they were stronger and the weather was truly warm, covering the box of chicks with a dish towel and listening to their chirping as she worked. When their sounds of panic rose she rushed to rescue those buried by others crawling on top of them. She didn't want to lose even one. The chickens and their eggs would be her only personal income.

She asked her husband to purchase geese for her care also. Goose grease was good for colds and coughs; she liked the birds for roasting. Jake said that he'd avoided geese particularly, because they were so mean, taking after other foul and even his dogs, but Anna said that she had learned to handle them in her childhood. Her husband acquiesced.

The brothers' farming venture was now more complicated, with additional land to tend and livestock in two settings. Sows produced their spring litters of pigs and Anna quickly became a true farm wife. When Jake was alone and needed help with chores, she became his full partner, even though her size and pregnancy diminished her strength. The two evolved to speaking only Czech in their home and work; it was quicker, easier. Anna's English was practiced only when she went to market or dances.

Now, besides battling dirt, spider webs and insects inside the house, Anna often spent hours outside clearing shrub, feeding livestock and the chickens or tending to spring lambs as the men tilled fields for planting. But the young immigrant fell into the cycle of birth and rebirth around her; she had deeply felt the rhythm of the land even as a child. And the fact that her husband's family owned the farm they tended added pride to hard work that never seemed finished.

Jacob came into his wife's house to eat and sleep in clothes caked with manure and dirt, often with pesky trefoil seedpods stuck on his filthy socks. Anna quickly laid down rules about where his boots were to go, as well as his dirty clothes. She told him where he was to sit. She began to cut his hair and shave his wiry chin with a honed razor. Jake would sit on a kitchen chair, a towel tied around his neck like a bib, as Anna lathered his chin and scraped the shiny steel blade over his cheeks and neck. Then she'd dip the razor into an enamel pan of sudsy water. A joke between them grew. She'd hold the razor in her hand and gesture that she had him at her mercy, he'd better behave. He chuckled.

Anna discovered that her husband's feet hurt most of the time. When he came indoors he immediately removed his shoes and went barefooted. He cut chaws of tobacco with his pocketknife after supper, retiring to sit beside the lamp in the parlor to read a paper, or just sit with his aching feet in a pan of warmed water. Anna fussed to make him comfortable, but she soon ordered that he keep a coffee can with him to expectorate in her clean house.

The answer from Anna's family in Velký Lunec, that Anna had awaited so impatiently, arrived April 9, three days after her twentieth birthday. The letter had been delivered mistakenly to John Kubesch's new address. He brought it with him when he came to talk to Jacob briefly about a livestock matter. The brothers' mail was being erroneously mixed often, and this delay of her letter particularly frustrated Anna.

She quickly tore open the envelope and read Antonia's words before she sank into a kitchen chair in disbelief. Antonia's Czech letter was filled with excitement. The money had arrived safely; everyone could hardly wait to be in America. But the sister wrote of one problem.

Maminka wouldn't leave Velký Lunec without little *Anton* Procházka. The foster child had settled into the family, and the mother had become attached to him as one of her own. The authorities seemingly forgot him. Now that Anna had a rich American husband whose family owned land, it was written, *Marie Barbora* asked that her eldest daughter send more money so that *Anton* could accompany her to Iowa. "Send the money quick, *Aničko*," Antonia pleaded. "I can hardly wait to see you."

Anna read and reread the letter, shaking her head. She certainly was not a rich American wife. On the other hand, she realized that all eight of *Maminka's* family lived in a room not much larger than the kitchen she sat in. They existed with one window to look out of and a cold dirt floor to walk on. The immigrant's memory brought back the smell of the room's charred hearth, the unwashed bodies and the mold of the thatched roof. She could feel the discomfort of straw beds sometimes infested with fleas or lice, the stifling heat of summer and the aching cold of winter. She knew that by comparison her husband's clapboard farmhouse would seem like a castle to them.

Of course she must find a way to bring them all, including *Anton*, to America, but how would she do it. She had no wages. Her flock of chickens had been divided. It would take time for her new chicks to become good laying hens.

Jake found his wife with teary eyes when he answered her dinner bell midday. After Anna read him the Czech letter, he was as stunned and disheartened as she was. Money was very tight. He and John had already taken out a loan at the bank to fund the growing season. Only if the harvest was good in the fall would there be much left for the long winter.

But he hated seeing Anna so upset, especially with the baby coming. She had worked so hard to help her family. After an evening of trying to console his new wife and sleeping on the problem for a restless night, Jake announced at breakfast that he would sell two calves at market to get the money for *Anton* Procházka. "But will that be all, do you think?" he asked, his eyes worried.

"Mother of God, I hope so!" Anna responded with irritation, adding that if she didn't get her family here quickly, *Maminka* could be pregnant yet again, further complicating everything.

Within a week another international money order was on its way to the farming village of Velký Lunec. It was a very important trip to town. While at the Post Office Jake informed the Post Master that he was changing his name from "Kubesch" to "Kups"–pronounced "Koops"–because of the constant mix-up in his mail. He also changed the name at his bank and the newspaper office.

It was not unusual for immigrants to change their foreign-sounding names, but it was a problem for friends and acquaintances to keep it all straight for a time. Anna liked the simple sound of "Kups." It seemed so American.

The young wife also had written news of her pregnancy to her sister, imagining the excitement it would cause in *Maminka's* household. And she tried to explain her husband's new and different last name in the letter accompanying the money order. The Mrkvičkas hardly were used to "Kubesch." Now they had "Kups" to remember, not Czech-sounding at all.

As the young wife mailed the important envelope to Velký Lunec, she pondered further the impression her family seemed to have that she was "rich." She and Jake were working before dawn to after dusk, and there really was no extra money for other than that to keep farm production going. She hoped that she didn't receive a letter back from Velký Lunec asking for more money from her husband. She no longer had wages; her own egg money now had to go for coming household needs.

She would use the diminished egg income for diapers and clothes for the new baby, as well as items needed for the care of eight more people in the house, three of whom were small children. Louise was barely a year old. The frugal wife began to wander through second hand stores at market looking for useable blankets and pillows, towels, blouses, pants and dresses.

She tried to gauge sizes of the people she had not seen for six long years. Antonia, Mary and Frank were young adults already, ages nineteen, seventeen and fourteen. *Anton* Procházka would be about eight, while little Antone only five. Those two soon would need clothes for school. Anna knew that the whole family would need better clothing, remembering the ragged garments they all had worn when she lived among them.

Some days the housewife walked through the Kubesch rooms trying to envision where everyone would sleep and how she could keep them all clean—their bodies, their clothing, their bedding. At times their number seemed overwhelming, but nonetheless, Anna believed that she could settle things into place; excitement started to grow inside her with the baby in her womb. She hoped and prayed that all eight of the Mrkvička clan would arrive safely in time for this American birth.

May came to the Iowa prairies announced by sounds and smells of brisk damp winds and fields awakened. The sky seemed bluer to the expectant mother. The Kubesch men tilled fields, sowed oats and corn, sheared sheep and let ewes and new lambs into far pastures. A short-eared owl took up residence in the cottonwood tree near the chicken coop. Catbirds and meadowlarks trilled through trees that were bursting with yellow-green buds.

Anna asked her husband to enlarge the kitchen garden to twice its usual size, well beyond the wire fence Jake's mother had insisted on long ago. Speckled king snakes slithered around her as she planted seeds of lettuce, peas, beans, beets, cabbage and onions, all the while calculating how many jars of vegetables and jams she would have to have ready by fall. Pumpkin and squash plants were nurtured beyond the fence near hills of white and sweet potatoes humped across the far side of the garden.

The twenty-year-old whacked at the snakes with her hoe, hardly missing a step as she worked the rich soil. There were always many tasks she had to complete before nightfall, but she took precious time to plant a flower border around her garden plot.

Anna looked forward to the scarlet, gold and vivid blues of asters, petunias, zinnias and dahlias. They would soon provide colorful blossoms to lighten up her rooms, just as they had in the rambling Gilbert home. She'd place them in Mason jars on the kitchen table and on her bedroom dresser. She planted a pea vine in a jar and set it to climb a curtain in the east window upstairs, thinking of *Teta* Anna all the while. Her stepaunt had been right when she commented on the immigrant's green thumb.

The chicks had been put outside with the older Leghorn hens as soon as they developed feathers on their wings and could fend for themselves. But one lasted only two days before a red fox slunk away with it in its jaws, the other chickens screeching and cackling in fear. The din brought Anna running from the kitchen, but she barely saw a bushy red tail scampering away in the newly tilled fields. She was angry, raising her clenched fist as she swore at the thief. She counted her flock and the number of eggs laid every day, keeping a wary eye for bull snakes searching out her precious source of income.

Shortly Jacob shouldered a shotgun and killed a fox skulking toward the chicken coop yet again. He slipped away each day from Anna's strong coffee and *koláče* as dawn broke, and waited in outside shadows for the four-legged bandits. He continued to keep guard.

Jake bought six geese and a gander from a neighbor, just as he promised his wife he would do. The former owners had been glad to be rid of them; they had taken after their small children one too many times, nipping legs and buttocks.

The feisty birds claimed the barnyard space as their own quickly; dogs sped away from their angry wings and hurtful bills. Anna often shooed and banged them with her broom when they became too aggressive. Even though she had to admit that they were bothersome, she looked forward to roasted goose for the winter holidays, anticipated their grease for feverish chests and winter croup, and their soft down for more needed pillows for the family.

By late May Anna's struggle with morning sickness had lessened. She held squealing new pigs while her husband cut off their tails by lantern light. It was the only free time Jake had from the fields to do it; he asked his wife to help. As the knife did its work, the din was harsh to the expectant mother's ears. Other frightened livestock nearby made a terrible clatter in their uneasiness, stomping, lowing and whinnying. It was a noisy, bloody mess.

Following a full day of gardening and scrubbing clothes on the washboard, cooking and baking, Anna felt weak and drained by the added ordeal, and went directly to the house when it was over. When the piglets were back with the sows and Jake finally entered the kitchen, he found his young wife slumped at the kitchen table wiping tears from her face with her blood-spattered apron.

"*Aničko,* what's wrong?" he said, staring at her puffy face in the glow of the kerosene lamp. He seldom saw his young wife like this. She was not a soft woman; he had been pleased and surprised at the way she had shouldered the work load on the farm. "Is it the baby?" he asked, concerned.

Anna shook her head with a heavy sigh. "Will they actually come?" she said, not seemingly to him, but to the flickering walls closing in around her. "It would help to have them with me."

"We'll hear soon. It takes time for the letters," he said. Then he went to the pantry and brought out the whiskey he kept there by the flour and the sugar crocks, and he poured a portion of the drink into two tin cups.

Anna looked at her husband, still in many ways a stranger to her. His overalls were splattered with pig blood on top of dirt from the fields, as well as manure and grime from nudging livestock here and there. She already could feel the hardness of the washboard on her knuckles when she would have to scrub his shirt and pants and underclothes extra hard. And she never would get them completely clean. Not ever.

She searched Jacob's concerned eyes as they stared into hers. They were tired and bloodshot from his hours of never-ending farm work. He looked older than his twenty-eight years, his dark curly hair already receding from his forehead. Anna felt to her bones her husband's weariness; it matched her own. His blue-gray eyes whispered *I understand* even though his lips said not a word. Anna finally shrugged her shoulders and slowly reached for the drink. Her husband joined her.

The whiskey disappeared quickly. The exhausted two felt the brownish liquor burn all the way to make their innards tingle. It seemed to fortify them for another work-filled tomorrow. The two slowly climbed the wooden stairs to peel off their sweaty clothing and fall into bed exhausted. They fell asleep curled together like spoons, their arms intertwined. Jake's snores reverberated from the slanting dormers above them.

Soon after that day Anna's husband announced that they would take a break the following Sunday. All seed finally would be in the ground; they would go fishing. They could spare a day to relax and have a picnic around a campfire. The brothers and wives would join them. Shortly the Kubesches were following their teams in wagons bumping over miles of rutted roads to the nearest bend of a river. Anna had looked forward to the much-needed day away from the grueling work on the farm.

She packed her basket carefully with fresh bread, *koláče*, her iron frying pan and a Mason jar of lard to fry the fish. She playfully chided her husband that he had better have a good catch or they would all go hungry. She was not about to kill one of her chickens to back him up.

The three farm couples relaxed by the river that day under white billowy clouds sailing on a sea of blue. Jake caught the first bullhead, showing it with pride to a grinning Anna. Each time one of the men drew in a carp or catfish he measured his trophy to enter it into the competition of the day. It was brother Joe who finally nabbed the winner.

The women cleaned and prepared the fish, then set out their basket lunches on old blankets. By midday they all were picking bones from bullheads hot from the frying pan, crisp and succulent.

There was time to gossip. The brothers' wives asked how Anna was going to care for her large family in Jacob's house, if they actually came. It was clear that they already disapproved of the added burden to their brother-in-law. Anna replied that she would manage, that her forty-six-year-old father and young brother would help on the farm until they found work, perhaps on the railroad. Then she pointedly closed the subject and moved on to other news.

A neighbor child had been run down by a bicycle in Center Point, even though there was a new ordinance that cyclists must dismount as they passed pedestrians. The group decided that people weren't safe these days even walking the sidewalks, minding their own business.

A Czech neighbor with an aged husband had suffered a miscarriage. A Polish daughter at the edge of town was "showing," with no father in sight. Chicken pox was making its rounds among school-age children. An old Norwegian grandfather who'd just arrived to live with his son had been killed when he fell from a horse.

Then there was talk of the threat of war in Europe. Germany was building up arms. The U.S. Signal Corps had been directed to plan for aerial balloon defense of the Atlantic coast as protection from possible German U-boat raids. It worried Anna. She longed for a letter from Bohemia every day. None came.

By June Anna was herself at war, with rabbits devouring her precious yield of carefully tended lettuce, cabbage and carrots. She had to depend on provisions from her garden to see her family through the winter. To fend off the thieves she sprinkled urine from the night slop jars around the edge of her garden, and threw the hair cut from her husband's head on the lettuce. It seemed to do the trick.

Jake's twenty-ninth birthday was July 1. They celebrated it on July 4th, when the corn was knee-high, by traveling to a rip-roaring Independence Day celebration in Center Point. Farmers loaded wagons and buggies and wove to town to gather in community, to honor being American. They looked forward to softball and speeches and bunting draped everywhere. There would be fireworks. Anna pinned her little American flag from New York City to her loose, freshly ironed blouse. Her belly was beginning to bulge.

She packed another of her famous food baskets, this time chopping off the head of a hen with a poor laying record for fried chicken, to add to a bountiful lunch. Jake's horse and wagon soon carried them to join the exciting, crowded commotion on Main Street in the city.

Once the horse was anchored to a hitching post, Anna saw Libbie miraculously appear from the crowd to greet her, just as she had years ago. The young mother was carrying her new baby, a smiling little boy who had his mother's dimples. The two young wives hugged and eagerly shared stories of their pregnancies, their work, their hopes and plans.

Together they cheered as drums and fifes marched by leading a rambling parade that included decorated wagons and children waving flags from the backs of ponies. A few new automobiles putted along among horses and buggies. Aged veterans of American wars limped along the ranks in their faded, too-small uniforms, or sat in rocking chairs on front porches holding little flags.

Later the Kups met the Gilberts at the city park. John and Rose hugged their Annie as best they could, considering her growing belly, and chattered excitedly about new puppies on their farm. Claire was delighted to see the young wife looking healthy, browned from the sun, curved and round with her first pregnancy.

Near them boys on stilts dueled with wooden swords. Other children had hitched dogs to two-wheeled carts and were giving toddlers rides through the crowd. Hawkers at makeshift stands sold apples and oranges, homemade pies and needlework. A couple of stores had ice cream while it lasted. A salesman under a tree tried to convince anyone who would listen to buy his elixir, the world's best cure for boils, catarrh and constipation. A bellicose mayor shouted his speech from a gazebo; few listened.

As dusk blended into indigo night skies, fireworks exploded to squeals of "Ooooh" and "Aaah." Finally, when the sparkles died to ashes, murmuring crowds separated to find their buggies, wagons and horses. Families packed themselves for the trip home onto crowded seats beside baskets emptied of food.

Annie and Jake headed into the inky black of farm night with lines of other farmers. Horses clopped their way along dark roads and lanes bereft of light other than a moon, stars and the glow of an occasional kerosene lantern hung on a buggy or in a distant window. Gradually the wagons separated and sorted into different paths, some passengers calling out "G'night!" as they drifted away from each other on their singular journeys. The day was cherished and remembered long into the following days of early risings and routine chores.

Just four days after that celebration, the U.S. Congress passed the 16th amendment to the Constitution, making final a federal income tax on the earnings of American citizens. At first, however, it affected people much more affluent than Jake and Annie Kups. That was one thing they currently did not have to worry about.

Later that month the newspaper brought more unsettling news concerning immigrants like the Mrkvičkas. The U.S. Immigration Commissioner submitted guidelines to reduce "undesirables at Ellis Island." Aliens would be requested to pay $25 each to enter the United States and guarantee life-long independence from public and private charities.

Most of that night Anna tossed and turned. Still no word had arrived from Velký Lunec. If $25 were required of each member of her family, it would put a further financial burden on them. She hoped that somehow Antonia was finding out about new immigration restrictions and costs. The question "Will they come?" whirred even louder through her mind each night and day.

The good news during August was that crops were becoming amazingly abundant. It appeared, if weather cooperated, that 1909 would yield a record harvest from the breadbasket midlands. Jake and Joe and John were jubilant as hailstorms missed their fields and their rich soil grew crops to healthy green. The harvest would pay farm workers back for their labor that year, and they in turn could pay back their bank loans with some profit to spare.

But industrial workers in the United States were not so lucky. Their work and pay were problematic, their lives increasingly dangerous in factories and mines. It was estimated that at least one worker was killed daily due to faulty machinery. There was little legal protection for these workers. Battles between wealthy management and the working poor continued to rage.

When Anna heard that union strikes by Pennsylvania steel workers resulted in clashes with government troops, she thought of the sweatshops she had seen first-hand in New York City. *Teta* Anna had told her of not being allowed to leave her sewing machine to go to the toilet without losing a portion of her pay.

She thought especially of the desperate cigar makers, the Matějíčeks, and their hopeless life. She could still smell the stench of their filthy quarters and see the eyes of the pale little girl who hugged her legs when she prepared to leave. Someone needed to try to change the terrible conditions for common workers like *Teta* Anna and the Matějíčeks. Perhaps the unions could do it.

The immigrant's heart was warmed with the thought that her American baby would be born on a farm with fresh air and adequate food. She would see above all that no child of her womb would experience the hunger she had endured so many years in Velký Lunec and with the Valendas.

As late Iowa summer settled into steamy days and breathless nights, Jake and Annie attended the Linn County fair to see what new farm implements could make their farming more productive. The Extension Service from Iowa State Agricultural College in Ames had been established in 1906. It tried to help farmers improve production and use land wisely. Rotating crops was advised to replenish nutrients in the state's rich loam.

Jake and his brothers checked out fair displays of the latest horse-drawn hay loaders, disc harrows and corn planters. They wandered livestock barns that reeked of sawdust and pig and sheep manure, to examine new motorized equipment. They viewed blue ribbons in halls stacked with fruits and vegetables, comparing winning produce with their own yields of potatoes, apples and field corn.

A midway of carnival acts claimed some space. Fat ladies, tattooed men, specimens of two-headed dogs in jars of preservatives were on display, as were snake handlers who scared audiences with their daring. Sword swallowers and contortionists showed their stuff. Hawkers lured people to games of chance–throwing a baseball to knock over milk bottles, hitting a lever with a sledgehammer to shoot a metal ball upward to strike a bell. Steam-driven calliopes whistled their monotonous tunes.

Anna wandered tents to examine new treadle sewing machines, quilt and clothing displays. As a cook she sought out first-place cherry pies and cakes, as well as canning innovations. Of course she searched for exhibits of the latest cooking range.

New black cast iron wonders had porcelain-lined reservoirs to keep food warm; they burned hard or soft coal as well as wood and corncobs; they had a shiny nickel finish and rococo bases and trim. And they sold for under $20. What a far cry from *Maminka's* simple clay fireplace in Velký Lunec.

Everyone flocked to the judging tents where judges rated livestock, pig calling, and even the "healthiest baby." There also were political debates, watermelon spitting contests, baseball games, horseshoe tournaments and potato sack races. Local bands and hand-shaking politicians wandered dusty aisles through the simmering heat. Suffragettes handed out pamphlets from their booths.

The highlight of the day was the hot air balloon ascension as dusk fell. It was the first time Jake and Annie had seen such an event. Many in attendance were dandies dressed in their best and women in corsets and fancy hats, but everyone stood or sat on blankets among farmers sporting suspenders, their wives in cotton dresses. Barefoot children in pinafores and overalls squirmed near their parents.

The Kups couple joined everyone to bend their heads backward, their sunburned faces to the sky. The crowd hushed. They froze in awe. The huge round ball with a brave man in a basket below it rose to float quietly over trees and fields into the sunset. In a few years at fairs their eyes would be watching flimsy two-winged aeroplanes made of wood and canvas looping their stunts.

On the way home, the couple chattered about all they had seen. Jacob dreamed about new machinery and implements, and Anna, a fancy new stove. For days husband and wife talked about the mysterious balloon that had whispered through the air at the Linn County Fair.

It wasn't until September, as busy threshing season was about to begin, that another letter arrived from Antonia. "Mrs. Jake Kups" was carefully written on the envelope, so Anna knew as she ripped it open that her last letter had been received.

Once she had rapidly read through her sister's Czech message, she whooped with joy and relief and immediately dashed out through the barnyard, scattering the chickens until their feathers flew. Jacob was doing late day chores with the horses. He rushed to meet his wife, afraid that she was unwell or hurt, but his Annie was just breathless with final word from Bohemia that her family would be coming to America.

The group would depart Velký Lunec after crops were in from the fields. Anna explained to her husband that pay for the working out of Antonia, Mary and Frank would be collected in November. Her family, including foster child *Anton*, planned to leave for Iowa late that month, hoping to be with their *Anička* for her baby's birth. *Maminka* was determined to deliver her first grandbaby.

Antonia closed with "I can't wait to see you and your rich American house." Jake and Annie managed this time to laugh about that expectation. For days they would kid each other about being rich farmers, the irony of it sometimes sending them into peals of laughter.

After sharing every word of Antonia's letter with Jake, Anna abruptly turned on her fast-stepping feet to run back into the house to continue preparations. The leghorns parted again before her like the Red Sea, their cackling like the rush of receding waves, their feathers splashing away like ocean spray each side of her. A determined, twenty-year-old *Anička* was Moses preparing to lead her family into the Promised Land.

She muttered as she went, "I still need six blankets and four more pillows. I'll need four or six quarts of vegetables to open each day in the winter, to feed them all. I'll need more Ball jars. After threshing I'll need to scrub the house top-to-bottom . . . ."

Jake listened as her words faded away and the hens quieted down. He began to do some calculating himself. Brother John had made it clear when Jacob had sold two calves for the Procházka boy that that number should not come from John and Anna Rabik's share of livestock they jointly managed. Jacob, who shied from discord, was already wondering how to approach his younger brother about needing his help to butcher more than the usual of his share of the animals come fall. Anna would need more beef and pork for her table. The smokehouse would be busy.

Adding the new baby, there would soon be eleven mouths to feed in his household. He didn't see how they were going to find a place for them all, but Anna was set to do it in her headstrong way. He wondered if she fully realized the additional work she was taking on, but she was happier than he'd ever seen her. A smile spread over the husband's sun-browned face.

Nonetheless, as he returned to his horses that evening, Jake hoped to God that the harvest would be so good that he could buy the livestock needed to replenish his shrinking share of the Kubesch assets.

Threshing season that year of 1909 wove around Anna's canning blitz. She prodded her husband into finding time to build more shelves in the storm cellar for the quarts and pints she processed: vegetables and jams, pickles and sauerkraut. In her kitchen the juice of cherries and raspberries stained her hands and aprons. The room was hot and steamy from before dawn to past dusk. The smells of spicy cabbage, dill and cinnamon filled every corner of her house.

She also prepared bountiful baskets for threshing crews and communal meals as neighboring men and women traveled from farm to farm to collectively help one another. The threshers' wives quizzed Anna about her family's arrival from Bohemia as together they prepared mounds of potatoes and gravy, platters of pork and chicken. Some clucked and rolled their eyes about the number of people that soon would be filling the Kubesch house. The farmstead always would be the "Kubesch" place to them, notwithstanding the middle son's newfangled efforts to change his name to "Kups."

The expectant mother remained joyful that autumn, however, refusing to become discouraged about the added work her family was bringing. She continued to scout Center Point second-hand stores for bedding and clothes that would help the newcomers adjust to the harsh winter climate.

Eight-year-old *Anton* Procházka soon would need warm coats for his trek to school through the snow. It had not seemed so cold walking under the shadow of Saint Barbara's Cathedral as it did sometimes when north winds whipped across the howling prairies of Iowa. Frigid Midwest winter–December through March–seemed never to end.

And there was a layette of diapers and wee clothes to accumulate. Anna's feet often worked the rhythm of the old Kubesch treadle sewing machine by kerosene lamp long after Jake was sound asleep in their bed upstairs.

Sometimes when the twenty-year-old watched the autumn sunsets of an evening, pausing from her work to ease a back strained from the growing weight of the baby, her heart ached with the anticipation of seeing her family again. The long wait to see her sisters and *Maminka* beside her seemed to stretch behind and before her forever.

She began once more to regularly lift the pale pink rosary from its hook in her upstairs bedroom. She prayed that her mother and her brood would arrive safely, and that the baby growing heavy beneath her heart would wait for its grandmother's skillful midwife's hands to deliver it.

When it became obvious that the yield from Jake's green and golden fields at harvest was indeed to be a bumper crop, Anna was as thrilled as her husband about it. The young wife by now felt as one with the rhythm of Iowa land. Her work on the farm had helped bring impressive results and its bounty overwhelmed her; she smiled with pride. She and her husband talked of their success at every meal. In bed their conversations about it trailed mid-sentence to silence as they drifted into exhausted sleep.

The Kubesch brothers were ecstatic that year to know that they would be able to pay off their loans from the bank when all crops were in. And they would have money left over. Jake could increase his herd of cattle and his hog production. He wanted to have at least twelve to fourteen sows for breeding remaining after he butchered.

The number of farmers in Iowa was diminishing, making it more profitable for those like the Kubesch brothers who remained to work rich Iowa soil. At the same time the size of farms was increasing.

Countless men were trekking westward or moving their families from tilling the land to cities, often to nearby Cedar Rapids. That large urban center offered employment at Quaker Oats, packing plants and a starch factory. Some farm families chose regular pay over the worry of bad crops, drought, and fluctuating farm prices. Fifty hours of work in a factory left men and women evenings and Sundays free, something they had seldom known in farming.

Newspapers reported that the cost of living had increased over fifty percent since the 1896 Spanish-American war, and nearly eight percent in 1909 alone. Anna and Jake mulled the prices of basics like flour and salt, yard goods and shoes, each time they went to market. The twenty-year-old shook her head at paying seventeen cents a pound for coffee, six cents for sugar.

On the other hand, eggs were selling for twenty-nine cents a dozen in Center Point markets. Anna worked to candle and keep her eggs clean, and present them well to shop owners. She usually bargained to be paid eighteen cents a dozen. She had learned how to haggle over prices; her income helped her prepare for her family. She even opened another small savings account at the bank in her own name.

When the men were husking corn in October, Anna and her sisters-in-law gathered together at Joe and Ida's to put up apple butter. They peeled and cored bushels of apples they had shaken and picked from their own few trees and bartered from a neighbor's orchard. Some of the fruit had been pressed for juice already for a supply of cider. They were prepared to place the apples in the cider and to cook them in large cast iron kettles set over stones and fire in the barnyard.

The women took turns stirring the brew constantly to keep the mixture from burning, adding seasoning as it boiled down to the proper consistency. They finally were pleased to scoop the savory apple butter into five-gallon earthen jars and seal them with melted paraffin. All three wives smiled thinking of it slathered over fresh biscuits throughout the winter, but Anna especially could hardly wait to serve the luscious treat to her sisters and brothers. She knew that *Maminka* would smack her lips with pleasure.

It was during the apple butter making, when it was her turn to stir the wooden paddle in the kettle, that pregnant Anna felt the first movement of her unborn baby. She immediately put her fingers on the place the curled little body had stretched to touch. That night at supper she moved Jake's large callused farmer's hand to feel the new life stirring within her. They both grinned.

During the isolation of her workdays after that first movement of the unborn baby, she began to talk to the little one growing within her as though together they were a team finishing the never-ending farm tasks together. "*Bejby* (Baby)" she would say, "we filled forty-three jars with string beans and beets today. What do you think of that, eh? That'll fill our bellies on cold January days, won't it!"

Shortly another envelope arrived from Bohemia. Antonia wrote to her sister gleefully in her careful Czech that they all were eager to leave Velký Lunec for America November 27, hoping to arrive in Iowa December 6 or 7.

Otec was quarreling with the man Frank was working for over the amount of money the boy was owed for his work. The sisters had new linen dresses to wear, and heavy wool shawls to keep them warm. *Maminka* was worried about how to care for diapers for little Louise on the long trip.

Anna frowned, remembering too well the problems the Dutch mother had trying to keep her sick little *Jan* clean and changed in the dingy steerage of the Kronprinz Wilhelm. She knew the trip would be difficult for the family. They would have to fight seasickness and suffer cramped, smelly quarters. They most certainly would struggle with poor and tasteless food.

Antonia closed her letter, "I hope train robbers don't raid our train, *Aničko*. Don't forget to meet us. We can hardly wait to see you. Kisses."

That night the farm couple took the bank calendar down from its nail and placed it on the kitchen table by lantern light to count out the days that the Mrkvičkas would be traveling to Center Point. While train travel in the Unites States had improved greatly since Anna's long westward trip—by 1909 there was twenty-four hour rail service from New York City to Saint Louis—still the time required in the long lines of immigrants at Ellis Island was the big unknown. Anna's long wait at the immigration center made her wonder how many days her family would be delayed there, and what their actual arrival date in Iowa would turn out to be.

The following days the talk at the Kups' supper table concerned how long they actually would have to hitch horses to the wagon and travel daily to see if the Mrkvičkas had arrived. It was a guessing game.

Anna quickly wrote another letter to her sister, hoping that it would arrive before she departed Velký Lunec. She explained that she and her husband would go to the Center Point depot daily beginning December 6 unless she heard otherwise from the travelers, and that they would continue to meet the train each day until she had them safely in her care. She added, smiling as she wrote, "And you don't need to worry about train robbers, Antonia." Nightly her prayers became more urgent.

The week before Thanksgiving, preparations for butchering began. The Kubesch brothers would rotate among their three farms to help each other with the task. Jake had the most work to accomplish.

He had decided, after long discussion with his young wife, to kill a large steer and three hogs. Anna helped him collect hickory for the smokehouse and ready the large cast iron kettle and its fire for hog dipping.

It began to snow lightly the morning of the day allotted for the men to butcher at the Kups' farm. Jacob and Joe held the steer and hogs as John, the best shooter of the brothers, shot them in the head. Then the animals were lifted by block and tackle and their throats cut for bleeding.

Crystal white virgin snow soon was blotched with spreading crimson. Smelling the blood, the other animals in pen and barn became uneasy, squealing and groaning themselves. Anna's stomach became queasy. Often she turned away, holding her swollen belly as if to protect her baby from the violence.

Hogs next were dipped into scalding water so that a sharp knife could afterwards scrape hair from their hides until the skin was smooth. Then the animals all were hung head down, their entrails removed and the meat carved into workable sections.

But the work of the expectant mother was just beginning. All the meat had to be cooked for cold packing or smoked in the smoke house. Husband and wife both had to see that the fire was kept going, the smoke doing its work. Nearly every part of the animals was saved for food. Headcheese was preserved from brains and scraps; pigs' feet were pickled, as were snouts. Sausage making required many hours of processing.

Shelves in the root cellar groaned with the weight of quarts and crocks of pork and beef, pints of vegetables, jellies and jams. Pumpkins, squash and potatoes were stored in bushel baskets. Anna often took inventory of the results of her work, again counting aloud in both Czech and English to keep proving to herself that she could do it. "What to you think of that, *bejby*?" she would murmur, satisfied and proud as stores filled her pantry and stretched into every earthen corner of the underground cellar.

After Thanksgiving, which the Kubesch brothers and their wives celebrated with a bountiful meal together, the date of the Mrkvička arrival approached rapidly. The twenty-year-old turned in earnest to scrubbing her house from top to bottom. She would explain to *bejby* that Antonia would not be coming to the "rich" house she imagined, but at least the American rooms her sister would enter would be clean.

Appreciating the fact that her family for the first time would have wood, not dirt beneath their feet, she wanted the floors spotless. She scrubbed the worn linoleum on the kitchen floor, lined with wear over the cracks of oak wood under it. Oval rag rugs were placed throughout the rooms. They were mostly made from worn and ragged work clothes cleaned and cut into strips, braided, then sewn together. A dirty Jake sometimes was made to strip to his long johns at her back door before walking through his wife's cleaned house.

And the windows had to sparkle. From one grimy window in *Maminka's* room in Velký Lunec, Anna's family was coming to a house with glass panes in every room. The young wife labored to remove every smudge.

November 27, the day the Mrkvičkas departed from Velký Lunec, Anna's mind began to travel with them on their long trip to her. As she completed her chores, she envisioned where the group was along its journey. She relived the feeling of her seasickness on the days she knew they were at sea. In the frigid cold of early December she remembered with a smile how it felt to see the Statue of Liberty, the Grand Lady, rising from New York Harbor. Her family would not have the opportunity to wander wonderful New York City as she had. They would not see the Brooklyn Bridge or the huge dinosaur bones at the grand Museum, and she was sorry about that.

The twenty-year-old busied herself hanging out blankets and bedding, often removing them frozen stiff from taut rope lines. She willed herself to being ready within a week, her excitement mounting daily. Her feet flew through her chores. "*Bejby,* they'll be here soon," she told her unborn child countless times each day.

December 4 she muttered, "Today they could be seeking out which train to take to come to Iowa, *bejby.*" She double-checked the blankets and bedding for her brothers and sisters who would be sleeping on the floor in the dining room and parlor. They were stacked in corners of the rooms, along with goose down pillows.

Maminka and *Otec* would share the extra bed upstairs under the sloping roof in the other half of the space where Anna and her husband slept. The young wife pulled from her trunk the red and pink quilt from her wedding gifts. She knew her mother would be in awe to have it laid atop her bed to keep her warm in the unheated upstairs. Little Louise could sleep on two chairs pushed against the wall near her parents.

As arrival day approached, the busy housewife mulled what food to take along for travelers she knew would be exhausted and hungry. She didn't want to waste anything edible in case they weren't on the first train. She decided to take in her large threshing basket boiled potatoes, rye bread, smoked ham and *koláče*, which could be eaten three or four days after baking.

The night of December 5 Anna slept little. Her mind raced with rolling images of her own trip: the waiting at Bremen and the general confusion as to what to do, where to go. She relived the sickening rocking of the Kronprinz, the stifling wait at Ellis Island. She felt again how comforting the arms of *Teta* Anna felt when the woman finally came to collect her and Old Joe.

Then the train trip they were enduring at that moment would take them through miles of track in Chicago. The clickety-clack of the steel wheels would forever rumble through their memories, combined with images of the farms and rural towns of America, people waving at the passing train.

Anna knew that the short trip from Cedar Rapids to Center Point, the final leg, might be the most anxious for them all. They would be very tired and wary of this big country, just as she had been, secretly afraid that no one would be there to claim them at the end. "But we'll be there, won't we, *bejby*!" she murmured.

After lunch December 6, Jake hitched two horses to the wagon to help with the expected load, and he and his Annie loaded up to make the trip to the rail station for the afternoon train from Cedar Rapids. The husband carefully helped his pregnant wife climb into the wagon, and then he loaded the bulging basket of food. He packed horse blankets and extra old coats, too, to brace the travelers from the cold.

Then the couple rumbled over frozen, rutted roads to the train station, silent with anxiety. Anna braced her belly with her strong work hands, hoping that the jolting of the trip didn't cause her to deliver the baby in the wagon, stranded between Center Point and home. It was threatening snow, but roads were swept dry by prairie winds that bit at reddened cheeks and noses.

When the two arrived and the engine at last chugged into the station, the different eyes of the twenty-year-old searched every person stepping from each train car. Then her heart fell. Her family was not among the passengers this day. The two turned back to the wagon. Anna wiped tears of disappointment from her eyes most of the way home.

"Tomorrow, probably," Jake said, reaching over to hold her hand as he guided the horses homeward from the fruitless trip.

The following day Anna again awoke early. Surely this would be the day she was to feel her family's arms around her once again. Familiar questions crowded her mind. Would she recognize the children after six long years? They would have grown so much. And she was mindful of how she had changed. What would they think of her now?

Glancing in the mirror over her dresser that morning she saw a small, very pregnant farm woman with different, light brown eyes anxiously staring back at her—eyes older and much wiser than they were the day she had left Velký Lunec. Her dress was loose around her bulging body. The baby was growing more active by the day, its birth due soon.

Suddenly her eyes fell on the little American flag poked behind the dresser mirror, the one *Teta* Anna had bought for her that exciting Fourth of July in New York City. She quickly tucked it into her pocket. It seemed appropriate this day of her family's arrival. At least she hoped this would be the day.

When it came time to leave, she again donned heavy boots, a *bábuška*, neck scarf and wool mittens to ward against the cold. She again wrapped a woolen shawl around her shoulders because her coat would not button.

As she left through the kitchen door, she glanced back at her scrubbed and polished house once more. Day-old *koláče* and lard-crust pies were tucked under a clean towel on the kitchen table next to a bowl of fresh butter and bread. She hoped and prayed that she would have her family around the table to eat it all come suppertime.

Jake led his horses to Center Point once again; it was still threatening snow. Anna this time took her bed pillow to sit on, to cushion the jolts of the wagon from the baby. Once at the station they discovered that the train from Cedar Rapids was an hour overdue. When the engine finally did pull into the station, Anna and Jake stood stomping from the cold on the wooden platform, the young expectant mother scanning once more through grimy train windows, nervous hope in her eyes.

There was a moment when a certain group of people making their way from their seats looked familiar to the twenty-year-old, but her memory doubted that this could be the family she had left in Bohemia. They were worn and rumpled and incredibly older. Then her heart stopped and astonishment mingled with tears and grins as relatives in- and outside the train recognized changed faces grinning back at them. One by one the Mrkvičkas stepped from the train into Anna's arms.

Marie Barbora and *Karel* were six years older, their faces more weathered, their hands more calloused and bruised from their difficult field work. They were dressed in their best–worn patchwork clothing. *Maminka* carried one-year-old Louise on her hip.

It was Anna's sisters and brothers that shocked her the most. They had been stair-steps when she had left them. Now Antonia and Mary were young women, and they both were taller than she was. The head of brother Frank, fourteen, stood well above his father's, but little *Anton* Procházka, the eight-year-old foster brother, was short and squat, with broad shoulders that over-powered his stubby legs.

The youngest brother, Antone, whom Anna had never seen, was five. He shyly stood back as the others crowded around their *Anička* to cry and hug the stranger who had brought him over the big ocean to America. Members of the group pumped Jacob's arm in awkward handshakes one by one.

Forty-year-old *Maminka,* wearing the *bábuška* she would forever wear in public, was overcome when she saw her eldest daughter standing before her large with child. Tears rolled down her hollowed cheeks. She had kissed a fourteen-year-old good-bye under the shadow of Saint Barbara's Cathedral, and had sent her thousands of miles over the ocean to what she'd hoped would be a better life. Every day the mother had wondered whether she would ever set eyes on her daughter again.

Now *Anička* stood before her beside her new husband, a strapping young man who greeted the Mrkvičkas in their native tongue. That this Jacob could speak the language of the family was a relief to all the travelers after their struggle with English from the moment they arrived in New York.

The emotional reunion on that cold wooden platform in Center Point was mixed with exclamations of joy and amazement that the family was finally safely together again, this time on the rich farmlands of Middle America.

As for Anna, all the while she was dealing with her happiness, crying and hugging and kissing them all, she was saddened with how thin they were, and how weary. She quickly told them of the ham and bread in the wagon. The little boys, particularly, perked up at the thought of food for their empty stomachs. Even little Antone stepped forward eagerly.

Anna stooped to tweak his cheeks. Fishing the little American flag from her pocket, she placed it in his hand and explained that it was of America, his new country. Then she told him that he was just the right size to squeeze between her and Jacob in the front seat on the trip home. He at last smiled.

Jake led them to his wagon and helped them make room for each other and their scant baggage. *Karel* and his son had manhandled an emptied flour barrel filled with clothing and diapers the thousands of miles from Velký Lunec. The older sisters lugged a small worn suitcase that held their few belongings.

Once everyone was seated, the basket of ham, bread, apples and *koláče* rapidly was emptied by a flurry of cold hands grabbing for needed nourishment. Anna reached to rescue a hunk of bread and an apple for little Antone.

The horses strained with the load of ten squirming bodies as it began to move toward the Kups' farm. A barrage of Czech chatter surrounded the wagon. Frosty breath rose in poufs all around them and from the horses' nostrils as they bore their load. Tales of the trip and experiences at Ellis Island were shouted out at the same time from young and old alike. Neighbors who saw and heard the noisy wagon that day would gossip at suppertime about the loud swarm of Czechs they had seen headed for the Kubesch place.

Anna and Jake soon learned that *Otec* and Frank had had to be deloused at the Island, which had kept them there an extra day; their ship's mattresses in the men's area had been infested. Mary and Antonia somehow had escaped seasickness and had danced away their time on the ship as a Polish fiddler played. They were ecstatic with the showers at the Great Hall, but thought that the ones on ship were too filthy to use. Practical Frank was most impressed with newly discovered flushing toilets.

Suddenly, in the midst of it all, *Maminka* reached forward to feel Anna's belly with her expert midwife hands. "*Brzo. Brzo.* (Soon)," she whispered about the coming birth of her first grandchild, settling back in satisfaction. Anna smiled, relieved to her depths that her mother was with her to help her with the baby's arrival.

Then everyone roared with laughter as little *Anton* Procházka told of bypassing the checkout procedure at the Island by hiding in the barrel of clothing. *Otec* explained that they were afraid the authorities would wonder why an eight-year-old with a different last name on his Austrian papers was traveling with the Mrkvička family. They didn't want to draw special attention. Little *Anton's* eyes sparkled with the fun and the secret danger of it as he spun his story, giggling.

He had crawled into the barrel in the crowd as they were taken by tender from the ship to the Great Hall, and had stayed there quiet as a mouse for hours. He had even fallen asleep in the softness of it. When the Mrkvičkas finally were finished with the immigration authorities, *Otec* and Frank had found the barrel again in the mound of baggage waiting to be reclaimed. There was so much confusion in the luggage area that the lone guard wasn't even watching when the two huddled around the barrel to lift *Anton* out again.

Anna glanced down at Antone, his eyes big. He was fingering the little American flag. She could tell that he was questioning everything around him in this strange new land. The confusion and anxiety in those young eyes reminded her of her lonely trip with the Valendas the steaming August of 1903, six years before. She hoped that she would never feel so alone again.

She pulled her youngest brother to rest his head on her swollen lap and draped her shawl around him. At the same time she thanked the Holy Mother that her difficult first years in America were over and done with, that now her family was beside her again.

The travelers continued to pepper their sister and Jacob with questions. After passing a series of unpainted, ordinary clapboard farmhouses, straw or manure around their bases to keep out winter cold, the wagon came upon an impressive, prosperous farmstead. Its white house and front porch were large and inviting, much as the Gilberts' was. Mary quickly blurted, "Is your house like that, Jacob?"

The young wife looked at her husband, his hands as one with the reins to his horses, strong and steady. He was smiling faintly, but it was obvious that he didn't know how to answer the question.

Anna responded quickly. "No, but it's a sound house, and Jake's land is good. It gave us a big harvest this year. And just wait until you see my pantry. It's stuffed with potatoes and squash and cucumbers from my garden." The couple glanced at each other and chuckled once again at the new immigrants' unrealistic expectations.

When a one-room school house by the country road came into view, looking so different from the stone Catholic School of the good sisters of Kutná Hora, Anna went on, "*Anton*, you will go there to learn about America," at which the yawning Procházka boy wrinkled his nose with displeasure.

Anna turned to see that all the travelers were sagging from weariness, and she added to comfort them, "We'll be home soon, very soon. I'll build a big fire in the stove."

The mother-to-be suddenly was exhausted herself. As the familiar sound of voices from her past continued spasmodically behind her–the girls' comments about the simple clapboard buildings so unlike the stone structures of Europe, the sting of Iowa cold–Anna scanned the fields spread out around her.

She tried to think back at her own reaction to this strange, unfamiliar land when she'd arrived six years before. The houses had seemed plain and sparse on the prairie landscape. Even today winter fields seemed barren. Working the flat fields with the quiet husband sitting beside her was not easy, but she had experienced its bounty. She now felt at home in this Iowa.

The rich land of the plains had brought a new anchoring and satisfaction to the young wife. It was a feeling she had never known before. Together she and Jake had been able to bring forth wonder from its soil. Yes, it was home to her now, and it would soon feel like home to her family, she was sure. All the Mrkvičkas finally had pulled their roots from the shadows of Saint Barbara's Cathedral in Velký Lunec and replanted them anew in the heartland of America.

Anna's different eyes lifted from the fields to look upwards at a changing sky. The threatening snow clouds at last had swept off to the east, allowing a blaze of sunset to emerge on the western horizon. Indigo clouds fingered their way through a fiery sun slowly sinking from sight. Burnt red rays painted rosy orange and purple shadows on the scattered patches of snow in frozen fields around her.

Of all the breathtaking sunsets Anna had pondered on her lonely immigrant journey–as she bobbed with the decks of the Kronprinz on the Atlantic Ocean, as she tried to sleep in the heat of the roof with *Teta* Anna in the Lower East Side of New York City, as she stood among the lettuce and radishes in her own bountiful garden–this one, this day, seemed the most beautiful.

At that moment the new American life within Anna stretched an arm or a leg, making its mother move to adjust her weight in the uncomfortable wagon. Jacob smiled again as he saw his young wife brace the infant in her womb with her capable hands. Over the clatter of the creaking wagon and the horses' rhythmic hooves he barely heard her murmur.

"We did it, *bejby*, didn't we! You can come join us now."

Epilogue

N OTE: THE AMERICAN-IZED names used after Anna's family reached this country are noted in parentheses.

December 20, 1909: Anna's first child, Libbie Marie, my mother, was born. The hands of the baby's Czech midwife grandmother, *Marie Barbora* (Mary Barbara), helped her from the womb. Aunts Antonia and Mary wrapped swaddling clothes around their first-born niece.

Spring 1910: *Karel* (Charles or Charlie) Mrkvička found his first American job tending railroad tracks for the Burlington Line. He moved his family to a small clapboard house in Walker, Iowa.

Spring 1911: Jacob's parents sold the Kubesch farm and Anna and Jake began a series of moves from rental farm to rental farm. Crops usually made a profit; bank accounts grew. The Kups' goal was to own their own farm someday.

December 1911: Forty-two-year-old *Maminka* gave birth to her last baby, Joseph, her only child American born. The birth took place at Anna's rented farmhouse. *Marie Barbora*'s three oldest daughters assisted the delivery. Jacob and *Karel* stoked the winter fire in the stove so high that the chimney caught fire. Their bucket brigade from the well doused the fire about the time Joseph's first cry was heard.

January 29, 1913: Anna gave birth to her second child, Ivy, with the help of her midwife mother. The baby lived only nineteen days; she'd contracted whooping cough from Libbie.

1914: Austria's Archduke Ferdinand and his wife were gunned down by a Serbian nationalist. By August Germany declared war on Russia and invaded France, Luxemburg and Switzerland. World War I began to roll into everyone's lives.

1915: Libbie began to attend a one-room school, but was harassed because she could speak only Czech. She ran home repeatedly, only to have Anna walk her back to her classes. An understanding teacher took the child under her wing and soon the six-year-old became a model student, reading and speaking English well and writing it beautifully in careful Palmer script.

1917: Aliens like the Mrkvičkas were requested to register with the U.S. Government as the war worsened in Europe. Amid patriotic fervor, July 3, Anna's twenty-two-year-old brother, Frank, enlisted in the army. He shipped out of Iowa with the Rainbow Division, the 168th Infantry Regiment. Anna had brought her brother to America only to see him go back into the chaos of war-ravaged Europe.

Frank was engaged to Anna Marck, also an Austrian immigrant. Neither he nor his fiancée knew that Anna Marck's father had been conscripted into the Austrian army. Frank and the elder Marck fought on opposite sides of the conflict.

Iowa's Herbert Hoover was appointed by President Wilson to find ways nationally to increase food production. Farmers Anna and Jake tilled and planted every scrap of their rented land. They bought the Liberty Bonds championed by Hollywood's Douglas Fairbanks, Jr. and Mary Pickford. Even though farm prices were controlled, harvests were profitable. The Kups continued to save to buy land of their own, but farmland prices were rising dramatically.

September 19, 1917: Anna gave birth to her last child, Lloyd LeRoy. A doctor came to her rented farm home in his Model T to assist in the delivery, but strong-willed Anna threw the pills he gave her to ease her pain beneath the bed when the man wasn't looking. She was afraid they would hurt the baby.

May 27, 1918: The Rainbow Division suffered many casualties near

Baccarat in France. Anna's brother helped bury the dead, and then, June 18, Pvt. Frank Mrkvička was himself the victim of a phosgene gas attack and was seriously injured. Each breath painful, he gradually made his way back through various hospitals to Iowa.

November 11, 1918: World War I ended, but the world was fighting another war—deadly influenza. Its germs had traveled around the globe in but a few months, carried by railroad passengers and troops moving in close quarters during the war. Thousands were quarantined with flu in Iowa. While over twenty million died worldwide due to the outbreak, over six thousand died of the flu and another three thousand died of related pneumonia in the Midwest. No one in either Anna's or Jake's family became ill.

Summer, 1919: Jake's hogs were off their feed; most had diarrhea. Within two weeks the animals were listless and dying. A summoned veterinarian determined that the whole herd was infected with hog cholera and must be destroyed, burned and buried. Jake and Anna's farming operation was wiped out. Fall harvest helped pay off loans, but the couple was left nearly penniless.

Reluctantly, the two decided to leave farming, and they moved in with Jake's aged mother in Cedar Rapids. For the first time the two left the farming life of their ancestors and began the painful transition to try to make a living as urban workers. They joined the over fifty percent of farming Americans who already had migrated to cities.

1921: Eighty-year-old Mary Kubesch helped her son, Jacob, buy his family a small bungalow in the northeast section of Cedar Rapids. Anna's married sister, Mary, and foster brother, *Anton* Procházka (Tony Prochaska), lived nearby on the same street. Anna worked cleaning houses and at Quaker Oats. Jake, a farmer to his bones, never could adjust to fast factory production lines. He walked to odd jobs daily.

The roaring twenties: As a teenager, Libbie rebelled from her mother's old world beliefs and values. She insisted on being called "Marie," believing that it sounded more American, and she sneaked out at night to compete in Charleston contests. She won a few. Anna's foster brother and a brother-in-law flirted with bootlegging.

April 18, 1928: Libbie quit school six weeks short of high school graduation to marry divorced Jesse (Jack) Cohea, of Irish descent. He was thirty-four years of age, and already the father of five children. It was not the "nice 'Bohemie' boy" Anna envisioned for her Libbie. She had forbid the marriage, to no avail.

1930: Libbie and her husband had relocated to Waterloo, Iowa, and as the Great Depression deepened, Jack was laid off from his job on the tractor line at John Deere's Company. It was two years before the manufacturer was able to rehire Jack and hundreds of other line workers.

April 7, 1931: Anna's first American granddaughter, Joan Barbara, was born. The grandmother not only relented and made peace with the baby's father at that time, she tried to help the family through their financial distress. With her sister Antonia (Toni) driving an old Model A, Anna regularly made trips to take bags of groceries to her daughter's household sixty miles away. She still was determined that no child of hers would suffer the hunger she had borne during her young life.

July 5, 1933: Anna's brother-in-law (Antonia's husband, Joe Zickmund) accidentally drowned in the Cedar River in Cedar Rapids, along with his son, Harvey. Joe's employer, Penick and Ford, had ceased starch production for Independence Day and also the following day due to reduced business. Joe and his son had gone to the river to wade for clams for dinner. Harvey was caught up in the current; his father went to help him. Antonia became a widow at forty-three.

1936: Anna and Jake purchased a small house in Czech Village in southwest Cedar Rapids, renting their bungalow on the northeast side. The Village seemed like "home" to Anna, with its Bohemian bakery and butcher shop, its many residents of Czech background. Her brother, Frank, lived across the street. Foster brother *Anton* Procházka by then owned a nearby hardware and welding shop. The closely-knit family saw each other daily.

December 7, 1941: Two of Libbie Marie's stepsons were on a navy heavy cruiser outside Pearl Harbor when the Japanese attacked the United States. All four of Jack's sons soon were enlisted in the navy. Two survived the sinking of their ship and all four returned home safely. Anna bought stacks of War Bonds and traded food stamps to supply food to her family.

September 12, 1944: Libbie's husband, Jack Cohea, died suddenly. Anna encouraged her daughter to move to Cedar Rapids to be closer to family. Shortly Libbie Marie relocated to be near her parents.

June 21, 1955: Anna's first great-grandson, Kelvin John Smith, was born. Five generations of Anna's line were still living: *Marie Barbora* Mrkvička, Anna Barbara Kups, Libbie Marie Cohea, J. Barbara Smith (Alvord), and Kelvin John Smith.

May 1, 1956: Anna Kups, having been retired from Quaker Oats for two years, entered the hospital for the first time in her life, and died there alone in the middle of the night of heart congestion. She had been preceded in death in 1941 by her father, *Karel*, her brother Antone in 1947, and her brother Frank in 1952. She is interred near most of her family at the Cedar Rapids' Czech National Cemetery (*Český Národní Hřbitov*).

October 9, 1958: Jacob Benjamin Kubesch joined his wife in death. He lies beside Anna, his name Americanized on his tombstone as "Jake Kups."

Three generations, 1937: Top left, Libbie Marie;
Top right, Anna Barbara; Bottom, Joan Barbara

Acknowledgments

IN 1947 A very wise English teacher at West High School in Waterloo, Iowa, assigned her students to write about the lives of older members of their families. I wrote a thirteen-page theme entitled "Little Bohemian Girl" after conversations with my grandmother, Anna Mrkvička Kups. That paper, packed away for decades and now yellowed and dog-eared, became the backbone of this creative biography, *Through Different Eyes.*

I remember how pleased my little grandmother was when I sat down with her and asked a series of questions about her life in Bohemia and her long journey to America. Of course I now wish that I had asked more and different questions of her. As I began to write about her journey, long after she was gone, I realized how many details of her life have been lost forever. Nevertheless, that sophomore English paper provided me with facts that I would have had no way of knowing without it.

My mother, Libbie Marie Cohea, also wrote out answers to questions I asked of her, answers written in her classic one-room schoolhouse Palmer's script. And she shared with me throughout our years together countless snippets of incidents about her mother's life and her own. She told me of the difficulties the two encountered as first and second generation Czech-Americans adjusting to a culture different from that of Anna's native country.

One hot day in July 1997, I was able to find more answers to Anna's story as I visited my American-born great-uncle, Joe Mrkvička, in Walker, Iowa. At that time he was my grandmother's only surviving sibling, twenty-two years her junior. He was 86, with a clear memory, and fortunately he was able to identify both the farm village of Velký Lunec where the Mrkvičkas lived in Bohemia, and its nearby historic market town, Kutná Hora. I had not seen Joe for years, but I am thankful to have made the trip to visit him that sweltering Iowa day. He died in his sleep just two weeks after our conversation.

Before her death in 2001, my Aunt Gayle Kupps (Anna's son had added a "p" to the spelling of his name), widow of Anna's only son, Lloyd, provided me with information about the Kups family, along with valuable family photos.

I will forever be thankful to an Internet correspondent, Joan Bice Underwood of Atlantic, Iowa, who clarified important details about the "Gilbert" family that in 1906 hired Anna away from the frightening situation on the "Valenda" farm.

Statistical information found within resources at the Iowa State Historical Society and its library has been invaluable. I was able to identify the ship on which Anna sailed from Europe and to locate important land plats, clipping files and maps. Scouring collections of old Center Point and New York City newspapers helped me learn about the news and lifestyles that framed Anna's experiences.

My eternal gratitude goes to the patient editor of this book, Patricia L. Johnson, and my enduring Writers' Group. Without their unfailing encouragement Anna's story would not have been completed.

I must add that *Through Different Eyes* is the result of sorting through often differing and conflicting memories of various family members about some events in my grandmother's life. I expanded the scope of this creative biography to include many facets of the times in which Anna lived because it helped me to come to logical conclusions and calculated guesses about what must have occurred on her heroic journey to become an American.

Resources

Through Different Eyes

Alexander, Edwin. *Down At the Depot–American Railroad Stations from 1831-1920.* New York, 1970.

Anuta, Michael J. *Ships of Our Ancestors, Genealogical Publishing Company,* 1983.

Bed and Board (video). Arts and Entertainment, 1998.

Bennett, Mary. *An Iowa Album–A Photographic History 1860-1920.* University of Iowa Press, Iowa City, 1990.

Brownlow, Kevin; Kobal, John. *Hollywood, the Pioneers.* New York, 1979.

Blum, Jerome. *Our Forgotten Past.* London, 1982.

Camp Dodge records. *The Forty-Second Division, the "Rainbow Division"* and files.

Cedar Rapids Gazette. July 6, 1933. "Locate Bodies of Two River Victims Here."

Center Point Journal (later called *Center Point Independent*). 1903-1909. Iowa Historical Society files. Iowa City.

Cooke, Alistar. *Alistar Cooke's America.* Alfred A. Knopf. New York, 1974.

Davenport, Marcia. *The Valley of Decision.* U.S., 1942.

David, Clifton. Editor in chief. *Chronicle of the 20th Century.* New York, 1987.

Derks, Scott. Editor. *The Value of a Dollar.* Washington D.C., 1994.

Eiseman, Alberta. *From Many Lands*. Atheneum, New York, 1970.

Ellis Island (video). I, II, III, The History Channel, Arts and Entertainment, Interviews from "Ellis Island Oral History Project," 1997.

Encarta. "Bohemia, Czechoslovakia, Agriculture." Microsoft Encyclopedia.

Encyclopedia Britannica, Macropaedia #18. "History of Education" U.S.A., 1942.

Evans, Harold. *The American Century*. Alfred Knopf. New York, 1998.

Evans, Harold. *Front Page History (1900-1989)*. Yugoslavia, 1984.

Filby, Wm. Pl., and Meyer, Mary K. Editors. *Passenger and Immigration Lists*. Detroit, 1981.

Foerster, Norman. *American Poetry and Prose*. Boston, 1957.

Folsom, Franklin. *Impatient Armies of the Poor*. University Press of Colorado, 1991.

Frazier, Ian. Editor. *The Best American Essays*,1997. Sante, Luc. "Living in Tongues." New York, 1997.

Frazier, Joseph. *Iowa, Its History*. New York, 1978.

Gateway to Citizenship. Department of Justice. U.S. Immigration Service. U.S., Government Printing Office, 1979.

Glaser, Kurt. *Czecho-Slovakia, A Critical History*. Idaho, 1961.

Gold, Sarah. Managing Editor. *New York Public Library Desk Reference*, New York, 1993.

Gold Star Museum, Camp Dodge. Photo Files "World War I" and Displays.

Grenville. J. A. S. Editor, *Collier History of the World: 20th Century*.

Gue, Benjamin. *History of Iowa*. Century Historical Company, New York City, 1903.

A Guide to American Laws. Vol. 7. "Naturalization," Saint Paul, 1984.

Hampel, Patricia. *A Romantic Education*. Boston, 1983.

Harlan, Edgar Rubey. Curator. *A Narrative History of the People of Iowa (Vol. II)* Historical Memorial and Art Department of Iowa. American Historical Society, New York, 1931.

Harvey, Lois Gerstenberger. *The Life Saga and Stories of Harvey, Cisler, Gerstenberger and Mosher (and some related lines)*. The Print Shop, Historical Division, Library of Congress Catalog Card No. 79-90619. Illinois, 1979.

Heller, Charles E., Major, USAR. *Leavenworth Papers #10*: Chemical

Warfare in WWI: The American Experience, 1917-1918. Combat Studies Institute, Washington D.C., 1984.

The History of Czechs in Cedar Rapids. Volume I (1852-1942). The Czech Heritage Foundation, Inc. Cedar Rapids, Iowa, 1982.

The History of Linn County, Iowa. Western Historical Company, 1878.

Iowa Historical Society, Des Moines, Iowa. Clipping files: WW I 1914-1919-The Hospitals; Rainbow Division.

"Iowa's 1918 Flu Epidemic More Deadly Than WWI." *Des Moines Register*, August 8, 1976.

Johnson, Paul. *A History of the American People*. Harper Collins. New York, 1998.

King, John, and Nebesky, Richard. *Czech and Slovak Republics*, 1995.

Kerr, Daisy. *Keeping Clean: A Very Peculiar History*. New York, 1995.

Kimball, Donald. *Sesquicentennial History of Iowa (1850-1956)*. Historic Publications., Fayette, Iowa, 1991.

Krusina, Alois. *Say It In Czech (English-Czech Phrase Book)*. Prague. State Pedagogical Publishing House, 1963.

Levy, Leonard W. Editor in Chief. *Encyclopedia of the American Constitution*, "Immigration". MacMillan. London, 1986.

Martin, Pat. Compiler. *Czechoslovak Wit and Wisdom*. (no date).

McGuire, William. Editor. *Carl Jung, Collected Works*. vol 10. 1964.

McSorley, Joseph. *An Outline History of the Church of the Centuries*. London, 1949.

Mercer, Derrick. Editor. *Chronicles of the World (1889-1956)*. London, 1996.

Modelski, Andrew M. *Railroad Maps of North America (The First 100 Years)*. Library of Congress. Washington D. C., 1984.

Natural Advanced Geography. American Book Company, New York, 1901.

New York Times. July–August 1903. Iowa Historical Museum files.

Northern Iowa Today: 125 years. Summer, 2001.

Ogburn, Charlton. *Railroads: The Great American Adventure*. National Geographic Society. Washington, D.C., 1977.

Plat Book/Atlas. Linn County. 1895-1907. Iowa Historical Society.

Plotch, Botia. Editor. *New York Walks*. Henry Holt Company. New York, 1992.

Quaife, Elvin Lee, and Arthur L. Anderson. "The Hog in Iowa." *Palimpset*

33, 1952.

Rand McNally Standard Atlas of the World. Chicago, 1889.

Rand McNally Premier World Atlas. United States, 1975.

Reilly, Henry, Brigadier General O.R.C. *Americans All* (The Rainbow War, 42nd Division of the U.S. Infantry). Columbus, Ohio, 1936.

Riis, Jacob Al. *How the Other Half Lives.* Dover Publishers, Inc. New York, 1971.

Ročenka. A Yearbook of Czech Genealogy. Winter. 1992 Schlesinger, Arthur. "The Crisis of the Old Order". Riverside Press. Cambridge, 1957.

Saint Barbara's Cathedral, Kutná Hora. L. Publishing House. Libice. (no date).

Sherrow, Victoria. *Triangle Factory Fire.* Brookfield, Connecticut, 1995.

Sinyard, Neil. *Silent Movies.* New York, 1990.

"The Story of the 168th Infantry." *Palimpset.* The State Historical Society of Iowa. Iowa City, Iowa, 1967.

Tabor, John H. *The Story of the 168th Infantry.* Roster. p. 300. The State Historical Society of Iowa. Iowa City, Iowa, 1925.

Taylor, Henry C. *Tarpleywick, a Century of Iowa Farming.* I.S.U. Press, 1990.

"Tenant Farming in Iowa 1860-1900 (A Study of Terms of Rental Leases)." *Agricultural History 48,* 1974. pp. 130-150.

Thompson, W. H. *Transportation in Iowa: A Historical Summary.* Iowa Department of Transportation, 1989.

A Thousand Years of Czech Culture. Old Salem, Inc., 1996.

Uys, Michael, and Lovell, Lexy. *Riding the Rails.* The American Experience, Public Television, 1997.

The West: The Greatest Enterprise Under God. Public Broadcasting Network. IPBN, September, 1997.

World Book Encyclopedia. "Electricity," "Agricultural Revolution." Chicago, 1996.

Yeoman, R. S. *A Guidebook of U.S. Coins.* Western Publishing. Wisconsin, 1996.